150 Years

Couturiers
Designers
Labels

Charlotte
Seeling

FASHION

150 Years
Couturiers
Designers
Labels

*h.f.*ullmann

CONTENTS

YVES SAINT LAURENT

PAUL PARNES

ISSEY MIYAKE

JOHN GALLIANO

VIVIENNE WESTWOOD

DOLCE & GABBANA

ANN DEMEULEMEESTER

KARL LAGERFELD

THE IRRESISTIBLE ALLURE OF FASHION

Although all of us have to wear clothes, no one is obliged to follow fashion.

Yet, most people do so with great enthusiasm because of its thoroughly seductive nature: always introducing something new, always different, sometimes glamorous, sometimes shocking, futuristic one day, nostalgic the next... but never dull!

Fashion does not spring from the arbitrary whims of unworldly designers, but is always a sign of the times, and when it also happens to reflect our own desires, longings and dreams, we fall under its spell.

Fashion—be it jackets or pants—is far more than mere clothing. The key difference lies in whether a silhouette is attractive and correctly proportioned, or whether an unexpected mix of contrasting colors works well. Fashion can be as much about deception as about art. It is in any event a mark of civilization: the fact that we wear clothes sets us apart from animals.

In the beginning, we used animal skins to protect ourselves against wind and weather and to instill fear in others. Nowadays, it is considered a mark of moral superiority to refrain from wearing animal skins, but the transition from bearskins to techno fabrics has been long and tortuous.

Fashion as such did not become a fashionable concept until relatively recently. It was not until 1860 or thereabouts that Charles Frederick Worth, an English designer working in Paris, had the brilliant idea of attaching labels bearing his signature to any gowns he designed, just as if they were works of art. From then on, ladies of quality would only wear garments designed by a well-known couturier—these were classed as fashion, anything else was mere clothing.

Since then, the great masters of fashion have become legends in themselves and their numbers include colorful birds of paradise such as Paul Poiret and John Galliano, shy recluses like Cristóbal Balenciaga and Martin Margiela, highly sensitive, artistic characters such as Christian Dior and Yves Saint Laurent, as well as capable pragmatists such as Coco Chanel and Giorgio Armani. Regardless of whether their work has been inspired by a sense of craftmanship, art, or commercial considerations, they have all striven to turn their ideas of perfection into reality. They have put their heart and soul into each collection, which is one of the reasons we find fashion so fascinating.

This book charts the development of fashion as seen against the historical background of the different eras, beginning with the great couturiers. They were followed, during the 1960s, by a large number of new-generation designers, who were in turn elbowed aside during the 1980s by large, luxury conglomerates. Two decades later, these then found themselves increasingly challenged by chain stores at the cheaper end of the market. However, be it haute couture, designer or brand name, the world of fashion relies, as it always has, on creative design.

As long as this remains the case, fashion will always have a future and the Internet makes certain that it can reach the furthest corners of the planet. Fashion is, after all, a source of fascination to people all over the world.

Charlotte Seeling

For Eberhard Hauff—for everything

How fashion became

THE INVENTION OF HAUTE COUTURE

fashionable

French haute couture made its triumphant debut at the Paris Exposition Universelle (World Exhibition) of 1900. A select group of fashion houses including Worth and Doucet, who clothed star actresses like Eleonora Duse and Sarah Bernhardt, presented their flamboyant creations before a admiring crowd. One newspaper critic declared that "for all those who worship at the altars of elegance, glamor, luxury, and beauty, Paris was, is, and ever shall be the one true place of pilgrimage."

Paris had been seen as the fashion capital of the world from as early as the 18th century. The fact that the very first department stores opened in France in about 1850 contributed to the spread of French fashion, as did the World Exhibition, which received much coverage in the international press. As French fashions began to be increasingly copied, the realization soon dawned that it needed particular protection, and the Parisian tailors' union (Chambre Syndicale de la Couture Parisienne) was founded in 1910, with the principal aim of protecting copyright. The message was clear: fashion could only come from Paris!

At the beginning of the 20th century the few big names in fashion, who called themselves "couturiers," considered themselves the keepers of the Holy Grail of haute couture. Nevertheless, individual couturiers had to have something of the creator, artiste, PR genius, entertainer, self-promoter, and stage director about them if they wanted to rise above the ranks of gifted tailors.

Yet it was an Englishman, of all people, who was the founder of French haute couture. After a seven-year apprenticeship in the London textile industry, the 20-year-old Charles Frederick Worth arrived in Paris. In 1858, 13 years later, he founded his own fashion house with his Swedish business partner, Boberg, in Rue de la Paix. In 1871 he became solely in charge of the business. Worth was the first person to understand how to make himself a star; he simply began to sign his pieces of clothing as though they were works of art. He devised a small cloth label that was embroidered with his jaunty signature, and sewed it into every one of his designs. The brand name was born. Of course, all the other couturiers began to follow suit. Worth also launched a new

At the beginning

of the 20th century the fight over fashion was fierce and merciless; one side insisted on wide skirts and wasp waists, the other on their right to their true figure, here splendidly caricatured by Knud Petersen.

Streit der Moden

(Zeichnung von Bruno Paul)

„Das Reformkleid ist vor allem hygienisch und erhält den Körper tüchtig für die Mutterpflichten." — „So lange Sie den Fetzen anhaben, werden Sie nie in diese Verlegenheit kommen."

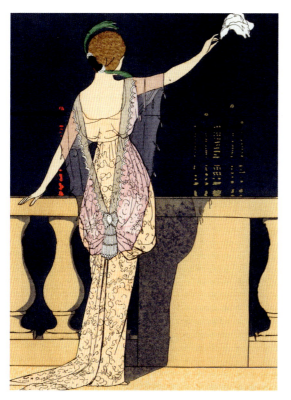

The high point and culmination

of the Belle Epoque was marked by the World Exhibition in 1900 in Paris (above right). Jeanne Paquin, who produced some pleasing fashions (above left and middle), was the very first woman to take a leading role in fashion. The trailblazer of haute couture was Charles Frederick Worth (middle right), who had also dressed the Empress Sisi (middle left), and whose studio (left) was filled with seamstresses embellishing his designs. Yet the showy features of his garments, including this German evening gown (left), were soon consigned to history; the Zeitgeist demanded greater freedom of movement for women.

collection once a year, thus introducing the concept of change in fashion as a means of driving sales—a ground-breaking innovation that designers still benefit from to this day.

His fashion line was, however, far less revolutionary than his marketing strategy. Monsieur Worth had done little but make the crinoline, which had become increasingly heavy, even more formidable: the skirt was flattened out at the front, while the bulk of the material was gathered at the back. This evolved into the bustle, which, like the hoop petticoat, soon began to take on ever more extreme forms, and provoked much ridicule.

Yet the origin of these styles and the inspiration behind them came not from the 19th century, but rather the 18th. No new fashion lines were presented at the World Exhibition in 1900. The real sensation was the upbeat feel for presentation exhibited by the new generation of couturiers, who all took Worth as their example. At the time of the Exhibition, Worth had been dead for five years and his sons Gaston and Jean-Philippe had taken over the business. The word "couturier" had been coined for Worth, who had understood how to combine English tailoring techniques with French flair; previously there had only been *couturières*, or simply seamstresses.

Jeanne Paquin, the woman who was given the honor of choosing the exhibitors for the Pavillon de l'Elégance, also identified herself as a fashion designer rather than a seamstress. She did not present anything new, but what she did, she presented with panache. A life-like wax mannequin, modeled on her own pretty features, was dressed in the finest lace and silks, and the sophisticated presentation meant that the lack of innovation went unnoticed. The fact that a woman was presiding over the fashion fair was shocking enough, as the world of couture was (and still is) dominated by men. They believed that the female body should be cinched and padded out to correspond with the ideal hourglass figure: vulnerable and fragile in the middle, generously rounded above and below. In profile, the line of the body resembled an S, the corset and bustle modulating the sharpness of its curves.

Jean Cocteau is reputed to have said that undressing a woman was a feat on a par with storming a fortress. The connoisseur of homoeroticism must have heard this from someone else; perhaps it was Colette, who was an ardent advocate of every kind of bodily pleasure, and equally interested in both sexes. Colette (1873–1954) was bold enough to try out various different lifestyles. Exploited and cheated when acting as a ghostwriter for her first husband, she turned toward the female sex and the stage. In 1909 she wrote a novel under her own name, following a hiatus of several years, and became famous overnight. Colette married twice more, the last time to a much younger man, and used all her experiences and emotions as material for her bestsellers. Her free-spirited adventures sent shivers down the spine of less audacious women.

Even in Worth's toned-down designs, women's clothes bore a certain resemblance to a straitjacket. High, narrow, banded collars, ideally made of stiff lace, forced the head upright, and a hat festooned with embellishments perched on top. Heavy ostrich plumes were much in vogue, and were a status symbol by virtue of being the most expensive kind of finery. The slender top half, cinched in by a whalebone corset, which was in turn hidden beneath a *cache-corset*, had enlarged sleeves that were often referred to as "leg of mutton" because they resembled one; they puffed out from the shoulder but clung closely to the arm from elbow to hand. The skirt was floor-length, loose around the hips, bell-shaped at the hem, and gathered at the back with ruffles and folds that often ended in a small train. To balance the silhouette the hat was used as a counterweight to the emphasized *derrière* by inclining it slightly forwards on pinned up hair. The matching ankle boots or shoes were pointed and had a slightly curved baroque heel. Essential accessories included silk stockings, which, of course, could only be guessed at, and narrow gloves ensured that outside the house not even the hands could be seen bare. When wearing a low-cut dress the gloves had to be so long that even the upper arms were "dressed." No wonder, then, that the merest glimpse of pale skin or a slim ankle was enough to drive men wild.

Materials such as linen, velvet, and wool were worn during the day, in muted, dark colors or pale pastel shades such as pink, blue, or mauve. Elaborate details were used to offset the unimaginativeness of the style: masses of braids, ribbons, piping,

Men's jackets were flattering for women, but only permitted *in pants roles* at the theatre

bows, appliqués, and flounces were deployed as decoration.

The evening look was one of silk, lace, muslin, tulle, chiffon, satin, and crêpe de Chine, elaborately crafted and embroidered, and often low-cut. Pearls were the jewel of the decade, whether worn as drop earrings, long single-row necklaces (*sautoirs*) or in multiple strands tight at the throat like a dog-collar. The society lady always looked as though she were heading out to a garden party—and she often was—whenever she was spending the Season on the Côte d'Azur, as was customary. In Paris, however, she loved to attend the theatre with dainty opera glasses and a sweeping fan.

Such were the accoutrements of the *femme ornée* of the Belle Epoque. Yet by 1903 the *femme liberée* stood on the threshold, and many people were working toward greater freedom in fashion—most of them women. Women were permitted to wear tailored suits for horse riding, so they knew that men could move much more freely by virtue of their clothing alone, and they increasingly began to adopt "Amazon clothes" as everyday wear. Pants were still frowned upon, but ankle length skirts were worn with jackets and shirts borrowed from men's fashion.

The "Gibson Girl," the creation of the illustrator Charles Dana Gibson, shows us just how becoming this style was. Between 1890 and 1910, Gibson regularly caricatured the reactions of bourgeois society to female emancipation in *Collier's Weekly* magazine. The main character was always a sporty and intelligent, yet beautiful and stylish, young woman who, as the Gibson Girl, soon became seen as someone to aspire to, bringing the plight of socially disadvantaged women to the attention of sympathetic readers with good humor and unpretentiousness.

The attractive Gibson Girl, the product of a man's imagination, achieved more than many feminists. Back in 1851, Amelia Bloomer had earned nothing but ridicule for her first pantsuit. Everyone made fun of the baggy pants that bunched at the ankles and were not exactly flattering, and "bloomers" remained sportswear for cycling and girls' gymnastics until the First World War.

The only woman to cause uproar by daring to wear pants was Sarah Bernhardt. The star of the theatre was a sensation not only on the stage but also in her

private life, and she was the couturiers' best customer. The young Paul Poiret, then an assistant of Jacques Doucet, designed her costume for her first pants role in *L'Aiglon* in 1900. The young hothead let slip a few disparaging comments about the celebrated actress, who was then in her mid-fifties and more fashion-conscious than ever. It cost him his job at Doucet, a top couturier. The pants role was yet another triumphant success for Sarah Bernhardt. Even when she later had to have a leg amputated, she remained the big fashion houses' favorite customer, although she had the habit of changing the exclusive designs worn by its models to suit her own taste.

In contrast, the other great tragic actress of that era, the Italian Eleonora Duse, was unconditionally loyal. Her staple wardrobe was supplied by Worth, and on the one occasion when efforts of the fashion house were not to her taste she apologized for her rejection of the dress with a long, polite letter which contained at least fifty occurrences of the word "unfortunately."

Apart from actresses, dancers such as Isadora Duncan and Mata Hari had the greatest influence on fashion. Duncan was the first to dare to perform barefoot, uncorseted, and scantily covered. The Americans found this scandalous. She achieved fame in Europe, where she travelled in 1901 on tour with a troupe led by the great American dancer Loie Fuller. She made her solo debut in Budapest, but had her greatest success in Berlin.

Her flowing garments did not constrict the body and gave new impetus to the development of "reform dress." From the mid-19th century doctors and feminists alike were agreed that women must be freed from the corset. The former feared health problems due to the forcible cinching of the torso, while the latter fought for greater freedom of movement, both literally and figuratively. Since the pantsuit had not caught on in the USA or England, international efforts concentrated on the dress. Female-friendly fashion was being developed in several countries at the same time, mostly by artists from the Arts and Crafts Movement.

The first designs were so shapeless that most women rejected them as "reform sacks." In 1900 renowned artists such as Henry van de Velde were invited to the "German Tailors Day," where reform

1914

15

COLETTE.

Like no other
Colette was one of the first to free herself from the corset of bourgeois ideas: she appeared half naked on the stage,
kissed women, wore men's clothing, and made her most intimate thoughts into bestsellers.

Great egos

were the driving force behind fashion. Paul Poiret (above left) saw himself as the greatest artist of all. The highly theatrical Sarah Bernhardt (above right) could do no wrong in a pants role, while poor Amelia Bloomer was ridiculed for her practical suit (left). Maestro Jacques Doucet, here with dog, upheld the virtues of couture, which were also embodied by the "Gibson Girl," albeit with emancipatory aims. The Belgian actress Camille Clifford (right page) was the model for the illustrator.

"The divine"
Eleonora Duse (1858–1924) was the first to bear this epithet, before even Garbo.
The Italian actress modernized the theatre by forswearing pathos and appearing without a corset or makeup.

The mysterious woman

Mata Hari (1876–1917) was only the most famous of many pseudonyms used by the Dutch dancer who performed in revealing clothing, but always kept her cards close to her chest when it came to facts. She was executed for espionage.

Doctors and women fought alongside one another *against the corset,* one for health, the other for freedom

clothing designs were exhibited. Three years later the concert singer Anna Muthesius altered the austere "sack" and presented a flattering dress which was received enthusiastically in England, where she lived with her architect husband. The *Wiener Künstlerkleid* (Viennese artist's dress) appeared in Austria at around the same time—also a loosely hanging garment, but with softer lines and colorful patterns that set it apart from the extreme sobriety of the first reform dresses.

The purpose of all these efforts was not only to free the female body from the corset, but also to free the international textile industry from Paris's stranglehold on fashion. Yet fashion's step forward into the modern era was to take place in this city, the capital of elegant overstatement. No one understood better than Paul Poiret how to make the most of this revolution in couture.

The bicycle

did more for women's liberation than anything else, especially when it was as chic as this wooden-framed model (above). Despite emancipation, women did not want to go around in sackcloth and ashes, so the practical reform dress itself was jazzed up. The Viennese designer Emilie Flöge, a friend of Klimt, designed a version with a Chinese print (below), while the German concert singer Anna Muthesius (right page), who had come into contact with the Reform Movement in England, opted for flattering flounces and dainty shawls.

THE FIRST DESIGNER:
Paul Poiret

04.20.1879
–
04.28.1944

"Fashion needs a tyrant" proclaimed Paul Poiret, with clear insight into what was lacking in fashion at the turn of the century, and a vision of himself in the role of despot. So much indecisiveness and frippery cried out for someone with an eye for the bigger picture.

Poiret, the son of textile workers in the Parisian district of Les Halles, knew early on that his true calling was as an artist. The chubby, good-natured daydreamer was dotingly encouraged by his mother and three sisters. Only his father proved resistant to his charms, forcing his son to graduate high school. To teach him about life in the real world he then sent him to work as an errand boy for a renowned umbrella maker.

"Perhaps," recalled Poiret, "I may have forgotten to wash my neck every so often, but I changed my white collars every day." He was utterly convinced that there was nothing more important than appearance, a conviction that led him to take the only thing from his employer that held any interest for him: scraps of leftover silk. At home he conjured up extravagant couture creations which he draped around a small wooden doll, a present from his sisters, who were effusive in their admiration for his designs. He was to seek this same reaction from women all his life.

What is even more astonishing is the fact that he is celebrated as the liberator of women's fashion to this very day, given that his only concern was with his own fame, and that he considered his own taste the benchmark for everything. This sense of taste and his talent for drawing secured him an assistantship with the couturier Jacques Doucet. There the multitalented Poiret learnt first-class tailoring and how to appreciate the finer things in life, and also the promotional value to be gained by flattering the stars of the stage.

After completing his military service, in 1901 Poiret secured a position at the leading fashion house of the day—Worth. However, the successors of the founder of couture did not allow Poiret's star to shine.

It was just as well, then, that there were women who believed in him unconditionally. Mama Poiret handed over 50,000 francs so that her son Paul could set up his first fashion house in 1903. The idolized actress Gabrielle Réjane defected from Doucet to become Poiret's first customer. The apprentice had well and truly surpassed the master when it came to charming the stars. Wherever Réjane appeared with her white donkeys, a present from the King of Portugal, she was like a magnet for others.

The man with the mask
Paul Poiret always presented himself as cheerful and confident, but no one knew what was going on inside. Poiret wanted to make the world a more beautiful place, and chose to escape from reality, especially with masked balls, for which he made himself up at his own dressing table.

Skin-colored *silk*
gave the illusion of naked legs

Within three years Poiret was a star himself, with all Paris at his feet. He partied and worked with Paul Iribe, George Lepape, Erté, Mariano Fortuny, Vlaminck, André Derain, and Raoul Dufy, and considered himself their equal. "Am I a fool because I claim to be an artist?" he asks in his 1930 memoirs, knowingly entitled *En habillant l'époque* (Dressing the Era). Yet by that time his fame had long faded, and other stars were shining brightly in the firmament of fashion.

Poiret was indeed justified in his boast that he had "declared war on the corset," but this revolutionary act had been based on purely aesthetic motives. He found the bisection of the female body into an outward-surging bosom and a protruding *derrière* utterly laughable. In 1906 he designed a simple, narrow dress, with the skirt beginning straight underneath the bust and reaching the ground. He had created the line that would make him immortal. He christened it *La Vague*, as it played around the body like a gentle wave. Compared with the corseted beauties of the Belle Epoque, the Poiret woman appeared outrageously agile. Who knows whether Poiret would ever have dared to produce this sensational design had he not married the svelte and lovely Denise Boulet in 1905, making her the mother of his five children and also one of the most elegant women in Paris.

Poiret generously promised that every woman who "felt despondent and enslaved by her old-fashioned clothes ... will now give a whoop of joy..." Women could feel younger and more daring not only by abandoning the corset, which Poiret replaced with flexible brassières and light garters, but also by wearing bright colors and bold patterns. He rejected the customary black stockings and gave women (and men) the illusion of naked legs by encasing them in skin-colored silk.

But from simple beginnings, things can soon get out of hand. In 1910 Poiret devised the infamous hobble skirt, which was so tapered at the hem that the wearer was forced to take tiny steps. He found this amusing: "I have liberated her upper body, but I am binding her legs." His enthusiasm was, however, misplaced; his *jupe entravée* did not catch on.

The fashion dictator cared not one jot, as he had long seen himself as a sultan, dressing the ladies of his harem in the most splendid Oriental garments. His slaves were ordered to wear kaftans, baggy trousers, and turbans, and they enthusiastically complied, arraying themselves in flamboyant embroidery, gold and silver lace, sumptuous brocade, tasseled trims, pearls, and the feathers of rare birds—the last word in exoticism. Everyone had been enamored of all things Orient since the sensational performance of the Ballets Russes on their first visit to Paris in 1909.

In 1911 Poiret threw one of the most famous fancy-dress parties of the 20th century, the "1002 Nights." The boundaries between clothing and costumes became blurred as the effusive and extravagant Poiret sought to present life as one great party. He traveled all over the world, drawing inspiration from everywhere he went. Taking his cue from the Wiener Werkstätte, he founded a school for applied arts, teaching furniture and textile design. He became the first couturier to create his own perfume, and in 1911 he managed to generate further interest with a scandal when his culottes were denounced by Pope Pius X. In the same year he established a workshop where designs by the painter Raoul Dufy were printed on the finest couture silk—a revolutionary moment for the textile industry. As he traveled, he saw how he was copied everywhere and so was prompted to set up a trade union that would protect independent creations.

Total provocation
A woman without a corset was bad enough, but a woman in pants? And a loosely belted ensemble at that, reminiscent of the comfortable loungewear sported by pashas when they were at home. Who but Poiret could have launched this fashion in 1925?

A world apart
The "Poiret woman" wore flowing garments with an Empire waistline and lived among velvet-covered interiors.
Poiret presented his world at the boutique Martine in 1924: fashion, furniture, accessories and his perfume, "Rosine."

Poiret was the first to pursue the idea of a complete artwork—everything surrounding him was cast according to individual (his!) taste

He could no longer be described as a mere couturier; he had become the first real designer, making his aesthetic mark on everything from accessories to interior decoration. Eight decades later, designers are still drawing on this concept, presenting their home collections including everything down to scented candles. Poiret had long been doing that very thing at his Oriental-themed balls.

Yet for all that, he was no visionary, but a man of his time—the time before the First World War, when life still seemed to be good. When Poiret returned from the front in 1918 he found that everything had changed. Having been celebrated as the liberator of women, he could not comprehend that the war had done more for women's independence than fashion ever could. He still believed that women were simply waiting to be persuaded into astonishing creations by the maestros of fashion: "First they demur, then they obey, and finally they applaud." But now they simply laughed and did as they pleased.

Poiret believed that his old customers could be won back if he threw a few big parties. Within six months he had accumulated debts of half a million francs. He found financial backers to profit from his genius, but they also wanted to make it subject to market principles. Poiret felt humiliated and held out for the first opportunity to re-establish himself spectacularly as the king of the couturiers. He thought that the time had come with Paris's Art Deco exhibition of 1925, and rigged out three boats on the Seine with his designs—the first a luxury restaurant, the second a couture salon, and the third a boutique for perfume, accessories and furniture. As always, the decor was grandiose, as was the cost. His financial backers refused to pay. Poiret was bankrupt, but continued to live in grand style. Seeing other couturiers achieve success with his ideas made him bitter. When his wife Denise left him, Poiret withdrew to Provence in a sulk to become a painter. He died in 1944, impoverished and forgotten.

Disconnected from reality
Poiret's wife Denise (left) bore him five children and was his favorite model.
He liked to dress her—and others—as a lady of the harem, in gorgeous material,
with her hair hidden, Oriental-style, under a turban, installing her in an opulent boudoir (right).

AN ALL-ROUND GENIUS:
Mariano Fortuny

05.11.1871
—
05.03.1949

Mariano Fortuny was no couturier, yet he managed to create the only truly timeless dress: the Delphos dress, a wisp of pleated silk which, when twisted like a skein of wool, could be squeezed into a tiny box. Today it is still worn by the world's most sophisticated women (provided that they can get their hands on one of the few originals at an auction). His 1907 design never goes out of fashion because it was never fashion in the first place; connoisseurs recognized it immediately as a work of art—a dress that revealed nothing, but that hid nothing, either.

Like the ancient Greek chiton robes, the dress fell towards the ground without shaping seams, pads, or gathers on the shoulders. It gave every woman who wanted to dispense with the corset the freedom of movement that she desired, and the Delphos became the dress of choice for contemporary dancers, from Isadora Duncan to Martha Graham.

Many designers have drawn inspiration from Fortuny's stroke of genius: first his friend Paul Poiret, and more recently the American Mary McFadden and the Japanese designer Issey Miyake, with his Pleats Please collection.

Mariano Fortuny was the second child of a highly successful painter in Granada, Spain. He was three when his father died of malaria at the age of only 36, yet he was strongly influenced by him. He inherited not only his father's paintings, but also his talents and interests, and even his taste. Like his father, he loved to travel and was especially fascinated by the exotic, particularly the Arab world. The similarities between his studio and that of his father were astonishing. Lengths of velvet adorned the walls or divided the room as enormous curtains, forming a backdrop for paintings by both father and son, interspersed with weapons and objets d'art from all over the world that had been collected by Mariano Fortuny senior. There were also pieces of art, religious artifacts and curiosities gathered in glass cases and cupboards, including the death masks of Beethoven and Wagner.

The artist as a young man
Mariano Fortuny y Madrazo—his full name—was only 16 when he painted himself in the costume of a Venetian nobleman from the 16th century. His models, both in painting and in life, were always the classic artists.

His ideal of beauty lay in the past,
while his sense of curiosity was excited
*by **technological progress***

No, this was not the studio of an avant-garde artist! His mother moved to Paris as a widow, taking the young Mariano to live with her brother, a popular portrait painter of the Belle Epoque, who taught the boy from the age of seven. In later years, the adult Fortuny followed all the art trends of his time, but he did not become an iconoclast. He preferred to discuss the masters of the past with his grandfathers and uncles, all of whom, on both his mother's and his father's side, were prominent artists. Right up until his death Fortuny was in the habit of visiting museums so as to perfect his style by copying the great works of Tiepolo, Rubens, Velasquez, Titian, and Tintoretto.

He was interested in every technological innovation, and particularly fascinated by the invention of electricity. He began by designing individual lamps, and later whole lighting systems. He was an ardent admirer of Wagner, and having attended the Bayreuth Festival at the age of 21, he strove to create the perfect work of art, developing a remarkable range of skills in the process. He was successful as a director and architect, as a stage and lighting designer, and especially as an inventor; he received almost two thousand patents for his innovations in lighting technology and in the printing and processing of fabric and paper.

Fortuny also trained himself in sculpture, copper engraving, and especially in photography. Critics say that his etchings and photographs, which he often created merely as source material for his paintings, generally surpass the latter in expression and originality. Yet Fortuny, ever his father's son, saw himself only as a painter.

His talents fully blossomed only when he finally managed to leave the oppressive family fold at the age of 31. Thirteen years earlier his mother had moved to Venice with him and his older sister, as Paris had become too noisy and expensive for her. At first, the family lived together in an old palazzo, where the veneration of his dead father continued. Eventually, in 1902, Mariano set up his studio and transferred all his work to the Palazzo Orfei—and horrified his mother and sister by installing the Frenchwoman Henriette Negrin there as his official companion. By that time Henriette had already been Fortuny's secret muse in Paris for five years. Another 16 years later, in 1918, Fortuny legitimized their relationship by marrying her, prompted by the horrors of the First World War. Mariano remained close to his family, but they never acknowledged Henriette, although she remained at his side until his death.

Fortuny loved plump women, not quite as ample as those of Rubens, but well-rounded all the same. His greatest fascination was with thick, loosely pinned manes of hair, which he thought the key to female beauty, and he always drew them. His very first portrait of Henriette shows more of her hair than her face. Later, he began to paint her in different Delphos dresses, with the Knossos shawl that often accompanied his designs. The sari-like shawl made of crushed silk was Fortuny's first fashion design, and became a versatile and popular costume for the stage, worn for Mata Hari's dance of the veils, among others.

Working alone in the enormous Palazzo Orfei, Fortuny came to the conclusion that all his activities had the same intrinsic value. Whether he was painting or taking photographs, or creating

The Delphos dress

This dress is timeless. The Ancient Greeks themselves lauded it as the ultimate garment, and Fortuny made it into a timeless work of art. How the silk was dyed and pleated by hand remains one of Fortuny's great secrets.

*Fortuny was an **artist, craftsman, and alchemist**, and the magic formula of his silken marvels works its spell to this day*

exquisite materials and clothes, everything he did could be described as art. He developed his own colors and pigments, printed his lithographs on his own press, manufactured the photographic paper for his prints, designed lamps and furniture, and constructed whole stages. Today, however, he is remembered for his clothing.

Unlike other fashion designers, he was not always coming up with something new. On the contrary, for 40 years he produced the same design with the same pattern in the same materials—only sheer silks from Japan and feathery velvet from Lyons. Prominent women who eschewed the diktats of fashion loved his Delphos dresses and were always willing to be photographed in them. The foremost of these was the eccentric patron and art collector Peggy Guggenheim, who spent her last years in Venice, not far from Fortuny's Palazzo Orfei. Yet his fans also included film stars like Lillian Gish and Dolores del Rio, actresses like Eleonora Duse, dancers like Isadora Duncan, and influential society ladies. The latter included the wife of the American publisher Condé Nast, who founded *Vogue*, which remains the most important fashion magazine in the world to this very day. The elegiac literary genius Marcel Proust immortalized Fortuny (with his real name!) and his delicate creations in his multi-volume work *À la recherche du temps perdu* (In Search of Lost Time). The fragile writer saw Fortuny's pleated silk dresses and shimmering velvet capes as the epitome of elegance, and female beauty in general.

Fortuny's garments were made in the studio in the Palazzo Orfei with all the care normally lavished on works of art. There were, in fact, only a few basic designs, but every dress was unique, as the material was dyed, printed, pleated, and sewn by hand, and each one had its lining, thread, silken cord, belt, and even the label dyed to match. The entire process was overseen by Fortuny himself, who, as alchemist and craftsman, mixed all the colors and produced all the prints himself. How he achieved the finely folded pleats remains a mystery. Only the decorative glass pearls (mouth-blown, of course) which weighted down the sleeves and seams, holding the ethereal garments in shape, were manufactured, in nearby Murano.

After the First World War Fortuny experimented with cheaper materials for the decorating trade, setting up a factory and developing new machines that processed Egyptian cotton. He was particularly successful in kitting out museums and private homes, particularly in the USA, where Elsie Lee (née McNeill) became his business partner, deftly marketing his exclusive robes and inexpensive furnishing fabrics. Elsie later married Count Alvise Gozzi of Venice and helped to preserve the Palazzo Orfei as a museum. It can be visited in Venice to this day.

When Fortuny died on May 2, 1949 Henriette was his sole heiress. She lived on in the Palazzo Orfei and tended to her husband's legacy until her death in 1965.

The world of Fortuny
His wife Henriette, in a portrait painted by Fortuny in 1920. He was fascinated by light, and designed many lamps covered in muslin, hand painted with Chinese motifs, and adorned with silk tassels. For capes and coats he used shimmering velvet. These can be seen alongside his trademark designs and old skeins of silk in the Fortuny Museum in Venice. He designed cotton upholstery fabric specifically for the American market, including this grapevine motif on a green background.

Classic beauty

Unchanged for a hundred years, and still perfect: This outfit of apricot-colored silk, with a short tunic,
weighted at the seams with Murano glass pearls, can be admired at the Victoria and Albert Museum in London.

They defined their era

Charles F. Worth	Jacques Doucet	Jeanne Paquin	Emilie Flöge

Charles F. Worth
Two empresses made this English tailor famous: the tragic "Sisi," Elisabeth of Austria, and Eugénie, the elegant wife of Napoléon III, at whose court Worth (1825–1895) began his rise to prominence.
Both are immortalized in portraits by Winterhalter wearing Worth's silk tulle designs, embroidered in gold. The term "haute couture" was coined for Worth's luxury fashion.

Jacques Doucet
Fashion left him cold, but luxury fascinated him. Jacques Doucet (1853–1929) covered his pastel-colored garments with lace, embroidery, and appliqués. "Doucet dresses us like decent, respectable mothers," wrote Liane de Pougy, one of the most famous *demimondaines*. He kept the same approach when respectable mothers and soldiers' wives wanted to dress like *demimondaines*.

Jeanne Paquin
"I did not invent anything, I simply left things out," said Jeanne Paquin (1869–1936) of her fashion. In 1906 she introduced the Empire dress, one year before Poiret established his reputation with this line, and she was also a year ahead of him with her kimono-inspired coat. In general, however, she made only gradual and subtle changes, so as not to alienate her international customers.

Emilie Flöge
Together with her two sisters, in 1904 Emilie Flöge (1874–1952) founded a couture salon completely decorated in black and white and committed to the aesthetic concepts of the Wiener Werkstätte—supplanting rampant *Jugendstil* ornamentation with simpler, geometrically abstract shapes. Her (supposedly platonic) lifelong friend Gustav Klimt helped her to come up with the design for the reformed "Viennese artist's dress."

The female body
HOW DANCE EMANCIPATED WOMEN'S FASHION
liberated

However much fashion moguls such as Paul Poiret were able to claim credit for having liberated the female body from all its restrictions—that is to say, from the corset—it was in fact women themselves who cast off these restraints in their enthusiasm for pursuing sporting activities such as tennis, golf, and skiing. Their greatest passion, however, was for dance. For two whole decades the Ballets Russes touring company was instrumental in dictating the fashions of that hedonistic generation—its influence extending all around the world from Paris and Berlin to South and North America.

The very first appearance of the Ballets Russes in Paris in 1909 paved the way for radical changes in the world of fashion. Subtle shades, delicate pastels, feminine reserve, and youthful modesty became a thing of the past—swept away by a whirlwind of movement, color, and breathtaking opulence.

After attending a performance of the Ballets Russes, Helena Rubinstein, founder of the first international cosmetics firm, was so electrified by the rich shades of purple and gold that she returned home determined to change her entire interior design color scheme. No sooner had she arrived home than she began tearing down the white brocade curtains from the windows of her salon, ordering new ones "in the brilliant colors I fell in love with yesterday evening."

All of Paris was captivated by the visual fireworks of a Ballets Russes performance. It seemed as if Serge Diaghilev, the impresario genius, was not only designing the stage sets for the Russian ballet company but also dictating the fashions and makeup, in fact the entire lifestyle, of decadent Parisian society. "Surprise me," he would urge his staff—and year after year the whole of Paris looked forward to, as he did, the surprises contemporary artists such as Léon Bakst and Alexandre Benoît contrived to produce in the way of designs and costumes.

It is true, of course, that the overwhelming success of the Ballets Russes was also due in part to innovative music and, more especially, to dancers like Anna Pavlova or Vaslav Nijinsky, but it was the exotically baroque, artistic spectacle as a whole that bewitched European elite society and prompted the *beau monde* to develop an interest in the fine arts. Women especially became consumed with a passion

Exhibiting a Tartar-like wildness and fieriness, the Ballets Russes took the West European art world by storm and in doing so changed our concept of dance and beauty forever.

Décor d'Henri Matisse

LE CHANT DU ROSSIGNOL

The song of the nightingale

Although the nightingale's song is sweetly seductive, it could also be harmful—the painter Henri Matisse,
a member of a group of artists known as the Fauves (French for "Wild Beasts") designed this set for the "wild" Ballets Russes.

Firebird and swan

Vaslav Nijinsky gave a provocative performance in *L'Après-midi d'un faune* (Afternoon of a Faun), becoming the first male dance idol to rival the supremacy of the prima ballerinas—a fitting partner for Anna Pavlova, unforgettable in her role as the "Dying Swan."

The painted face

Polish-born Helena Rubinstein (right) emigrated to the USA where she set up the first-ever international cosmetic empire. Not only did she develop and market her products but also she offered treatments in her own salons. (Below) Louise Brooks, whose distinctive short haircut and heavily made-up eyes and lips established her as the quintessential flapper. Born in Kansas, she began her career as a dancer before being brought by director G. W. Pabst to Berlin, where her starring role in *Lulu* made her a film legend. She was regarded as the archetypal seductress.

New departures in art

"My work expresses only dreams," commented Erté, a Russian-born artist, who was to become the most sought-after fashion illustrator and costume designer of the 1920s and 1930s. Other artists turned their attention to realism and worked, like Marc Chagall, for the Galerie Der Sturm in Berlin. During the 1930s, the Ballets Russes company, some of whose posters were designed by Jean Cocteau, faced a challenge from the USA when the Charleston craze swept the world. Isadora Duncan, famous for dancing barefoot and dressed in scarves, was one of the first dancers to demonstrate the liberating potential of dance.

While some danced, others demonstrated

Inspired by Serge Diaghilev (circular photo) and his Ballets Russes, creative artists such as Paul Poiret and Josephine Baker were living the high life at fancy dress balls. Elsewhere, mass demonstrations were being held in protest against outdated social structures. Throughout Europe, women were taking to the streets to fight for their rights, sometimes landing themselves in jail like Emmeline Pankhurst, an English suffragette (below right). The end of the war heralded the birth of modernism, a movement in which the Bauhaus, founded in Weimar in 1919, played a key role. This new approach to architecture simplified all the construction elements into their basic geometrical forms. In New York, meanwhile, the nervous atmosphere of the Jazz Age around 1930 manifested itself in towering skyscrapers, such as the Chrysler Building, built in a highly decorative Art Deco style.

for anything Oriental—it was as if a spark of color was all it took to liberate them not only from the corset but also from all conventional restrictions. This wholesale emancipation erupted into opulence and luxury. No sooner had fashion turned its back on the overly ornate style of the Belle Epoque and begun to embrace a move to new-found simplicity of style than it fell under the spell of exotic splendor. At this point, Paul Poiret was still setting the tone in the fashion world and his influence remained unchallenged until just after the First World War. It was he who introduced feather-trimmed, jewel-studded turbans and brilliantly colored harem costumes, featuring pantaloon-style pants and fur-trimmed tunics. His odalisques, for the sake of authenticity, often went barefoot, but their lingerie was trimmed with valuable fur—something they owed to their Russian roots.

Even Isadora Duncan, who was notorious for her liberated style of dance performance, offstage chose to dress in Poiret's lavish and brilliantly colored designs. It was her white, nightdress-like stage costumes that had provided Poiret, by his own confession, with the inspiration for his revolutionary, softly flowing *La Vague* range. She too loved to surprise and had hatched a plan to conceive a child with the incomparable Nijinsky on the occasion of the famous "1002 Nights" ball organized by Poiret. The much-coveted offspring failed to materialize, however, and her ambitious plan to bring a new dance god into the world came to nothing.

Artists and other creative individuals, and others who inhabited the circles they moved in, allowed themselves all kinds of additional liberties. The high, stiff collar, for example, was replaced with a more décolleté style even for daytime wear. Even though this consisted of no more than a modest V neckline, it was enough for the clergy to start issuing warnings of the devastating decline in moral standards. A few daring women went a step further and were soon applying so much makeup that it was barely possible to distinguish them from "ladies of the night." And what is more, consorting with such *demimondaines* suddenly became regarded as fashionable. What, after all, was the difference between an uninhibited dancing star, a kept woman, and a pampered spouse? The latter could certainly learn quite a lot from the others regarding how to make her appearance alluring—and in fact she quite often did so. As a result it became increasingly impossible to identify accurately the social grouping to which an individual belonged. In terms of appearance at least, this hedonistic trend had negated all the differences within society.

While the love affair with Orientalism in all its exotic forms was flourishing in the hothouse atmosphere of heavily perfumed boudoirs, a new fashion had begun to emerge in the fresh air of fashionable spa resorts. This was a fashion that introduced women to a world beyond the nearest bazaar and that reflected their growing enthusiasm for sporting activities. How, after all, were women supposed to cycle, play golf and tennis, or go horseback riding in their customary everyday outfits of tight-fitting jackets and narrow, ankle-length skirts? Admittedly, culottes and even ladies' pants existed even then but they were frowned upon as being so improper that they often had to be concealed beneath a skirt. Furthermore they were made from heavy, rough fabrics, guaranteed to chafe.

It was at this point that an unassuming *modiste* arrived on the scene. She observed that a free spirit could only thrive in a free body and hit upon the simple yet inspired notion of using soft, elasticated fabrics for her designs. In 1913 in Deauville, Gabrielle Chanel introduced her first sportswear designs made of jersey. Though the cut of these was only slightly larger and looser than normal, the stretchy fabric permitted considerable freedom of movement.

For most women, the war drove all preoccupation with fashion from the mind and forced them into working clothes and uniforms—and of course mourning garments. Fashion magazines, such as *Le Style Parisien*, featured designs for appropriate widows' clothing: always high-necked, always black, always shaped to disguise the contours of the body, consisting of full skirts and accessorized with hats, often with veils. However, the longer the war continued and the number of victims mounted, the rules surrounding what constituted correct mourning dress gradually relaxed. In the end, only a very few women spent an entire year dressed in black and limiting their jewelry to the wearing of black jet. Gray and even mauve soon became acceptable alter-

While the rich and beautiful danced,
politicians were arming for war—
the First World War had become inevitable

natives and widows once again began accessorizing their evening wear with diamonds and pearls.

With the men busy fighting at the front, women took over many of their jobs. They found jobs in agriculture and the construction industry, they worked in munitions and other factories, became conductors and drivers on buses and trains, and even took over the running of many firms. Those who volunteered for military service in some cases found themselves right on the frontline where they served in a variety of roles, including nursing. Women thus became accustomed to wearing uniforms.

The severe style of military garments was quickly embraced by the world of fashion. Coats, in particular, came to resemble uniforms and were now designed to completely cover the garments underneath. Before the war, coats were always worn shorter than skirts, allowing a tantalizing glimpse of whatever was underneath. Extravagant shawl collars, often luxuriously lined with fur, were now replaced by severe lapels. Clothes in general became more functional: Narrow pencil skirts were replaced by calf-length pleated skirts, hats became smaller and were worn without decoration, and the wearing of jewelry also became virtually taboo.

Many couture houses, Poiret and Vionnet among them, closed down during the war. Chanel, on the other hand, whose practical jersey ensembles were so well suited to the times, was considered to have done rather well out of the war. After Deauville, she opened another boutique in Biarritz. Parisians, desperate to escape from the city, arrived in these seaside spa resorts with "absolutely nothing to wear" and would stand in line to purchase her new, simply styled outfits, which were worn without the addition of jewelry or any other ornamentation whatsoever.

Initially, fashions in Germany remained untouched by what was happening on the Paris fashion scene. The year 1916 saw the founding of the "Association of German Fashion Designers," an organization concerned less with economic considerations than with the artistic aspects of fashion. Ideological principles in themselves were enough to prevent the fashion-conscious ladies of the German Reich from embracing the soft, fluid styles so popular in France and Italy. Although skirts had been exposing a little ankle since pre-war days, the overall style remained severe. German women preferred well-defined waists, tightly constrained by corsets.

When peace returned, many women were reluctant to relinquish the liberties thrust upon them by the war. Morals had altered along with fashions. Both had become more relaxed. Shorter skirts allowed women more freedom of movement and were more popular than pants, which were still too closely associated with hard work and privation. People were desperate to have fun and to dance. It was the simplest style of dress that eventually provided the greatest freedom of movement—a straight, tube-like shift, which had the additional advantage of being easy to copy: Anyone could reproduce the design at home on their own sewing machine.

Fashion designers needed fresh ideas and new clients. The aristocracy and bourgeoisie were a declining breed, and the Paris scene was now dominated by the *nouveau riche* and dollar-rich Americans, along with actors, artists, writers, and *demimondaines*, all of whom had traditionally helped spin the carousel of fashion. This flamboyant social group hankered after a fashion style that epitomized the rhythms of the incipient Jazz Age.

The time had come for Chanel to say goodbye to the seaside resorts and establish herself in Paris, the fashion capital of the world. In 1919 she opened her first studio in the Rue Cambon where her empire is still based to this day. The same year, Molyneux and Patou also opened major fashion houses in Paris.

The decade that followed was known as the Roaring Twenties, an era famous for the Charleston and jazz, bobbed hairstyles, red lips, free love, cigarettes, birth control, and short skirts, and which ended in the Great Depression. This, at least, has become the collective memory of this period. In reality, however, the *années folles*—the wild, crazy years—did not begin until 1924 and came to an end just five years later, but life was no doubt lived at double the normal pace during this time.

After the horrors of war, people were intent on having fun and this overwhelming desire to make up for lost time happened to coincide with some unlooked-for opportunities. Technological advances and inventions, such as the automobile, household appliances, the telephone, radio, and gramophone, all conspired to make life easier and pleasanter, at

1918

1919

Women on the move

French tennis champion Suzanne Lenglen left a whole generation gaping in astonished admiration and desperate to follow suit.
Remarkable not only for her performances on court but also for her
style, she was the first woman to appear on Wimbledon's
Centre Court with a plunging neckline and bare arms and legs. This
scandalous behavior was only tempered by the fact that she won 81
championships, including 25 Grand Slam victories. One person who
profited from the fame of this tennis legend was fashion designer
Jean Patou, who designed her clothes and was the first couturier to
develop a modern range of sports clothes, ranging from swimming
costumes to ski outfits. Madeleine Vionnet's designs for women
golfers and aviators were not quite so revealing but likewise focused
on allowing the wearer freedom of movement.

L'ESSAYAGE A PARIS (CROYDON-BOURGET)
COSTUME POUR TOURISME AÉRIEN, DE MADELEINE VIONNET
TRAVERSÉE A BORD D'UN AVION DE "L'INSTONE AIR LINE"

The Flapper with her scanty dresses and casual approach to morals epitomized the youth culture of the Roaring Twenties

the same time strengthening the belief in a better future. A whole series of new doors began to open up for women. Having successfully filled a variety of roles during the war years, no one could now expect them to return uncomplainingly to more menial tasks.

They pushed their way into occupations that were more highly regarded and better paid than domestic work. They spent the money they earned at their own discretion, investing it largely in their appearance. After all, what was the point of spending it on anything else, considering that they had just experienced first-hand how one could lose everything from one day to the next? The key was to live for today—while you were still young and alive.

Youth culture was an invention of the 1920s. The events of the Sixties were merely a later revival. In order to be part of it, you had to be fit and reckless. Life was lived in the fast lane, the automobile took the place of the old-fashioned horse and carriage, people depended on alcohol to fuel their bodies and staved off their gnawing hunger or any twinges of guilt by means of nicotine and opium, and then danced the night away. There was no better way than this to keep one's weight down and being slender was vital for the flapper—or *garçonne* as the French call this 1920s fashion look.

The French name originated from a novel entitled *La Garçonne* by Victor Marguerittes, published in 1922. Despite the book being censored as pornography for depicting women who wore their hair short, had careers, wore mannish clothes, and practiced free love, it quietly became a bestseller and for many years its eponymous central character remained a role model for androgynous young women who, as a matter of principle, enjoyed doing whatever was scandalous or forbidden.

In all fairness, they would not otherwise have had much fun at all since there was a complete dearth of men, with women outnumbering men by three to one and even four to one in some cities. Given such a state of affairs, what woman was going to continue harboring idealistic dreams of finding a man to provide for her in return for her devotion as a wife and mother? It was viewed as far better, therefore, to embrace the role of man-eating vamp, a figure whose portrayal in movies was causing such a furor. Consequently, women employed dramatic makeup, began shaving themselves, and wore perfume, as if they were all stars of the big screen.

Apart from these aspects, they appeared somewhat boyish, having none of the usual distinguishing features of their sex. Their hair had, of course, been cut short—but where had breasts, bellies, and butts disappeared to? Exercise, diets, and spa treatments were all part of a modern woman's obligatory routine and the new-style stretch girdles flattened those parts that the corset had once accentuated. However, the old-fashioned matron could hardly reinvent herself as a modern-day flapper girl. In truth, the specter of old age—just like inflation, starvation, unemployment, and political unrest—has simply been edited out of the perceived memory of the 1920s that has been handed down to us. What remains instead is a glittering image of privileged youth, who for a short time made the most of this period of economic and cultural prosperity by turning it into one long party.

At first the Roaring Twenties were characterized by a period of uncertainty among fashion designers. When the couturiers finally agreed on a new direction, the aim was to try to turn the wartime "working girls" back into ladies, which meant, in their view, a return to long skirts. Although hemlines never again brushed the ground, they did drop back to ankle length, only to rise again soon afterwards. The fashionable style of this period eventually settled at calf-length and consisted of a sack-like shift, with a belt or scarf fastened around the hips. The upper part consisted of a loose, blouson-style bodice above a dropped waistline. The overall style was certainly comfortable if not necessarily flattering.

By 1925, hemlines were still just below the knee but two years later they rose for the first time ever to just above the knee. This heralded the typical 1920s silhouette associated with the *années folles*—a simple, straight shift, held by two narrow straps, as worn by that "sweet young thing," the flapper girl.

For the first time in fashion history, evening wear skirts were just as short as daytime wear. It took a lot of imagination to produce a spectacular gown out of such a small amount of fabric. The solution then was the same as it is now: allow a hint of the naked body. This was achieved largely by using transparent fabrics, embellished in strategic places with glass beads or silk fringes, which, while dancing, served

1925

50

to accentuate what they were supposed to be concealing. Legs were covered with fine, sheer stockings, almost like a second skin, only more beautiful. They were made from silk or artificial silk, another name for the newly developed fabric called rayon. In addition, a good deal of bare flesh was also left on show as décolletés continued to plunge almost to the waist, revealing—absolutely nothing.

Anyone whose chest was not in need of flattening wore teddies or combination garments made of silk or rayon. Stockings, blouses, and daytime dresses were also made from artificial silk, an inexpensive, but, above all, washable fabric, which made life so much easier. Thus unencumbered, the flapper was able to dance the nights away, wearing dresses that weighed next to nothing. Ultimately, this act of shedding what amounted to pounds of heavy clothing was of incalculable importance in contributing to women's emancipation.

Since the dress weighed next to nothing, the coat had to be a lavish affair designed to keep out the cold. It was draped around the body like a heavy kimono and anyone with style held it closed with just one hand; alternatively it was fastened with a single large button. The voluminous shawl collar and wide cuffs—or, ideally, the whole coat—were generally made of long-haired fur.

With regard to accessories, it was not value that was important but their shock value. The infinitely long cigarette holder, for example, which could be employed so provocatively and to such lascivious effect, was even more indispensable than a long chain of pearls, which did not even have to be the real thing. Cigarette cases and powder compacts in matching designs—extremely flat and decorated with geometric patterns—were another novelty. Feather boas and fans made from dyed ostrich feathers were essential evening wear accessories and were useful for exploiting any flirtation opportunities.

A *garçonne* needed only one eye to spot her potential prey; the other eye—in true pirate fashion—was kept hidden: by evening beneath a lavishly decorated headband, often made of bead-studded tulle, and by day behind the brim of a cloche hat pulled right down over the face. This type of small hat became increasingly fashionable once long hair, both real and false, had given way to short, cropped styles.

If only one eye was on show, then it was important to make as much of this as possible. Erté, a famous fashion design illustrator who began his career under Poiret, was the first to realize that a thin, fine arc over the eye was the best way to enhance a slender appearance. He recommended that eyebrows be carefully plucked—a procedure that continues to be one of the basic elements of any beauty treatment.

Shoes in the "wild, crazy years" were designed for dancing. They could not be cut too low at the sides or else they might fly off during the Charleston or Shimmy and they were fastened by means of a buttoned ankle strap. The heel was of medium height, waisted and sturdy. It was regarded as the height of elegance to have one's dancing shoes and evening dress made out of the same fabric.

The short, straight skirt only remained in fashion for a few summers, after which handkerchief hemlines, floating scarf and train effects were added to give the illusion of length as well as elegance. Daytime fashions were increasingly influenced by sporting activities. Skirts remained just below the knee, slightly flared, or pleated. Lightweight wool and cotton, or jersey, an increasingly popular fabric, were the most popular materials of the day and sweaters also began to make their first appearance in the world of fashion. The shirtdress, albeit made of silk, also became an essential item of the sporting wardrobe. Unlike the straight lines of the flapper's dress, it accentuated the waist, a style many women, who lacked the benefit of a boyish figure, found more flattering. Towards the end of the decade, the waistline had more or less returned to its natural position and skirts had become longer. The world was heading toward more serious times.

In January 1929, the Ballets Russes performed in Paris for the last time. Its impresario Serge Diaghilev died in August. Diaghilev and his dance creations had survived the First World War, two revolutions in Russia, and constant financial problems and exercised a pivotal influence on art and fashion throughout the world. "Black Thursday," when the New York Stock Exchange crashed on October 24, 1929, finally marked the end of the Roaring Twenties era. Money suddenly became worthless, making the poor even poorer and causing many wealthy citizens to lose their entire fortunes overnight.

1929

FASHION VISIONARY:
Madeleine Vionnet

06.22.1876

–

03.02.1975

Although Vionnet's visionary designs were as slow to gain acceptance as the notion of women wearing trousers, they are now regarded as an equally essential part of women's fashion. Without them the Hollywood glamour of off-the-shoulder gowns, floating around the body like liquid silk, would not exist. Madeleine Vionnet invented the bias cut and was famous for her incomparable skill in creating elegantly draped designs. Designer Azzedine Alaïa, himself a cutting artist of great skill, took months to unravel the secrets of Vionnet's tailoring and he remains the only designer who has succeeded in working out the mysteries of an ivory-colored evening gown from 1935. Now the gown can be admired, as it should be seen, on a mannequin at the Musée de la Mode et du Textile in Paris. Previously it was regarded as an uncompleted draft design. It is one of those masterpieces of design in which a perfect fit depends entirely on a single seam. This was always Madeleine Vionnet's ultimate objective and an art, which no one else has ever equaled.

It must have been her love of geometry that enabled Madeleine Vionnet to create such sophisticated designs from simple basic squares and triangles. Despite her gift for mathematics, Vionnet, who was born in 1876 into a poor family, had to leave school at the age of 12. She was apprenticed to a seamstress, worked for a while in Paris and then, aged 16, went to work in England, where she earned a living for a time working as a washerwoman.

At the age of 20, after a short-lived marriage and the death of her young daughter, Vionnet was put in charge of the studio of London dressmaker Kate Reilly. She returned to Paris in 1900 and joined Callot Soeurs, one of the most important fashion houses of the day. She became the chief assistant to Marie Callot Gerber, the oldest of the three sisters, who was in charge of the firm's artistic design. For the rest of her life, Vionnet felt deeply indebted to her mentor: "It was she who taught me how to make a Rolls Royce—without her I would have only made Fords."

In 1907, Jacques Doucet entrusted her with the task of rejuvenating his couture image. Vionnet did so by banishing corsets and shortening hemlines. Such new creative trends in fashion continued to be resisted and her ideas were unpopular with both clients and sales staff alike. Vionnet realized that in order to put her proposals into practice she would have to set up her own business, but it took another five years before she could do so. By 1912, she was ready but, despite the fact that her incredibly sophisticated designs offered women the freedom of movement they so craved, she was not initially a resounding success. Her—predominantly—naturally colored

Madeleine Vionnet
created all her models around a wooden mannequin. She was a gifted mathematician who put her faith in the geometry of the body itself. Her clothes were designed to follow all the contours of the female figure—a revolutionary concept in its day.

DE LA FUMÉE

ROBE DE MADELEINE VIONNET

Smoke signals

Madeleine Vionnet's gowns were ethereally light. One of the House of Vionnet's models, Sonia, poses here for a famous *Vogue* photo in a design entitled "Bas Relief" which was inspired by the robes worn by dancing nymphs in a ceiling frieze in the Louvre (left page).

"When a woman smiles, her dress should *smile with her*"

clothes were judged to be too plain in comparison to the splendors of Orientalism, which owed its popularity to the Ballets Russes. It was not until after the war—she closed her fashion house during the war years—that Madeleine Vionnet began her rise to greatness.

Vionnet approached the female body like a doctor, intent on preserving its natural beauty. With surgeon-like precision, she began to experiment with the artful use of seam lines that allowed the fabric to follow the curves of a woman's figure. This was a revolutionary departure, as up until then the body had always been expected to adapt to the current fashion. In order to achieve her goal, Vionnet worked much like a sculptor, modeling her designs around wooden mannequins rather than sketching them. This enabled her to drape the fabric around the whole body in order to check how best to accommodate the contours. Her skills in doing this and use of the bias cut, an invention that had previously only ever been used for collars and never for a whole dress, were great assets.

Putting on a Vionnet dress was no easy task, however. Her cutting style was so unusual that many clients found it difficult to find the correct way of getting into the dress. It was not uncommon for women to call on Vionnet in hysterics just before an evening engagement to ask for instructions. In later years, some heiresses had no idea how to wear these valuable gowns and left them to decay in boxes and chests.

The second most important element of the "Vionnet miracle" was the fabric. Only soft fluid material was suitable for following the body's movements which is why she only used silk fabrics like crêpe de Chine, muslin, velvet, and satin. In order to be able to cut her designs on the bias, she always ordered fabrics two yards wider than strictly necessary. In 1918, her main supplier, Bianchini-Ferier, went so far as to develop a fabric specially for Vionnet: crêpe rosalba, an early synthetic material made from silk and acetate.

Vionnet was not particularly interested in color and was content to keep to the various shades of white, one factor in making her gowns resemble Grecian-style robes. Embroidery, rose motifs, and knots were the main forms of ornamentation but even these were not purely decorative, as they served the purpose of gathering the fabric at a strategically important point, removing the need for a seam. Vionnet always ensured that any decorative features did not make the garment too heavy and any embroidery detail was placed along the line of the seam so that it could follow the wearer's natural movement. And when the dance fanatics of the 1920s wanted fringes on their dresses, Vionnet was the only designer who did not use ready-made lengths of fringe trimming. Instead, each fringe thread was individually attached to the garment and knotted one strand at a time in order to preserve the fabric's elasticity. Her garments were intended to be more than mere clothing; they were meant to be a second skin. To quote Madeleine Vionnet: "When a woman smiles, her dress should smile with her."

Madeleine Vionnet was aware of how unusual her techniques were and so she made every effort to prevent them being copied. To this end, she photographed each of her models from the front, from the side, and from behind. These were stuck in a "copyright album" and eventually she accumulated a collection of 75 such designs, which now form the basis of the UFAC (Union Française des Arts du Costume) collection.

Fringe by fringe
While other couturiers sewed yards of these popular fringes onto dance dresses in ready-made lengths, Madeleine Vionnet attached each strand individually. In this way, the dress reflected the tiniest movement of its wearer as if it were a second skin.

*Vionnet's female workforce
did not have to fight for their rights as she looked
after their **social needs** like a mother*

However, Madeleine Vionnet was even more concerned with justice than with the legal rights. She provided her staff with the kinds of welfare benefits that did not become enshrined in law until much later. These included short breaks, paid holidays, and assistance in the event of illness or other emergencies. She also provided a canteen, a resident doctor and dentist, and even an in-house travel agency, which dealt with vacation arrangements for her one thousand or so employees.

She remained very discreet about her private life. She divorced her first husband when she was still quite young, and only close friends were aware that she later married an exiled Russian, Dimitri Netchvolodoff. Known as "Netch," he had joined the household to care for her beloved father when he was terminally ill, and she married him shortly after her father died in the spring of 1923. Netch was at least 18 years younger than Madeleine Vionnet, and was tall, slim, good-looking, and completely unreliable in every respect. The marriage between this white-haired matron, who never made any attempt to look younger than she was, and her kept "beau" lasted 20 years. Vionnet herself, who was possibly the greatest couturière ever, certainly of her time, wore a kind of uniform that lent her a timeless and inconspicuous elegance.

Vionnet's successor in the creative sense was Jacques Griffe, who, as a young tailor in Toulouse, had admired the gifted designer from afar. In 1936, he arrived in Paris, where he managed to obtain a position as a cutter in the House of Vionnet. He remained in that position for three years without ever personally encountering his revered boss. He invited her to the opening of his own couture house in 1946 and a respectful friendship blossomed between the two of them, despite Vionnet being 39 years his senior; their relationship is documented in a comprehensive correspondence. Later on, he bought her country house in Fontainebleau and preserved it exactly as she had left it. Remaining true to everything his mentor had taught him, Jacques Griffe tried out all his designs on a wooden mannequin that Vionnet had given him—a lifelike copy of the one that she had used to create her designs for so many decades.

Madeleine Vionnet never really understood how to market herself successfully. Although the silhouette she developed was characteristic of the elegance of the 1930s and the blossoming era of Hollywood glamour, she herself was completely detached from worldly things. She hated traveling and avoided fashionable society. Consequently, once her fashion house closed down in 1939, she was virtually forgotten, even though she lived to be almost 100 years of age and continued to take an active interest in fashion trends right until the end of her life. Without Vionnet's "copyright albums" and many of her original designs, the Musée de la Mode et du Textile in Paris would never have been founded. Unfortunately it was not opened until after Madeleine Vionnet's death at the age of 98. Then, if not before, the world began to appreciate what leading fashion icons such as Dior, Alaïa, Miyake, Yamamoto had understood for a long time: "The art of couture had never reached a higher standard."

Compared with Chanel, Vionnet remains still relatively unknown to this day, perhaps because she was more concerned with producing Rolls Royces whereas Chanel's reputation was based on her popular little black "Ford of the fashion world," as *Vogue* in the US once commented.

The sphinx of fashion
No one produced more bafflingly intricate cutting patterns than Vionnet. For many years after her death, this 1935 dress of ivory crêpe was regarded as an unfinished design until Azzedine Alaïa, himself a gifted cutting technician, managed to work out the correct way of wearing it.

THE PRAGMATIST:
Coco Chanel

08.19.1883
–
01.10.1971

Mademoiselle Chanel was responsible for modernizing fashion. For the first time ever, the focus was on functionality and comfort rather than impact. This liberating change of direction made Chanel irresistible in the eyes of her admirers. With her boyish appearance and active lifestyle, and her sharp tongue, she represented a welcome challenge to men who had grown used to their own success. Gabrielle Chanel had nothing to lose; she only stood to gain.

She was born on August 19, 1883, in Saumur in the Loire valley, the second child of unmarried parents, who did not get married until 15 months after her birth. The union between her father, a totally unreliable street vendor, and mother, a hard-working farmer's daughter from the Auvergne, proved anything but happy. Following her mother's death when Gabrielle was just 11 years old, her father abandoned her and her two siblings to the care of a convent-run orphanage and disappeared from her life, never to be seen again.

Chanel was taught to sew by the nuns who ran the orphanage and at the age of 18 she was taken on as a salesgirl in a lingerie shop in Moulins. In her spare time, she worked for a seamstress, mending the uniforms of army officers stationed in the nearby garrison, and also sang in a local cabaret. Her great ambition was to become a famous variety singer but according to one singing teacher, she had the "voice of a crow." Despite her limited talent for singing, she nevertheless became a favorite with the officers. The two main songs in her repertoire were "Ko Ko Ri Ko" and "Qui qu'a vu Coco?" and these led to the nickname "Coco," by which she was to become internationally famous.

She was just 20 when she took the next step in her career, openly becoming the mistress of an infantry officer, Etienne Balsan, and living at his country estate near Paris. The ladies of the *demimonde*, who visited with their aristocratic escorts, admired Chanel not only for the way in which she sat in a saddle like a man, but also for her simple straw hats, which she designed and made herself. She soon found herself inundated with commissions.

However, it was not until she met up with Arthur "Boy" Capel, an English coal-mining heir and polo player, that she had the idea of opening her own business. She moved to Paris, where she lived in Capel's apartment whilst running a milliner's shop from Balsan's apartment. She was obliged to accept that Boy Capel would never marry her but managed at least to persuade him to invest in her enterprise. In 1919, thanks to his assistance, she was able to open her own couture salon in the Rue Cambon. That same year Boy Capel died in an automobile accident, on his way from Paris after a rendezvous with Chanel to join his English wife in the south of France. He had

---

Coco Chanel

had a gift for showing herself off to the best advantage. Over the years and despite her provincial origins, she came to be known as an icon of Parisian elegance. With her thin, elegant figure, 50-year old Coco Chanel posed for the well-known photographer Horst P. Horst wearing a simple sweater with ornate jewelry and a bow in her hair.

Chanel's timeless elegance

The photo shows the "little black number" designed in 1926 which immortalized Chanel. Her first perfume Chanel No. 5 was the only thing Marilyn Monroe wore in bed... Be that as it may, both these creations remain bestsellers to this day.

Chanel found inspiration for her fashion ideas among her *lovers' wardrobes*

married a woman of his own social standing but had continued his relationship with Coco, who apparently never again met anyone she loved as much as Boy Capel—though it was not for want of searching.

Chanel became involved with the Parisian circle of trendsetting artists. She met Diaghilev, impresario of the Ballets Russes, as well as Jean Cocteau, an all-round genius, whose rehabilitation treatments for opium addiction she later paid for. Her seduction skills succeeded in capturing Igor Stravinsky, but failed to have the same effect on Picasso. She travelled to Venice with her best friend and patron of the arts, Misia, holding court there like a queen. One of her suitors was the Russian Grand Duke Dimitri whose dubious role in the murder of Rasputin, the Russian mystic and faith healer, had forced him into exile. Dimitri lavished opulent Byzantine jewelry on his beloved and introduced her to Ernest Beaux, former perfumer to the Tsars. It was Beaux who created the perfume Chanel No. 5 in 1920.

Chanel's penchant for anything masculine became the driving influence in her life and fashion designs. Beginning with canotiers, charming little straw hats that resembled circular saws in shape, she continued with loose-fitting outfits made of jersey, an "inferior" material which had hitherto been used mainly for men's underwear. Coco was constantly raiding her lovers' wardrobes, pulling out a tweed jacket here, or a pullover there, making it fit by means of a belt around the waist and finishing it off with some striking jewelry. Chanel was regarded as an expert in fashion jewelry—yet considering how she had had real jewelry showered upon her by Grand Duke Dimitri, and also by his successor, the Duke of Westminster, she had no scruples about wearing strands of fake pearls or other costume jewelry. Ideally, she liked to combine the generous gifts her lovers gave her with jewelry she had created herself, both in order to be provocative and to emphasize her independence.

But Chanel's life was not always happy. She would have liked a more permanent relationship with the Duke of Westminster, whose friendship meant that she could count Churchill and the Prince of Wales among her circle of friends. Already in her mid-forties, she tried to provide him with an heir. Despite surgical intervention and "humiliating acrobatics," her efforts came to nothing and she lost the richest man in England to other women half her age.

It was certainly not his vast fortune that she hankered after. Chanel had, by her own efforts, become the richest businesswoman in the world. Yet it was once again her hunger for the unconditional love that had been lacking during her childhood that could not be appeased. Consequently, she continued to entertain a succession of all kinds of would-be lovers. The tall, genial British aristocrat, Westminster, was followed by a stocky, difficult, and "demonic" illustrator, Paul Iribe, from the Basque country. Their relationship almost led to marriage, but Iribe collapsed from a heart attack before Chanel's very eyes, leading to his death just a few hours later.

The next, and perhaps last, on Chanel's long list of lovers was German secret service officer Baron Hans Günther von Dincklage, who was her junior by a good few years. She called him "sparrow" and put her honor at risk on his account, going into exile in Switzerland with him when she was accused of being a collaborator. Later, she used to joke about the "enemy in her bed," who had indeed cost her a great deal in every respect: "A woman of my age cannot be expected to demand to see a man's passport if he wants to sleep with her." This sentiment was something the French could empathize with and they forgave her.

The chic world of Coco Chanel

It was not the outfit the mannequin modeled in 1958 that created such a stir but Chanel's own costume of light tweed, which remains a classic to this day. Chanel liked men and their fashions and men also liked Chanel: she was even permitted to go hunting with Winston Churchill. On the beach (below right) with Serge Lifar, star of the Ballets Russes, she wore men's trousers and espadrilles, complemented with pearls and a turban! No sooner had Chanel been seen wearing this light, yet elegant ensemble in Biarritz (below left), than it became hugely popular in other fashionable seaside resorts and no amount of unkind caricatures could alter that fact. Chanel and her friends, such as pianist Marcelle Meyer, moved around with casual ease in their jersey outfits.

Karl Lagerfeld
took over the reins to continue Mademoiselle Chanel's legacy in 1983 and even this rough sketch shows how well
he grasped the essence of her style. Thanks to Lagerfeld, the House of Chanel is even more popular today than ever.

Chanel returned to Paris early in 1954 at the age of 70. Her first collection was considered a flop by the French but the American press greeted with enthusiasm her new classic tweed suits, featuring boxy, braid-trimmed jackets with gold, lion's-head buttons. To this day, elegant, style-conscious women still wear Chanel and "the little black dress" which immortalized Chanel even before the war. Her stroke of genius in 1926 was to transform the working clothes of poor servant girls into the simplest and most stylish fashion statement of all time—substituting the apron for a rope of pearls. She herself wore this new evening uniform with incomparable allure—as befitted someone who, throughout her lifetime, had always been the best model for her own emancipating style of fashion.

They defined their era

Jean Patou	Edward Molyneux	Lucien Lelong	Jeanne Lanvin

Jean Patou (1880–1936), leading exponent of the "garçonne look," was famous for his pale, pastel-colored, pearl-embroidered dresses for dance-mad flappers. His main contribution, however, was to sportswear. He designed a spectacular "uniform" for tennis champion, Suzanne Lenglen: short narrow-pleated skirts in white silk, teamed with white, jersey knitted cardigans and practical headbands. Simplicity and comfort, combined with elegance were the hallmarks of his daytime ensembles.

After Princess Marina of Greece commissioned him to design her wedding dress and trousseau for her marriage to the Duke of Kent, Edward Molyneux (1891–1974) became popular with aristocrats and film stars alike. He modernized the Empire look by giving it a severely tailored cut. He was also a master of practical daytime outfits and was hailed as the inventor of the three-quarter length coat.

Lucien Lelong (1889–1958) was probably the most innovative of all the great couturiers of the pre-war period. He had studied economics and introduced the idea of *editions*—a reasonably priced alternative range. He also sold lingerie and stockings as designer goods. One of his main achievements, however, was to ensure that during the German occupation, the fashion houses remained in Paris and were not transferred to Berlin.

Jeanne Lanvin (1867–1946) began her career when she gave birth to her only child at the age of 30. Her love for Marguerite inspired her to design delicate, colorful clothes—miniature versions of the embroidered, ankle-length *Robes de Styles*, which were proving a delightful alternative to the provocatively short and flimsy flapper costumes. In 1926 she also began designing clothes for men, thereby providing fashion for the entire family.

Madness
versus
FASHION IN HARD TIMES
Reason

The stock market crash of 1929 marked the beginning of uncertain times, characterized by mass unemployment and political turmoil. In 1932 there were 14 million unemployed in the USA, 6 million in Germany, and 3 million in the UK. Many of the American couture buyers did not make the trip to France, and even the big US fashion houses, which customarily bought the rights to a range of designs every season so as to reproduce them in the States, now took on only one or two licenses and copied them endlessly. In the French fashion industry alone, 10,000 people lost their jobs.

People who had managed to hang on to their fortunes were no longer ostentatious about it. Rather than being a sign of sensitivity toward others, this was often simply because they were in tune with modern times; Art Deco and Cubism had sparked a trend for geometric lines, while revolutionary architects like Le Corbusier and influential interior designers like Jean-Michel Frank had changed the

look of the home by reawakening a taste for functional design. Chrome, mirrors, and glass were the new look for the home, the antithesis of coziness. Towering skyscrapers like the Rockefeller Center in New York and bridges like the Golden Gate Bridge in San Francisco were acclaimed as technological marvels and encouraged a belief in progress.

Yet not everyone could tolerate this severe modernism for long. Within a few months, the socialite Carlos de Beistegui had transformed the famous "living machine" which Le Corbusier had designed for him on the Champs-Elysées into something out of a neo-Baroque fantasy. After a short apprenticeship with Le Corbusier, Horst P. Horst, one of the stars of fashion photography, also found that he could no longer make any headway with the austere diktats of the Modern, remarking, "Everyone longs for beauty—why should the working man live in a prison cell?"

Despite their poverty, ordinary people wanted to maintain a certain status. Good clothing was never

---

Farewell to the Old World
In 1938, the year before he emigrated from Paris to New York, Horst P. Horst photographed French elegance in front of an old map of the world: a waisted jacket made of nubbed wool with carnations on the lapels, and a pleated skirt, suede gloves, and a hat.

Women's weapons

Marlene Dietrich gave herself an androgynous look with a tailcoat, top hat, and a cigarette in 1930. Society ladies liked to appear casual in pajama pants and hand-knitted tops. Ginger Rogers, on the other hand, was soft and affectionate in the arms of her partner, Fred Astaire. He put a brave face on it when she tickled him under the nose with her ostrich feathers, setting off his allergy, as she did in the 1935 film *Top Hat*.

Edward Steichen, the patriarch of American fashion photographers, documented the elegance of the prewar era with two evening dresses from 1933, both featuring the plunging backs so popular at the time. Women had to wait until after the war for stockings in different colors.

Elegance at any price

Whether pieces were exclusive and expensive, like the fox fur stole worn with one of Elsa Schiaparelli's white-lined black dresses (left), or inexpensive and youthful, like cork sandals and fashionable charm bracelets, in 1937 the fashion world was still in good condition.

The more demure the outfit,
the crazier the hat, *always sitting*
at a jaunty angle on the head

more highly prized than during the Depression. The woman of the 1930s always wore long dresses in the evening, and it was silk or nothing, as only this, the most expensive of fabrics, fell on the diagonal in such a streamlined way, flattering the body without exposing it. Madeleine Vionnet's brilliant new technique of cutting the material on the bias was universally copied. The ingenuity of this lay in the way the cut gave the material elasticity, long before the invention of lycra. These evening dresses of shimmering silk satin needed no fastenings, but could simply be pulled on over the head or stepped into. The generous necklines also made this easier, particularly the deeply plunging backs. Many attribute this development to the prudish American film censors, who concentrated only on banning expanses of cleavage. So Hollywood showed bare backs, something which, like everything else from that dream factory, was copied everywhere else. These low-cut necklines were often simply yet effectively emphasized with a single dangling string of pearls.

Dancing became hugely popular. Swing was in, and everyone danced to the sound of the big band. Foxtrot and rumba were up-and-coming trends, and the tango remained a firm favorite. Fred Astaire and Ginger Rogers were the prime dancers in the movies, and from 1934 to 1939 their eight musicals, including *Swing Time*, sent out the message that a couple only had to dance in time to the music in order to be happy. Ginger Rogers designed many of her own costumes, much to the irritation of her partner, whom she almost knocked out with her heavy, pearl-encrusted sleeves. She also had a penchant for ostrich feathers; Fred Astaire was allergic.

The best thing for bare shoulders was, of course, fur, especially silver fox, and laying two whole skins about one's shoulders was seen as particularly chic. The height of glamor, however, was an entire cape made of white fox fur. Anyone who could not stretch to that went for a velvet cape or a brightly colored chiffon wrap. And for those who could not even afford silk, Coco Chanel had the answer; she reckoned with the economic crisis by including woolen dresses in her evening collection.

Women knew how to make the best of the downturn. Those who could not afford to buy new dresses would simply lengthen the ones that they had. At the time, very short hemlines were no longer in fashion in any case, but fell to about mid-calf, and anything shorter was artfully made into the correct length with ribbons, panels, and extra material, or fur. Using the very smallest pieces of fur at the neckline or as cuffs gave clothing a hint of luxury.

Wealthy women wore fur during the day, too. Persian lamb, broadtail, beaver, and otter were also made into three-quarter-length coats and worn with the obligatory princess dress. This was cut from a single piece of material, and the waist was emphasized with a narrow belt. Film costumes also featured a slender silhouette with a clearly defined waist. The lapels were wide and the necklines plunging, at least in summer, and a blouse was worn underneath.

A ladylike outfit always included gloves and a hat. The sensible fashions of the 1930s were paired with the most outlandish headpieces. At first the trend was for small, flat hats pinned high on top of the hair, and then came a vast array of berets and caps, boaters, cloches, porkpie hats, and every kind of fantastical creation. The only thing they had in common was that they were all worn at a jaunty angle, tilted over the forehead. The foremost hat designer was Elsa Schiaparelli, who had studied the craft of neither the milliner nor the couturier, yet who largely shaped the fashion of the 1930s.

The trend for tiny waists gave new impetus to the bodice industry, now using very light materials like Lastex, which exerted only slight pressure, and only below the bust, which was supported separately. The American company Warners introduced the first bras with different cup sizes. As before, stockings were made of skin-colored silk or artificial silk, and were only superseded by "nylons" in 1939.

Accessories, for many the only affordable kind of adornment, were essential for updating a woman's wardrobe. Slim, envelope-shaped bags were carried under the arm (later to be reincarnated as the clutch, the "It bag" of the 1970s). The alternative was a small purse with snap-shut clasps, made of silver or—a real novelty—plastic. Costume jewelry was accepted everywhere, again thanks to Chanel's bold step of merrily interspersing real and imitation gems.

By now pants, especially silk evening pajamas, were to be found in the wardrobe of every elegant city woman. Yet in a way they went unnoticed; they were not seen as acceptable in public. It is significant that the fashion magazine *Vogue* presented pants with sweaters as women's clothing for the first time in only 1939.

Sport was a great leveler of political differences. Physical training and gymnastics associations mushroomed all over Europe, nudist camps opened, and the trendsetters and the affluent indulged in driving automobiles and flying. Cycling, tennis, and golf remained popular pastimes. At long last, bathing became a pleasurable activity, due to the invention of Tampax and new fabrics that allowed bathing costumes to cling to the body without the risk of losing their shape in the water.

Germany had a well-established international profile in fashion, but politically the National Socialists were moving further and further away from the rest of the world. Gradually the Allies were forced to realize that Hitler's promises of peace were not to be trusted, and the threat of war loomed ever more threateningly on the horizon. Resistance began to gather, and, as is common in dark times, sparked a great longing for opulence and beauty. In the early summer of 1938 the British king and queen visited France, setting off a wave of new romantic fashion. Even Chanel, the inventor of modern chic, suddenly began to design evening dresses that, with their padded skirts and lavish embellishments, were greatly reminiscent of the supposedly long-forgotten hoop skirts. Everyday fashion, on the other hand, became increasingly austere. By 1934, shoulders had become wider, and four years later they were further enhanced with excessive pads, disrupting the proportions to the point that only a shorter and wider skirt looked good with them. Shoes also had to have greater "volume;" women wore wedge heels, and later platform soles.

1939   In 1939 Hitler provoked the outbreak of the Second World War. Fashion seemed to have already foreseen the catastrophe as, toward the end of the decade, clothing took on an almost uniform-like appearance: square shoulders, frog fastenings, narrow skirts, plumed hats, gauntlet gloves, shoulder bags, and flat walking shoes. The most important thing was an immaculate appearance, as though every woman were an eager recruit. Fashion took its cue from perfection rather than innovation.

War and couture are seemingly completely at odds with one another; on the one hand the destruction of the world, on the other the creation of beautiful things. And yet fashion, this utter frivolity, provided a natural outlet for the defiance of the French citizens. No matter how scarce material was or how strict the rules and regulations, even during the Second World War French women lived up to their reputation as the best dressed in the world. Against all the odds, they expressed their independence by cultivating an extremely extravagant look. Everywhere else women saw it as their duty to dress as inconspicuously and modestly as possible, but their French counterparts nailed their colors to the mast; blood-red lipstick and colorful clothing, preferably in blue, white, and red, strengthened morale and resistance.

Hats and shoes became higher and higher. Women teetered on platform soles or wooden or cork wedge heels, and on their heads they balanced exuberant creations made of every imaginable material, from newspaper with a veil to flowers, velvet, and feathers. Milliners were the only sector of the industry that was not rationed on materials.

Between the flamboyant head and the clumpy footwear, the thin body no longer warranted much attention, even when the skimpy garments in which it was clad were made of pure silk. This was seen as a scandal. "While we wear artificial silk, French women swathe themselves in meters of the real thing," complained American *Vogue*. Yet French women held true to the saying that "all's fair in love and war," and gave their imagination free rein. This meant provocation—proving to the *Boches*, as the French disparagingly called the Germans, that Paris alone had the flair for creative fashion. The Nazis thought that Berlin or Vienna should be the home of haute couture, the most French of institutions.

Lucien Lelong, the president of the Chambre Syndicale de la Couture from 1936 to 1946, had to use all his powers of persuasion to keep the luxury industry in Paris. He managed to negotiate certain guarantees for haute couture, thus ensuring both his own survival and that of houses including Lanvin, Fath, and Rochas.

So it came to pass that Paris reveled in extravagance while extreme thrift ruled fashion in every other country. In 1941 all the German fashion

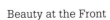

Beauty at the Front

Even in wartime, women want to be chic. Female soldiers selected their perfume carefully, and Lady Mountbatten had her uniform tailored on Savile Row so that she could appear at her husband's side. Those who did not go to the Front could at least look pretty, wearing espadrilles while cycling, and pairing a smart hat with a narrow skirt. At the end of the war everyone flocked to the cinema to see *Les Enfants du Paradis*.

A fight for survival

In 1937 the star photographer Cecil Beaton portrayed the dread of war with a model airplane on the wall. A few years later protective suits for the bunker were recommended for the elegant lady instead of Molyneux outfits. Was Uncle Sam happy with women going to the Front in shimmering artificial silk? A Frenchwoman would never have responded to the call without applying lipstick. Marlene Dietrich donned the uniform of a marine officer in 1940 for the film *Seven Sinners*, while the handsome Jean Marais played the "Beast" in France's seminal film *Beauty and the Beast*, released just after the war.

Frenchwomen lived
by the saying
"all's fair in love and war"

houses were incorporated into the Berliner Modell-gesellschaft, with production solely for export. In Britain, rationing from 1941 led to painfully exacting regulations: purchase of material per item of clothing, maximum skirt length and width, maximum number of pleats, buttons, and accessories—everything was regulated. Wearing silk was considered absolutely taboo among the civilian population, as it was used to make parachutes. But, conversely, it seemed wonderfully frivolous to make underwear out of parachute silk—preferably retrieved from a shot down enemy pilot—even though it rustled and chafed.

Norman Hartnell, the dressmaker to the British queen, along with Charles Creed and "Captain" Edward Molyneux, who had both learned their trade in Paris but had returned to England following the outbreak of war, were tasked with designing uniforms for women in the army. Lady Edwina Mountbatten, a member of one of the richest families in England, preferred to have her uniform altered by one of the famous gentleman tailors on Savile Row—to make it a little more flattering, a little shorter, and much more chic.

Six and a half million British women saw active duty during the war, and four of them managed to rise to the rank of General. In the US there were two million voluntary workers in 1942, which soon became a paid labor force of four million. From telephone operators to female engineers, this new "women's power" was widely applauded. Only a decade earlier, women who had become accustomed to independence during the First World War had struggled to devote themselves once again to home and hearth, but now willingness to engage in the war effort outside the home was once again seen as a feminine virtue. The brave little soldier's wife was diligent, thrifty, efficient, and resourceful.

When the US government made it a national goal to reduce production of fabric by 15 percent, there was a "freeze" in fashion. They conjectured that if styles did not change, then available clothing could be handed down. In fact, between 1941 and 1945 there was no significant change in fashion, but the Americans moved ahead with sportswear. Elsa Schiaparelli said proudly, "it is astonishing how inexpensive and tasteful sportswear is in America."

Ironically, it was during the war that many people first developed a feel for quality. They learned to appreciate durable material that also felt good against the skin, such as cotton, wool, and linen. The way in which it was processed also suddenly became important. Once women began to produce everything themselves, they were able to tell good craftsmanship from bad.

The war had the effect of ensuring Hollywood's status as the factory of dreams. This was where the role models for millions were created. There was no longer an international society, art, and theater scene with a press to report on it; almost everywhere cultural life was in disarray, and if there were any developments in individual countries, such as France, they went unnoticed by the rest of the world. Only film could still spread the idea of utopia among the masses.

In 1939 the role that all the Hollywood beauties had been hoping for went to an actress from England, of all places; Vivien Leigh was cast as Scarlett O'Hara in *Gone with the Wind*. She proved that she was the right choice with a passionate performance that won her an Oscar. A year later she was awarded another Oscar for another iconic American role, Blanche Dubois in *A Streetcar Named Desire*, thus establishing her place in the history of film.

Other big stars came from abroad, including Greta Garbo, the mysterious "divine woman," and Ingrid Bergman, both from Sweden. German Marlene Dietrich became a style icon with her liking for men's suits. The American star triumvirate of the time was made up of Joan Crawford, Bette Davis, and Katharine Hepburn, all strikingly independent, powerful women—as the war and so-called women's films demanded that they be.

After the end of the war no one wanted to give way to feelings of triumphalism; the memories were too bleak and the cost of the conflict too ghastly. Yet people's zest for life could not be repressed. Interest in theater, film, and music blossomed, particularly in Germany, where people were now able to discover plays by Jean-Paul Sartre, Arthur Miller, Thornton Wilder, and Tennessee Williams, along with works written in exile by Bertholt Brecht. Cultural life had survived without interruption in France. Jean Anouilh's first plays were staged with great success

New horizons

The war was scarcely over before upscale fashions were being shown once again. In September 1945 the US designer David Crystal made the coveted new material rayon into a very sophisticated cross between a blouse and a jacket.

The theater of fashion

At the end of the war the illustrator and designer Christian Bérard (1902–1949) created the backdrop for a "theater of fashion." Due to the shortage of fabric the haute couture creations were shown on small wire puppets, with minimal expense. It was spectacularly successful.

Longing for a happy ending

The splendid weddings of kings and queens excited the war-weary public as much as films with a happy ending. The British crown princess Elizabeth married Philip Mountbatten in 1947 and wore a satin dress made by her court tailor, Norman Hartnell. The Cannes Festival, founded in the same year, made the Croisette (below) into an annual Boulevard of the Vanities.

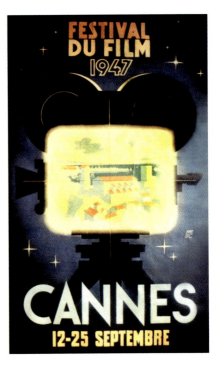

during the occupation, and the Comédie Française performed Paul Claudel's *The Satin Slipper*, directed by Jean-Louis Barrault, to a full house every night during the war. Yet film held the greatest interest for the French. A total of 278 films were completed during the war, including unconventional works like Jean Cocteau's poetical fairy tale *Beauty and the Beast*. The consummate masterpiece of that time was Marcel Carné's *Les Enfants du Paradis*, which stunned the world in its final version in 1945.

The French enthusiasm for film led to the founding of the Cannes Festival in 1947. Year after year, cinema devotees from all over the world gravitate to the Côte d'Azur during the beautiful month of May.

Social life did not bounce back quite as quickly as cultural life. There was an enduring sense of shame which forbade simple amusement. Instead of evening dresses, *Vogue*, for instance, recommended the more discreet "ambassador's dress," which owed its name to embassy receptions. It was a narrow sheath dress with long sleeves and a high, square neckline. Jewelry and flashy embellishments were frowned upon.

An unusual spectacle restored haute couture to the public consciousness in 1945. Due to a shortage of fabric it was impossible to put on big shows, so the idea of a "theater of fashion" came about. The couturiers demonstrated their great craftsmanship on small dolls made of wire, which required only a small outlay on material. With their pretty little plaster heads and hair made of thread, the 200 dolls served as ambassadresses for fashion. The all-rounder Christian Bérard, a talented painter, outstanding illustrator, and gifted designer, created the perfect stage for this original fashion extravaganza. After a successful launch in the Musée des Arts Décoratifs in Paris, the Couture Show went on tour across America, winning back former customers and enticing new ones.

Although America had been effectively free of fashion during the war, and had learned to live in casual, everyday clothes, it succumbed to the fascination of haute couture, which cared nothing for practicality or cheapness, but offered a feast for the senses. This fulfilled the prediction made by the exclusive fashion magazine *Harper's Bazaar* at the end of the war, looking optimistically to the future:

"We are waiting for birds of paradise, not little brown hens." Yet the colorful feathers were a little while longer in coming. It was as if imagination was being reined in. Even the younger couturiers felt bound by duty during the difficult postwar period, not daring to be extravagant.

They drew on the memory of the artistic creativity of Elsa Schiaparelli and the glamour of the Hollywood stars dressed by Adrian.

THE SURREALIST:

Elsa Schiaparelli

09.10.1890
–
11.13.1973

Elsa Schiaparelli inscribed the words "For Sport" on the door of her first fashion salon in Paris. Yet she earned her place in the history of fashion not for her sportswear, but for the most flamboyant creations of all time.

She simply wanted to dress the modern American woman, who had no need for complicated bespoke clothing, but rather functional separates that could be worn in a variety of different combinations. Elsa's very first knitwear collections were the forerunners of *prêt-à-porter* (ready-to-wear), which had not yet come into existence. She had her first success with a small, practical sweater which set itself apart from anything else with a large white bow design, like a butterfly, on a black background. It was bought by a working woman, Anita Loos, who had come to fame with her novel *Gentlemen Prefer Blondes*. Providentially, she worked in Hollywood, where her becoming top did not go unnoticed. The American department store Strauss promptly ordered 40 of the sweaters, and Schiaparelli's customers suddenly included half of Hollywood—Katharine Hepburn, Joan Crawford, and Greta Garbo among them.

At some point, it is inevitable that even the most practical woman will want to shed her work clothes and slip into an evening dress. In 1933 Elsa designed her first long gown, a narrow column of white crêpe de Chine, complemented with a dress coat with tails that crossed at the back. The design was a smash hit, and formed the launch pad for Schiaparelli's haute couture career.

Schiaparelli's golden period was the five years from the opening of her salon in the Place Vendôme, opposite the Ritz, up until the outbreak of the Second World War. Influential customers such as Nancy Cunard and Daisy Fellowes, both heiresses of substantial means, defected from Chanel and Patou to Schiaparelli. The press was full of rave reviews and praise for her creativity, boldness, and uniqueness, and artists felt magically inspired by her. Elsa's collections brought Surrealism to fashion by employing the movement's basic principle of uprooting familiar objects from their normal surroundings and placing them in a quite different context. Her shoe hat is famous, its red sole pointing pertly upwards. Other creations included gloves with golden fingernails or the "tears" dress with a print that suggested severe wear. The matching cape caused scandal with its real rips, just as punk fashion would do four decades later.

Salvador Dalí helped to create the "ripped" material, and also designed a black velvet bag for Schiaparelli in the shape of a telephone with a golden dial. He also painted the giant lobster onto the white evening dress for which "Schiap," as she was known to her friends, became famous.

Critical distance

Elsa Schiaparelli often treated new acquaintances with aristocratic aloofness, captured in this 1937 portrait by Horst. She was a generous friend to artists, but those who worked with her feared the tantrums of this temperamental Italian.

Inspired by art

Baron de Meyer, who created a theatrical shoot for her quilted red Peking cape in 1933, was Schiaparelli's favorite photographer. Her friend Salvador Dalí provided the template for the "tear" dress with headscarf, which foreshadowed punk fashion, and for her appetizing lobster-painted evening dress in 1937. Cocteau drew two profiles that formed a vase filled with roses, and Vertès painted caricatures of people from the 1890s for a nostalgic evening gown.

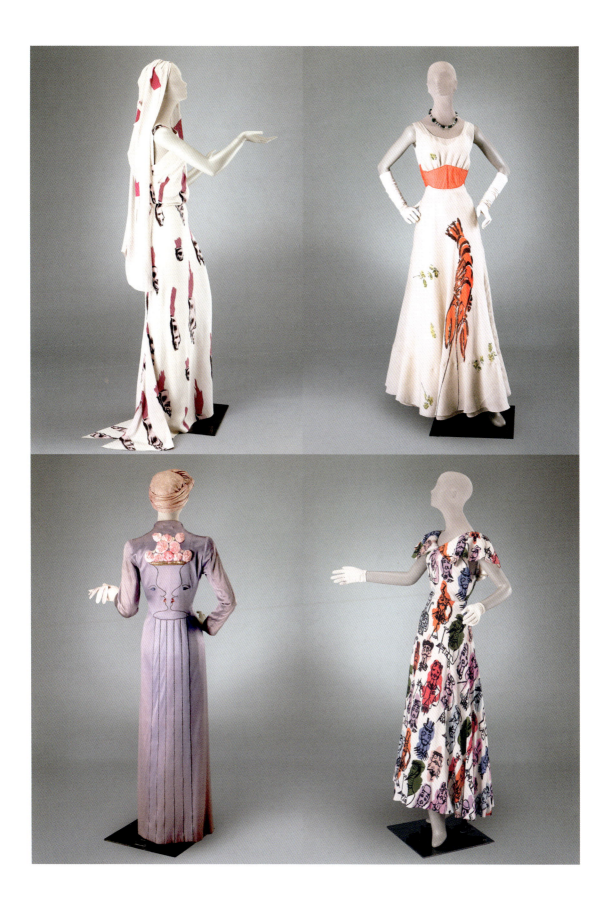

*Schiap's love of surreal jokes
and **desire to shock** made her
an ideal collaborator for artists*

Her instinct for surreal jokes and desire to shock made Elsa the ideal partner for artists. Picasso inspired her to print material with newspaper articles, and Jean Cocteau sketched poetic designs for embroidery. The House of Lesage rose to every challenge that Schiap set its embroiderers, resulting in pieces that rivaled works of art found in museums.

Surrounded by the most exciting artists of her day and with the ability to make them enthusiastic about fashion, Schiap was spurred on to create the most audacious collections in terms of both the designs and their presentation. Every show was a theatrical spectacle, an idea only taken up much later by Kenzo, Gaultier, and Galliano. Unsurprisingly, she became the darling of the press, much to the chagrin of Coco Chanel, who vied with her for the patronage of the richest customers and the approval of the best artists.

Elsa's upbringing had given her certain advantages. Born in Rome as the second daughter of a well-off, cultured family, she studied philosophy and wrote a volume of poetry before traveling abroad. In London in 1914 she fell head over heels in love with the shadowy mystic Count William de Wendt de Kerlor, and married him in haste, against the wishes of her parents. The five years that followed were not recorded in her memoirs. In this time we can assume that she lost her whole dowry and the scales fell from her eyes. We only know that Elsa traveled first to Nice and then to New York with Count Kerlor, who had virtually no money of his own. There, under very difficult circumstances, she gave birth to her only child, her daughter Yvonne, nicknamed Gogo. Her husband embarked on a passionate affair with the dancer Isadora Duncan, and Elsa was granted a divorce.

After a brief fling with an Italian tenor who unexpectedly died of meningitis, Elsa was on her own with her daughter once again, and in financial straits. In June 1922 a friend helped her to move to Paris, where the maestro Paul Poiret encouraged her to go into fashion herself. Elsa inherited her love of color from her renowned mentor. She gave the name "shocking pink" to the strident hue that she used for everything from packaging and lipstick to richly embroidered evening capes.

She wanted to shock at any cost, calling her last collection in 1952 "Shocking Elegance," and her 1954 autobiography *Shocking Life*. Her most successful perfume, launched in 1938, was, of course, given the name "Shocking," and has a good anecdote attached to it. The story goes that the artist Leonor Fini modeled the bottle, in the shape of a female torso, on the tailor's dummy with the dimensions of the Hollywood star Mae West that stood in Schiap's atelier. Supposedly West had given it to her instead of turning up in person for a fitting, and Schiap decided to put this gift to her own use.

Nothing was impossible for Schiaparelli. Aspirin tablets were made into necklaces; bits of plastic, beetles, and bees were used as materials for costume jewelry; "vulgar" zippers adorned haute couture evening gowns, and whole dresses were made of new synthetic materials such as cellophane and Rhodophane. Schiap found buttons boring, so she made little sculptures out of them: crickets, circus horses, trapeze artists, crowns, or sugar cubes. She had an inexhaustible talent for invention, but her greatest achievement was perhaps the way in which, despite her complete lack of experience, she "revolutionized fashion from 1930 to 1940," as the actress Arletty, who once worked as a model for Schiaparelli, wrote in her memoirs.

A study in lighting
In fashion shoots Horst P. Horst liked to keep a certain distance from his subject, a technique ideally suited to Schiaparelli's designs and her attitude. In this 1940 shoot in New York, this famous lighting technique perfectly emphasizes the decorative bow on the back of her dress.

Shades of Dada

Schiap's idea to use a shoe as a hat caused a furor among the Surrealists, as did her "peephole" and diamante eyebrow on an evening cap. Others found her Dadaesque designs simply shocking, including her little tulle hat, which resembled a hairnet, or costume jewelry made of guinea fowl feathers. Aware of this, she named her perfume, which came in a bottle modeled on the bust of Mae West, "Shocking."

Buttons are boring until they are transformed into **tiny sculptures**

Despite her showmanship, which ensured that all eyes were on her, Schiap's fashion was essentially simple and wearable. The cut of her knitted outfits and pantsuits, which often featured boxy jackets without fastenings, was often reminiscent of uniforms, but the lines were softer and more rounded, and she always added a witty detail. Her famous boleros were also more than a mere luxury accessory; they cosseted the breasts and shoulders, which Schiap considered the most sensitive parts of the female body.

When war broke out Schiaparelli fled to the US, and only returned to France in 1945. She was increasingly plagued by financial problems, as she saw no reason why she should rein in her imaginative ideas on mere economic grounds. Yet her surreal creations were no longer in tune with the Zeitgeist. She retired from fashion design in 1954, the year that her old rival Coco Chanel returned to Paris after 15 years away.

Elsa did not resent her newfound success. She had something that Chanel never did: a family. Gogo and her second husband, an Italian like Schiap, and her two grandchildren cared for her greatly. Elsa lived and died in the certainty that "birth is not the beginning, and death is not the end."

Her instinctive feel for beauty, art, and style lives on in her granddaughter, Marisa Berenson, who is renowned worldwide as a model, film star, and style icon.

Monkeying around
Schiaparelli liked to season her fashions with humor. The best example is her monkey fur shoes. You only notice on a second glance that her neat white collars, stockings, and even her gloves have been hand-crocheted.

THE AMERICAN COUTURIER:
Gilbert Adrian

03.03.1903
–
09.13.1959

While Paris was arguing over whether Chanel or Schiaparelli was the greatest fashion designer, in faraway Hollywood one man's influence overtook that of French couture altogether. Adrian Adolph Greenburg, who had called himself simply Adrian since the age of 18, rose to become the most expensive and sought-after dresser of the stars of the screen. His designs for the goddesses of celluloid were bought and increasingly copied all over the world. Hollywood's factory of dreams made possible the kind of success that Paris could only dream of.

Costume designers were only rarely known outside their field. This meant that they never simply copied the Parisian masters, but rather transformed every design so that it fitted a particular star like a second skin, sometimes literally. When Adrian adapted the "long white dress," which looked much better on screen than the "little black dress," for Jean Harlow, it was stuck to her body in the literal sense, and could only be removed with a flat iron. Underwear never even had a look-in. The bias-cut day dresses that Adrian designed for the sex bomb also clung to every curve of her body, and sold like hot cakes.

The director George Cukor, who was behind most of the glamour films of the era, said of Adrian's work, "If an actress has a fantastic figure, Adrian allows all its assets to shine." Clearly, Adrian also saw good features where others saw none. He devised a style for Joan Crawford that greatly accentuated her shoulders. Hollywood insiders believed that he did this to provide a counterpoint to her wide hips, but in truth he was simply impressed with her unconventional body shape; "she has shoulders like Johnny Weissmuller," he marveled, and built them out as though she were in fact the original Tarzan, albeit a far more feminine one. He piled frills upon frills onto her shoulders for the 1932 film *Letty Lynton*, and this white puff pastry-like organza confection was such a hit with the cinema-going public that Macy's sold 500,000 copies for a mere 20 dollars each. The "power suit" that Adrian invented for Crawford made her into a style icon and was to prove a real hit in the 1980s. Most importantly, however, he realized something that few had grasped before: Bodily imperfections can be played down with clothing, but they can also be emphasized and made into a personal strength, and perhaps even a new trend. Adrian's big-shouldered designs sold so well in the 1930s and 40s that he joked, "Who would have thought that my whole career would rest on Joan Crawford's shoulders?"

Adrian had taken the idea for padded shoulders, which made a nipped-in waist appear even smaller, from Elsa Schiaparelli. He knew the French fashion scene inside out, having spent the second year of his apprenticeship in Paris in 1922. By contrast, none of the French couturiers,

---

The secret king of fashion
The costume designer Adrian Adolph Greenberg, who made his career under the name of Adrian, became more influential than any European couturier, as all cinema-goers wanted to look like the big Hollywood stars that he dressed.

The best-selling dress
Half a million women were so thrilled with this white organza creation with ruched sleeves that they bought a copy of it.
Adrian had designed the dress for Joan Crawford in her 1932 role *Letty Lynton*.

A second skin

Jean Harlow, who made her name in Hollywood as a platinum blonde bombshell, owed some of her success to Adrian;
he tailored her flowing silk dresses exactly to her figure, leaving little to the imagination.

He styled Greta Garbo as the "divine woman"
and made the eight stars of The Women
into much-imitated **style icons**

not even Coco Chanel, ever managed to gain a foothold in Hollywood. Their problem was that they styled themselves as stars in their own right, while costume designers had to be wholly at the service of the film stars.

Adrian understood this better than anyone else. He designed his first costumes in 1925 for Rudolph Valentino, at the behest of the star's wife, Natacha Rambova. The costume had such exaggerated embellishment that the great Valentino was ridiculed. Yet it was Adrian who restored Valentino's reputation as a real ladies' man, with clothing to fit the part. He had an even greater rapport with female stars. Mae Murray, Norma Shearer, Marion Davies, Joan Crawford, and Greta Garbo all owed a great deal of their fame to his talent. Adrian dressed every actress in such a way that her figure was shown off to its best advantage and her costume also brought expression to the character that she was playing. This won him the trust of the bosses at MGM, who gave him an almost unlimited budget.

Adrian achieved cult status with the 1939 film *The Women*, for which he dressed Joan Crawford, Norma Shearer, Rosalind Russell, Joan Fontaine, Paulette Goddard, and Hedda Hopper. This wonderful comedy, directed by George Cukor, revolves around men and clothes, and often seems to centre on which man can get the woman the right clothes, rather than the other way around. The film was in black and white, but there was one breathtaking sequence in color: the big fashion show with its vibrant Adrian designs, from dramatic evening dresses to bathing suits that were far too glamorous for actual bathing.

Adrian showed real genius in devising the pared-down style of Greta Garbo. He fiercely resisted the kitsch frippery that MGM wanted the Swedish actress to wear: "Nothing phony should ever distract from this noble creature!" In doing so, he helped the breakthrough of androgynous beauty, which was unprecedented in flamboyant Hollywood. The slouch hat, which he paired with Garbo's trench coat in 1930, remains an iconic look. As an outfit, it respected the actress's desire for privacy, and has never gone out of style.

Adrian, who married the actress Janet Gaynor in 1939, had the rare gift of being able to design both historical costumes and fashionable clothing that could be worn in normal life. By 1937, 90 million Americans were going to the cinema every week to admire their favorite stars, and they wanted to imitate them. Adrian's designs were the most sought-after and the biggest sellers in the big department stores. French couture meant little by comparison. By serving the stars Adrian rose to stardom himself, becoming famous, rich, and even a little eccentric; he built himself a kind of throne in his studio. In 1941, when his mentor George Cukor turned down his costume designs for the first time, due to their expense, Adrian felt he had to take action. He was now being asked to dress Greta Garbo in cheap sweaters for *Two-Faced Woman*. "When the glamour ends for Garbo, it also ends for me," he is reported to have said. He and Garbo bade farewell to Hollywood.

In 1942 Adrian set up his own couture house in Beverly Hills, and many stars came to be dressed by him. He also developed a ready-to-wear line that was only sold in America's most exclusive boutiques. Yet he was able to bask in his success as the great American couturier for only ten years; he died in 1952 at the age of only 59.

Adrian: the genius behind every star

From Valentino, worshipped by Nita Naldi and millions of other women, the divine Garbo and the eight stars of George Cukor's hit comedy, to Norma Shearer, who favored long skirts, Adrian dressed all of them to show off their best features. The young actress Janet Gaynor (below right) even married the sought-after costume designer. He fulfilled his wish to design a hat for his friend Greta Garbo; here she laughs in the guise of *Ninotchka*.

A desire for change
Adrian called this two-piece silk dinner outfit, which he had designed for Joan Crawford, "change," as this word was already a famous campaign promise in 1946. This fashion was to recur in later years, just like his wide shoulder pads.

They defined their era

Jacques Heim

In 1923 Jacques Heim (1899–1967) took over his parents' fur business. Only two years later he caused waves at the Art Deco Exhibition with his casual, youthful designs. In collaboration with Sonia Delaunay, who put color and light at the center of her geometrical, abstract art, he developed a colorful, boldly patterned style that was exactly in tune with the Zeitgeist. He was also ahead of his time with the invention of the bikini that made Brigitte Bardot so popular in 1946.

Marcel Rochas

Schiaparelli was not the only one pushing the boundaries of fashion with elements of whimsy; Marcel Rochas (1902–1955) was more than a match for her in terms of originality. His clothes had stuffed robins perched on the shoulders or were printed with tiny books. Instead of conventional silk evening pajamas, in 1932 he designed a gray flannel pantsuit for daywear, and the curvaceous silhouette that he came up with for the film star Mae West anticipated postwar style.

Mainbocher

First an illustrator, then a fashion journalist, and finally, in 1930, the first American to have his own haute couture house in Paris, Mainbocher (1890–1976), born Main Rousseau Bocher, was successful from the very start. His meticulously ladylike style meant that he was destined to become the designer of choice for one Wallis Simpson, who married the Duke of Windsor in 1937. He designed her wedding dress: a bias-cut, dove-colored silk gown.

Nina Ricci

The Italian dressmaker Nina Ricci (1883–1970), who settled in Paris in 1932, loved patterns and soft colors. She wanted to make women look feminine, elegant, and beautiful, rather than provoking and shocking the public with new trends. Her low-key elegance was just the right thing in times of crisis, and Ricci, who had started off with 40 employees, had 450 seamstresses by 1939. The House of Ricci is one of the few fashion houses from this era to have survived to this day.

The well-dressed woman

1947

The 1950s were the last great decade of haute couture before it began to falter, a state of affairs from which it has never really recovered. Never before and never again since then have there been so many independent couturiers, and so great was their influence that their exclusive designs and extravagant ideas had a worldwide impact on fashion for the masses. One of the leading figures in this respect was Christian Dior, who launched his New Look in 1947.

The fashion world was ripe for a radical change of direction. After years of clothes being austere and in short supply during wartime, women now yearned for soft lines and extravagantly full skirts, even if this ran counter to all common sense. Naturally enough, there were numerous critics of this new style, who—with every justification—viewed it as an unnecessary, if not downright outrageous, extravagance to produce a dress costing 40,000 francs when most women could not even afford milk for their hungry children. And feminists, including English MP Mabel Ridealgh, realized immediately that the new style was not a sign of progress, complaining that: "The New Look is too reminiscent of a bird in a golden cage."

However, that was exactly what many women wanted after the horrors of war: They longed to be pampered and protected without having to shoulder responsibility for anything. This was why the New Look caught on so readily, even if it marked an explosion of suppressed desires rather than a move towards a better future. The New Look symbolized a sense of optimism and opulence, a prospect many people must have viewed with cynicism when the style was first introduced in 1947, but which seemed a matter of course just a few years later. The economic miracle removed any final doubts. This was largely thanks to the Marshall Plan, also introduced in 1947, which brought about a general economic upturn.

Since it was only the very wealthy who could afford the New Look fashion, it actually served to emphasize class differences. Despite this, it was still welcomed, because it promised affluence, elegance, and good times to come and consequently acted as a spur to social advancement. It also sparked the emergence of a new sector of society: the middle classes. When women began taking down their old blackout curtains and turning them into their first long, full skirt in the new style, they were embarking on what was to become their unstoppable quest for beauty.

The ultimate color coordination

The society lady of the era coordinated her appearance from head to toe, from her hair to her fur trim. This model's blond hair is echoed in the Paul Parnes suit with its mink-trimmed collar, and even the Afghan hounds tone beautifully with the elegant palette of colors.

Casual clothes for leisurewear

US society demonstrated that it was acceptable for a lady to attend a social function wearing a simple ribbed wool jacket and blue-gray knitted skirt—the prime consideration was that she should radiate the necessary allure (never without a cigarette!) and have correct accessories.

My house, my car, my telephone…

The Fifties were a decade for proudly showing off one's newly acquired affluence (clockwise from top left): A bungalow in its exotic location provides the perfect backdrop for this green Irish linen dress; immaculate makeup, consisting of Revlon's bright red lipstick and nail polish, complements this pearl-beaded jacket; a cigarette is an obligatory evening-wear accessory to this long, checkered coat worn over a silvery-white sequined gown; a 1953 "Form 2000" coffee service by Rosenthal illustrating the narrowly waisted New Look design; mohair coat, silk chiffon dress, and multi-strand pearl necklace in the lightest, most luxurious color; sporting a sable stole in front of one of the first fashionable pink Lincoln "Premieres."

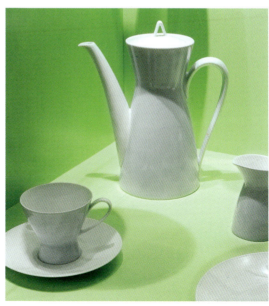

Cinema, curves, and careers

It was sex kitten Ava Gardner who was Clark Gable's co-star in the movie *Mogambo*, while Grace Kelly, later Princess of Monaco, played a supporting role. Elizabeth Taylor made the transformation from child star to voluptuous woman and was able to continue in her career (pictured above right, aged 18). The bikini was Brigitte Bardot's "working outfit" (right) and Italian star Sophia Loren (below left) was famous for her perfect hourglass figure. Rita Hayworth in her role of *Gilda* was idolized as a "love goddess" before she married Prince Ali Khan. Jayne Mansfield was and still is famed for her remarkable cleavage (below right). But it is the exception that proves the rule: Audrey Hepburn with her boyish appearance swept to stardom for her role in *Funny Face*, starring alongside supermodel Dovima (facing page), and as Holly Golightly in *Breakfast at Tiffany's*.

Thanks to the economic miracle,
even ordinary mortals can now aspire
to the lifestyle of movie idols

And this brave new world was indeed beautiful! The austere lines of modernism, in which form was dictated by function, gave way to attractive designs in a fashion geared towards seduction. The hourglass silhouette, which became a hallmark of the New Look, was echoed in every aspect of life, ranging from architecture, to interior design, to the most insignificant household object. Kidney-shaped tables, bucket seats, tulip glasses, two-headed lamps, hourglass-shaped vases, and curved glass ashtrays all mirrored the sculptural lines of the New Look. The "New Look" name was even adopted by the Rosenthal company in 1955 as a label for its new "organic" coffee service. It is no wonder that Christian Dior, witnessing the reaction to his latest fashion innovation, remarked: "What have I done? What on earth have I done?"

What he had done, in fact, was to tap into the prevailing mood of the 1950s, a mood which for the first time was not confined to one country, or a single social class. What seemed like some sort of revolution to many people sprang from a global desire for a restoration of old values. There was a widespread longing for things to return to how they used to be when men and women still had clearly defined roles—with the proviso that everyone now wanted a share in the good life and in the double standards enjoyed by the landed classes. There was as yet no sign of rebellion in the 1950s; material desires were still the main priority. Three new inventions—department stores, synthetic fabrics, and ready-to-wear clothes—enabled people to copy the fashions of the rich. In this way, haute couture fashion found its way to the High Street.

The main role models were supplied by Hollywood. Grace Kelly, more than any other movie star, was the embodiment of the 1950s' ideal of immaculate perfection. She had a naturally aristocratic manner long before her marriage to Prince Rainier of Monaco made her a princess. The director Alfred Hitchcock, whose three movies *Call M for Murder*, *Rear Window*, and *To Catch A Thief* made her an international legend, described her as one of those most desirable of women: "the drawing room type, the real ladies, who become whores once they're in the bedroom." In terms of fashion, she personified the "genteel" look, consisting of pearls and twinset accompanied by short, snow-white gloves and—of course—the Hermès purse, which became Kelly's signature.

Audrey Hepburn came to symbolize the decent, clean-living teenager of the decade: innocent, doe-eyed, dance crazy. *Roman Holiday*, *Sabrina*, and, above all, *Love In The Afternoon* made her a fashion icon. Audrey's fringed hairstyle and heavy eyebrows, her black turtleneck pullover, capri pants, and ballet pumps were copied by millions.

The new era of sex goddesses dawned right after the war, introduced by Rita Hayworth in *Gilda* and Ava Gardner in *The Killers*. Virtually all they needed to excite the fantasies of men who had been away at war were off-the-shoulder, black evening dresses, long gloves, and cigarettes, smoked in a seductive manner.

Marilyn Monroe, who combined an aura of innocence with the appearance of a sex bomb, became the idol of all those who could not quite decide between the nice "girl next door" and the exciting vamp of the movie screen. Elizabeth Taylor was in a class of her own. She began her career as a child star, then somehow blossomed into womanhood overnight. Brigitte Bardot likewise represented an explosive combination of childlike innocence and shamelessness, and became famous for popularizing the bikini after its invention in 1946.

Sex bombs were the perfect shape for the hourglass silhouette introduced by the New Look. Curvaceous actresses from both sides of the Atlantic, including Jane Russell, Jayne Mansfield, Kim Novak, Sophia Loren, Gina Lollobrigida, and Anita Ekberg, quickly rose to movie stardom.

The movie screens were responsible for popularizing a lifestyle—represented by refrigerators, automobiles, vacation trips, parties—that suddenly seemed within everybody's reach. The man in the street spent his money trying to emulate glitterati in the way they lived their lives, even if this was not easy. Not only did people have to work hard to sustain the economic miracle, but it also imposed additional pressures of its own which many people found it hard to keep up with. Once you were on the consumer carousel, you had to work harder and harder to keep it turning; you were duty bound to acquire the latest invention and, what was worse, were obliged to be *au fait* with all the ins and outs of proper etiquette. The rule of terror generated by this preoccupation with "good taste" was the cause of many sleepless nights.

1950

Why, for example, were bungalows and kidney-shaped pools acceptable, when garden swinging hammocks and cars with the new shark's fin design were not? Social advancement did not signify an end to class-based society; on the contrary, the differences were just more subtly defined. To help cope with this insecurity, a strict moral code was devised: "The done thing" soon became the hard and fast yardstick for all social climbers.

Unsurprisingly, this had more ramifications for women than for men. During the 1950s, they returned, both literally and figuratively, to the constraints of their tight corsets. After standing their ground all through the war, women now wanted to go back to feeling completely feminine. In doing so, however, they inadvertently surrendered a good deal of hard-won ground and went back to tending the domestic hearth. It was just all too tempting: the man as absolute master and breadwinner, his wife keeping house in the suburbs—a home filled with modern, functional furniture in light, bright colors, easy to keep clean, comfortable, and packed with technological aids to relieve her of much of the hard work. Men felt that loyalty and a well-maintained house were not too much to expect in return for all this, nor was it asking too much for a wife to appear immaculately groomed from morning until night. It sounded like an excellent bargain—but women paid the price.

French writer and feminist, Simone de Beauvoir, who was herself always elegantly and stylishly turned out, exposed what had become the new cult role for women, calling it the "bondage of elegance." She recognized that women had now become mere advertisements for their husband's success, constrained by new corsets and old conventions. Most women, however, did not realize what was going on. Even if they were aspiring to a career of their own, or were obliged to go out to work to help finance or, indeed, improve the new lifestyle, they still followed the rigid rules of female respectability. For instance, a woman would always take a hat and gloves when going out, a matching purse and shoes were obligatory, accessories and makeup had to be color-coordinated, high heels and stockings were "de rigueur"—except for sporting activities, plunging necklines were not acceptable until evening, and the fabrics worn were

dictated by the time of day—brocade, for example, could never be worn before 6 p.m.! Nor was it considered seemly for a society lady to buy herself flowers or perfume— her husband was expected to give her these as a gift, presumably as a reward for always keeping herself looking beautiful for him. A woman who had to perform social commitments alongside her husband was required to change her outfit up to six or seven times a day, altering her accessories, makeup and hairstyle accordingly.

Women's magazines tried to help their readers by suggesting the correct clothes for every occasion. For lunch at home, a narrow-skirted velour dress, matching stockings, and suede pumps would be considered the ideal outfit. If lunching out, however, the correct attire would consist of a gray flannel dress and matching coat, a little hat, gray suede gloves (which should be kept on during the initial greeting), a gray, patent leather purse, and a slim, gray umbrella. The suggestions, or rather instructions, continued in this vein for eveningwear, with a description of every detail, ranging from the correct type of collar to the appropriate jewelry and perfume, and finished by outlining the proper etiquette to be observed—and the lists grew longer and longer...

Not even the mailman, let alone her husband, ever glimpsed the "economic miracle" woman without her makeup. She would rise an hour before him in order to apply her heavy makeup, then curl, back-comb, and spray her hair until she was barely recognizable. Some husbands apparently never got to see their wives' natural features, since they postponed removing their makeup until their men were peacefully slumbering, or else—after a complicated cleansing procedure—they applied a special night-time makeup to wear during intimacy. It goes without saying that fingernails and toenails likewise were kept immaculately manicured and painted, and even the clothes worn for housework had to reflect the latest fashions.

Only the wealthy, who were free of the additional burdens of childcare and cooking, washing and ironing, shopping, and household chores, could resist the pressures of such a rigidly defined lifestyle. They, for their part, derided the social climber's obsession with perfection and, as usually happens when the masses begin to copy the behavior of their betters,

Spruced up at all times

Most women dreamt of having a home of their own out in the country with a modern built-in kitchen to make their lives easier. This meant they could still look smart and attractive—should visitors arrive unexpectedly—even when they were doing the housework.

the latter quickly retaliated by introducing a different set of standards. The whole business of coordinating colors and accessories, which until then had been slavishly followed to an excessive degree, was now suddenly scornfully dismissed as being bourgeois—besides which, it was much more fun to flout all the existing rules. Good taste was eschewed as something for the masses, while the higher echelons amused themselves by breaching all the previous style rules.

They derived their inspiration for this in Paris. New clients, particularly from the USA, flocked to the salons. Royal queens and movie stars came to view the collections of Christian Dior, the king of fashion. Rita Hayworth, Ava Gardner, Marlene Dietrich, Ingrid Bergman, and Lauren Bacall all sat crushed together in the front row along with the Begum Aga Khan, Empress Soraya of Iran and her successor, Farah Diba, the Duchess of Windsor, and Barbara Hutton. Every new show was a feast full of surprises since Dior went to great lengths to keep his audience's interest in fashion alive. During the 11 years of his reign, he introduced 22 different styles, raising and lowering hemlines (but only between the knee and ankle), contouring the female body with a figure-of-8 style, before introducing his H-, A-, and Y-line styles, then finally enveloping it in a sack dress. And the women lapped up his ideas—not just his clients, but the whole world.

There was actually little anybody else could do. Despite the large number of different couturiers, the overall line remained surprisingly uniform. Dior set the tone and the rest followed suit. Even the latest *prêt-à-porter* mode, newly introduced into France and modeled on US ready-to-wear outfits created by Lempereur and Weill, unhesitatingly embraced whatever emerged as the current seasonal trend. This brisk exchange of products and ideas within the Atlantic community also played a role in democratizing and internationalizing fashion—for the first time in history, women all over the world joined forces in following the same fashion dictum.

The New Look and subsequent variations were characterized by soft shoulders, rounded hips, and wasp waists. It was not until the end of the decade that geometric shapes, reminiscent of the 1920s, began to reappear and hemlines crept upwards to just under the knee. This new fashion silhouette was dubbed the "string bean look" by the press, nicknamed after the exceedingly fine green beans used in haute cuisine.

The shoes of this decade were narrow, pointed, and supported on medium-high or, ideally, very high heels, which gradually became narrower and narrower until they mutated into the famous "pencil heel," or "stiletto." Shoes with the tips "cut off" and ending in a square peep toe were another variation of this period. Peep-toe sandals in silk or brocade were the most popular style of evening footwear and these were often embellished with paste gem clasps to augment their extravagant appearance. The leading shoe designer of the era was Roger Vivier, who provided the footwear for all Dior's collections. For the coronation of Queen Elizabeth II of England in 1953, he designed a gold leather sandal, the heel of which was generously studded with rubies. In 1955, Vivier introduced the *choc* heel, which curved inward toward the toes in such a way that it looked as if it could easily break off at the heel—an unpleasant occurrence which had already befallen many women wearing high heels.

Hats of this period were generally small with a flat crown, even if they sported wide brims. They gradually developed into little caps known as "Bibi" hats, which were decorated with flowers, feathers, or veils and perched on top of the head around hair that had been carefully pinned up or styled. Sometimes the "hat" consisted of nothing more than a silk headband which could be decorated for eveningwear with a long feather.

Leisure was such an extremely important feature of the affluent Fifties that a fashion was created specifically to cater for it. No one would have dreamed of throwing on some comfortable item of old clothing—leisure activities were, after all, an extremely stylish affair. People attended garden parties or cocktail parties, played tennis or golf, and, as soon as they could afford it, went to the Riviera, Capri, or even Jamaica. The proper attire for such occasions demanded youthful styles and bright colors.

The 1950s witnessed an explosion of colors—a backlash after the gloomy years of war. Dior became renowned for his optimistic reds, although this seemed rather conservative in comparison to the multicoloured "blot" designs which fabric manufacturers were borrowing from modern art. The rising star and hero of the art scene was Jackson Pollock, or "Jack the Dripper" as he was known. In a very energetic style of action painting, he splattered his colors apparently at random onto giant canvases laid out on the floor. His short, wild life ended in 1959 when, under the influence of alcohol, he was killed when his car veered off the road. The manner of his death turned him into a cult legend like James Dean, who also died in a fatal crash at the wheel of his Porsche—as did Jack Kerouac, one of the Beat generation, who both lived and wrote *On the Road*. Young people were fascinated by these tragic American heroes.

In Europe, it was the Theater of the Absurd, the main proponents of which were Samuel Beckett and Eugène Ionesco, and the existentialism of Jean-Paul Sartre which provided the counterbalance to the dreary image of the beaming, clean-cut, typical "nice guy" of the 1950s. Intellectual young people of that time demonstrated their disenchantment with life by adopting the black clothes favored by beatniks and existentialists, who idolized Juliette Gréco as their muse and fashion icon.

No one could have guessed that Marlon Brando's appearance in a T-shirt in *A Streetcar Named Desire* could trigger a craze that a decade later would sweep away the old social order. The role of "angry young man" became fashionable but the white T-shirts, black leather jackets, and blue jeans that Marlon Brando wore in *The Wild One* and James Dean wore in *Rebel Without a Cause* became a uniform which expressed a particular attitude: namely, a sense of dissatisfaction and emptiness. Over the course of time, it became clear that the apparently unlimited opportunities the consumer society provided were unable to heal the sickness of youth.

Rock 'n' roll music, which swept the world, thanks to Bill Haley, and then Elvis Presley, gave the first hint of things to come. As long as young people were still cavorting about on the dance floor, all was still well with the world. All these manifestations remained simply a fashion trend—the rebellious behavior did not start until a decade later. Lulled by consumerism and frightened by the Cold War, which dominated this decade of contrasts just as much as the belief in unlimited growth, the new breed of teenagers seemed, for the most part, fashionable and elegant, and—more importantly—respectable. Petticoats and petting tended to lead with all due haste to womankind's highest goal: marriage.

The youngest, most famous bride of the era was Ira von Fürstenberg, who married Prince Alfonso zu Hohenlohe in Venice at the age of 15. Dream weddings of this kind served to fuel people's romantic yearnings. In 1953, Jacqueline Bouvier, more commonly known as Jackie, became one of the most prominent fashion icons of the century when she married John F. Kennedy, senator and later president of the USA. In 1956, Hollywood star Grace Kelly turned into a fairytale princess when she married Rainier of Monaco and in 1960, thanks to Balenciaga's gifted couture, shy Fabiola of Spain was feted as a beauty on her wedding day when she married King Baudouin of Belgium. And the striking Soraya, who was half-German, became an empress as a result of her marriage to the Shah of Persia.

Anything seemed possible and everything was possible. Girls from the lowliest of backgrounds became stars or models, like the Polish policeman's daughter, Dovima, who epitomized the aristocratic, immaculate, and cultured lady of the 1950s. In the film *Funny Face*, with Audrey Hepburn starring in the leading role, Dovima played herself and she could not have been given a more perfect role—her fame as a mannequin had brought her everything she ever dreamed of. All she lacked was the right husband. This was not usually a problem for models since they could have virtually anyone they chose. Eliette became the wife of Herbert von Karajan and her friend, Simone Bicheron, married Curt Jurgens. Fiona Campbell-Walter married Baron Hans Heinrich von Thyssen-Bornemisza, while Anne Gunning became Lady Nutting. Anne Cumming, meanwhile, became the Duchess of Rutland, while Balmain's star mannequin, Bronwen Pugh, married Lord Astor.

1957

Tradition and rebellion

Even successful women, like film star Grace Kelly (above center) or press photographer Jacqueline Bouvier (above right), kept a lookout for top-notch husbands. These two bagged Prince Rainier of Monaco and US President John F. Kennedy, respectively. Cabaret singer and muse of the existentialists, Juliette Gréco, (above left) and France's best-known intellectual, Simone de Beauvoir (below center) insisted on having careers of their own. As far as men were concerned, it was only the rebels that were of interest: Marlon Brando in his T-shirt, Elvis Presley with his forelock, James Dean, who was never without a cigarette and who died tragically young, and author Jack Kerouac, whose novel *On The Road* became the cult book of an entire generation. Grace Kelly's Hermès purse, known as the "Kelly bag" (facing page), likewise became a cult fashion item, still coveted to this day by high society ladies.

THE GENTLE DICTATOR:

Christian Dior

01.21.1905
–
10.23.1957

On February 12, 1947, Christian Dior showed his very first collection and although the temperatures outside were down to less than 10 degrees Fahrenheit, people were getting hot under the collar inside the salon on the Avenue Montaigne. How long had it been since people had last seen such soft contours, such tiny waists, and such extravagantly full skirts? Not since the Belle Epoque! Yet, now, two world wars later, this silhouette suddenly seemed new and refreshingly feminine. It was Carmel Snow, editor-in-chief of *Harper's Bazaar* who coined the name for this style that would go down in history: "It's quite a revolution, dear Christian," she congratulated the shy couturier. "Your dresses have such a new look."

So it was that the "Ligne Corolle," as Dior had christened it, became the "New Look" and Christian Dior, hitherto a relatively unknown designer, suddenly found himself overnight the unchallenged king of couture.

Who was this man who revolutionized fashion by bringing back fashions typical of the turn of the 20th century? When the fashion enthusiasts crowded backstage after the show, they encountered a short, 42-year-old man with a bald pate and a shy, sad smile, who looked like a "country curate made of pink marzipan," according to one of his friends.

This quiet, reserved Frenchman was moved to tears over the amount of praise that overwhelmed him from all sides. Carmel Snow remarked: "Dior saved Paris as Paris was saved in the Battle of the Marne" and couture, which had stagnated during the war years, did indeed flourish again thanks to Dior's overnight success.

Dior's winter collection, which was shown in August of the same year, featured gowns with full skirts, some of which consisted of 40 yards of material. Once again it proved a huge success. It was to Dior's great credit that he was able to inspire this kind of ecstatic reception on a regular twice-a-year basis through an entire decade. By 1949, Dior alone was accountable for 75 percent of the whole of French fashion exports.

How did this modest Frenchman achieve such success? His skills as a couturier were by no means superior to those of other contemporary designers. Balenciaga, who was acknowledged as the absolute master of his day and who was, generally speaking, extremely sparing with his opinions, confessed that he found Dior's use of fabrics appalling—all those multi-layered linings of

---

Creativity in seclusion

Twice a year, Dior would withdraw from the world and isolate himself in one of his country houses. Suffering untold anxieties, he would then begin working on a new collection. When he eventually emerged with his sketches, his staff would breathe a unanimous sigh of relief and set to work on his designs.

New Look and constant changes
The "Bar" suit (facing page) was the prototype for the New Look; sloping shoulders, nipped waist, padded hips, and full skirt. Later on, skirts became narrow again whilst a bustier-style bodice was introduced and worn with a shawl as additional embellishment.

Swirling elegance

Royal photographer Cecil Beaton was commissioned to photograph the widely acclaimed New Look, which enveloped women in extravagantly full skirts made of black wool, for the "fashion bible" *Vogue* magazine (facing page). All the designs shown in Dior's sensational autumn and winter collections of 1947 were characterized by their extremely feminine silhouette, featuring accentuated waists and full, swinging, calf-length skirts. Gloves and little hats were essential accessories for this style.

Behind many a great couturier
*is an **elegant and unapproachable mother—***
Dior was no exception in this respect

ticking, starched cloth, and tulle contradicted Balenciaga's main credo of "letting the fabric speak for itself." The harshest criticism came from Chanel, however: "Dior? He does not dress women, he upholsters them."

The truth is that the "New Look" tag is the greatest misnomer in the history of fashion. What was new, after all, about dressing women up as sex objects and status symbols for their husbands? The New Look was a counter-revolution which sent women straight back to the Belle Epoque. It reflected Dior's desire to revive the "tradition of great luxury" in French fashion. And precisely therein lay the secret of his success.

Despite his apparent reserve, he was nevertheless a genius at marketing. He introduced a completely new style of presentation to haute couture that represented a complete departure from the staid, peaceful shows typical of the pre-war era. Dior's models took to the runway with a theatrical presence, swept regally past the audience, swirled their full skirts provocatively, and turned on their heel with breathtaking tempo. The spectacle could last anything up to two hours without the least sign of anyone becoming bored. This was partly due to the fact that Dior launched a new range every six months. He was the first couturier to dramatically change his collection from one show to the next, be it with the length of hemlines or the entire silhouette. Not only did this tactic insure that his previous fashion styles quickly became outdated but, at the same time, guaranteed headlines in the media and boosted his turnover.

Christian Dior was born on January 21, 1905, in Granville in Normandy. One of five children, his father was Maurice Dior, a prominent fertilizer manufacturer. "It smells of Dior today," the villagers would often remark. Later on, this same remark was frequently heard in his exclusive salons, where the ladies were perfumed with Miss Dior, Diorama, and Diorissimo. Christian had been interested in fashion from a very early age and was very fond and greatly in awe of his extremely elegant mother. When his father lost his entire wealth following the crash of the stock exchange and some bad investments in the early 1930s, Christian, who had led a cushioned life, suddenly found himself having to earn his own living. Thanks to his artistic talents, the young Dior soon found a permanent position working for fashion designer Robert Piguet.

In 1939, he had to interrupt his new career and go to war. He returned to Paris in 1941, however, and was fortunate enough to be taken on as a designer by Lucien Lelong. A few years later, he caught the attention of Marcel Boussac, an extremely wealthy and influential textile manufacturer who was impressed with Dior's ideas for a fashion line featuring gowns made from extravagant amounts of material. Thanks to this partnership, the House of Dior was launched at No. 30, Avenue Montaigne, where it remains to this day.

Dior was a mother's boy—soft, gentle, timid and dreamy. Everyone who worked with him described him as modest and courteous. He would bow politely to the lowliest of apprentices, standing aside to let her enter the lift in front of him. He was renowned for the remarkable consideration he showed his many hundreds of employees and would spend months looking for the perfect Christmas present for each individual.

Dior loved elaborate meals and hated being alone. He was always surrounded by an intimate group of friends, which included Jean Cocteau, Christian Bérard, the composers Georges Auric

---

Cause for celebration
Whatever Dior created in terms of fashion was greeted enthusiastically by the press and his clientele. With his policy of constant change, he commanded the fashion scene throughout the 1950s. His designs were as much a cause for celebration as the economic miracle and well worth toasting—it goes without saying— in champagne, while wearing mink.

Change is as good as a rest

Dior's determination to produce a continuing
succession of new lines placed him under a great
deal of stress. Be it his X-, H-, Y-, or A-line look
with straight or curvaceous contours, he invented
a new silhouette for every season. With the aid of
tape measures and bamboo poles (facing page),
he kept a strict eye on proceedings to make sure
that his design measurements were followed to the
letter. Prominent clients, such as Hollywood star
Jane Russell (above right), whose career relied on
her large bust, finally gave into his coaxing and
adopted his "flat look," and Princess Margaret of
England (middle, right) was similarly bowled over
by this modest couturier. It was, however, his own
models who admired him most (below left).

and Francis Poulenc, and his *directrice*, Raymonde Zehnacker. He was prey to superstition and insisted on consulting his clairvoyant, Madame Delahaye, before making any major decision. It was she who advised him to launch the House of Dior with Boussac and also urged him to keep his rooms filled with fresh flowers at all times.

Twice a year, before creating each collection, Dior would fall into a deep depression, shutting himself away in his study in one of his country houses, either in Fontainebleau or Provence, and letting no one see him except his valet who brought him meals on a tray. Seated at his desk, Dior would sketch designs on a large drawing pad, becoming absorbed in doodling hieroglyphics and aimless scribbling until the moment of inspiration, when he suddenly saw with perfect clarity the silhouette of his new collection. For the duration of this tense, anxious period, half a dozen assistants were always on hand, waiting nervously for him to appear. When Dior finally emerged with hundreds of sheets of paper in his hand, a cheer would go up before his staff got on with the task of meticulously converting his sketches into models.

Dior's gentle, mild personality, which was so obviously plagued by artistic anxiety, easily masked the fact that he was also an extremely astute businessman. During his first visit to the USA in 1947, he realized straight away that this was a market with untold opportunities—and wasted no time in introducing the system of royalty payments whereby he received a percentage for every copy of his designs. This made the introduction of accessories and perfumes an extremely lucrative venture.

Dior was soon opening salons in London, New York, and Caracas, striving in each case to cater for the individual needs of the country. This meant producing about a thousand new designs every year. Such an intense production schedule must have been extremely grueling for someone whose goal was to create a completely new look every season. Dior's health began to suffer and by the mid-1950s he was showing visible signs of stress. His nerves were sometimes so bad that his personal clairvoyant and his chauffeur Perrotino, a former lover from his younger days, had to drive him round the block several times before he could work up the courage to face his staff. Madame Raymonde, his *directrice*, was sometimes woken in the middle of the night by a call from her boss, crying like a child.

Only Perrotino knew Dior's dark secret—that he had already suffered two heart attacks. And there was a further secret: Dior had for years been unlucky in love. Countless attractive young men had refused to offer him anything more than friendship. In 1956, however, Dior's affections were finally reciprocated by Jacques Benita, a good-looking young man of North African descent. In a bid to make himself more desirable to his young lover, Dior decided in the late summer of 1957 to undertake a rest cure in Montecatini in order to lose weight.

In mid-September, his clairvoyant, Delahaye, saw warnings in the cards and urged him to change his travel plans. For once, he ignored her advice and set off for the spa resort in Italy with his chauffeur, his *directrice*, and a young goddaughter. During the evening of the tenth day of his stay, on October 23, 1957, Christian Dior, one of the most influential couturiers of all time, collapsed shortly after a game of canasta and died of heart failure.

A bit of wild cat

Dior loved animal fur, whether spotted, speckled, or striped, real or synthetic. In the case of this belted New Look coat in green velvet with patterned trim, the fur element is limited to wide cuffs and a pillbox hat in leopard skin.

THE STRICT ARCHITECT:
Cristóbal Balenciaga

01.21.1895
–
03.24.1972

The whole world was talking about Dior and his New Look but the cognoscenti knew that the true innovator of fashion was Cristóbal Balenciaga. Fashion photographer Cecil Beaton once remarked that the couturier "created the future for fashion." Even Dior, himself the darling of the media, felt nothing but unadulterated admiration for him, referring to him as "the master of us all." In 1948 when Balenciaga, deeply depressed, wanted to close his salon following the death of his friend Vladzio d'Attainville, it was Dior who persuaded him to carry on.

Balenciaga could, without a doubt, have turned his couture business into an international enterprise, like Dior and others, but after visiting the USA and seeing the off-the-rack clothes there, he returned more determined than ever not to use machines. No amount of lucrative offers from would-be manufacturers were able to change his mind: "I will not prostitute myself," insisted Balenciaga with the pride typical of a true Basque who was daring in his designs and uncompromising in his standards.

Cristóbal Balenciaga was born in Guetaria, a village close to the elegant seaside resort of San Sebastián. His father was a fisherman and his mother a seamstress. After the untimely death of his father, Cristóbal, the youngest of three children, soon found himself helping his mother. Their best client, Marchioness de Casa Torrès, soon spotted the potential of young Balenciaga and became his patron. She threw open her closets and invited him to choose one of her gowns as a model to copy, a task which he completed with remarkable skill. Not only did he have great talent, but also a huge amount of self-confidence. On one occasion, he stopped the Marchioness in a narrow village street wanting to sketch her in precisely that spot. When asked why, he answered simply: "Because I can." He succeeded at everything he tried, mainly because he was prepared to work day and night to do so.

Balenciaga was only 24 when he opened his own fashion house in San Sebastián where, thanks to his great patron, the Marchioness, he was soon numbering the royal family among his clients. A few years later, he opened more salons in Madrid and Barcelona. The Spanish Civil War forced the closure of his three salons but in 1937, with the assistance of some Spanish friends, he was able to launch a couture house in Paris.

All the press talked about after his first collection was a coat sleeve, cut in one piece with the yoke. It was this sleeve design that served Balenciaga as the basis for many variations.

Proud Spaniard
Cristóbal Balenciaga was always immaculately turned out when meeting clients. In this photo he is 32 years old and already the owner of three exclusive fashion stores in Spain. Ten years later, he launched his legendary couture house in Paris.

Fresh perspectives

The pose of the model in front of the mirror shows off Balenciaga's "melon" sleeves to perfection. The fullness of the sleeves is drawn together in a wealth of pleats to end in a narrow cuff. A soft, wool velour fabric was particularly well suited to this style.

Bands instead of feathers

Hundreds of bands of silk chiffon, sewn onto a simple box dress, create a very feathery effect. The colors are typical Balenciaga: black coat over a brown cocktail dress.

His quest for the perfect sleeve
became an obsession that cost Balenciaga a great deal, including several friendships

Throughout his lifetime, Balenciaga was constantly seeking the perfect sleeve. If a sleeve failed to follow the wearer's every movement, Balenciaga rejected the design as a failure. His guests frequently had to return home without their coats because Balenciaga had removed the sleeves with the intention of improving them in his studio. One such victim was Hubert de Givenchy, himself a designer of immaculate elegance, who nevertheless deferred to the dictates of the master for whom he felt such admiration.

La manga, la manga! echoed like a battle cry on the part of this otherwise reserved Spaniard. He could work on a particular sleeve for days on end, first cutting it out—on a curved board on his lap—then experimenting with extremely complicated types of seams, which he personally sewed by hand. The list of Balenciaga's different types of sleeve is a long one: raglan, kimono, puff, batwing, balloon, melon... A 1951 suit made of black piqué was even dubbed *Les Manches* (The Sleeves) because it focused all the attention on the exaggerated lantern shape of the sleeves.

Balenciaga met with immediate success in Paris. All the women who appeared on the annual list of the world's best-dressed women became his clients: Mona von Bismarck, Barbara Hutton, Gloria Guinness, Pauline de Rothschild, the Duchess of Windsor, Marella Agnelli, and, naturally, film stars such as Marlene Dietrich and Ingrid Bergman. Thanks to such affluent patrons, Balenciaga, despite his reputation as the most expensive couturier, managed to survive the war without suffering financially. He was even able to reopen his Spanish salons.

The 1950s were Balenciaga's greatest decade, a period during which his succession of innovative ideas helped move fashion forward. In 1951, the media were shocked by his "half-finished" suits, the jackets of which were fitted around the figure in front, but hung loosely at the back. Only Carmel Snow, the perceptive editor-in-chief of *Harper's Bazaar*, correctly interpreted this as being a final departure from the wasp-waisted New Look and the first signs of a new casual look, remarking that this style would shake up fashion.

One year later, Balenciaga introduced the "sailor blouse" as the bodice element of a casual suit with a pencil skirt, an outfit that caused a sensation and was endlessly copied. Women loved it since it disguised the most critical parts of a woman's figure. As Balenciaga once rather pompously declared: "A woman does not have to be perfect or beautiful to wear my fashions, my clothes will take care of that for them."

He kept his promise in this respect when he launched the tunic in 1955. This garment had a long, narrow silhouette, was flexible like an elegant fencing foil, and could make even matronly women look as graceful as lilies. This was the opinion of Carmel Snow at least, who was herself frequently photographed in a red linen tunic.

The stand-away collar which Balenciaga invented for suits and coats proved a real gift to women. Fashion icon Gloria Guinness raved that this type of collar let women and their pearls "breathe." Nor was it any wonder that his flattering little turndown collar was particularly favored by ladies who wanted to draw discreet attention to their husbands' importance and wealth. Balenciaga, meanwhile, was less concerned with pearls than with the fact that many of his clients benefited because such a collar made their necks look longer.

Silhouette masterpiece
Balenciaga loved experimenting with different lengths and often tried out train effects, as in the case of this 1967 cross between a cocktail dress and evening gown made of gazar, a shiny, stiff fabric of loosely woven silk.

*In his studio **as bare as a monk's cell,***
  he spends entire nights sewing a "little black dress"
by hand

Balenciaga always tried to accommodate the needs of his clients. An example of this is his innovation of the shortened, three-quarter length sleeve, soon nicknamed the "bracelet sleeve," as it allowed women to display their bracelets and watches to their best advantage. At the same time, it protected expensive fabrics from coming into contact with jewelry that was liable to snag or pull threads.

Despite all his striving for perfection and his aesthetic tastes, Balenciaga never forgot his humble origins or lost sight of what was practical. His guiding principle was simply to do things properly, an aspiration which also explained his ritual of personally making a "little black dress" from beginning to end entirely by hand for every collection. Carrying out this obsessive ritual helped Balenciaga prove to himself time and time again that he was still the master of every procedure in the art of haute couture. Needless to say, he only ever used Spanish Galia black, the blackest black in the world of fashion, next to which all others appeared almost gray, or at least slightly dusty.

From his native Spain, Balenciaga had inherited a sense of drama, mysticism, and severity while Paris taught him modernity, extravagance, and elegance. Balenciaga's gowns were ideal for dramatic entrances, surrounding the wearer like a magnificent frame. This was partly thanks to expensive fabrics, which were so stiff and firm that they would remain standing in whatever silhouette Balenciaga created. In his efforts to create a pure form, he approached his work like an architect, creating perfect proportions around the female body and turning women into unattainable beauties of intimidating elegance.

The older he grew, the more this was the case. His techniques became more sophisticated with every year that passed and his fashions increased in simplicity until, eventually, his gowns resembled minimalist sculptures which were not recognized as masterpieces until a very long time afterwards. They were not in tune with the prevailing spirit of the age. Buyers from the major US department stores had begun to lose interest in his styles and the press had begun courting new kings of fashion, such as André Courrèges, who, like Emanuel Ungaro, had first learnt his craft from Balenciaga.

The fashion world no longer understood Balenciaga and he no longer understood the world. The revolutionary events of May 1968, the youth culture, the emergence of so many new designers creating street fashion—this was no longer his era. In 1968, Balenciaga closed his studios, disappointed by a world that, in his view, had sold out to mass production and vulgarity. His clients greatly mourned his loss. Mona von Bismarck took to her bed and cried for three days, in despair over how she would be able to maintain her high standards in future.

There was one last occasion when Balenciaga was persuaded to create a dress: for the wedding of the Duchess of Cádiz in 1972. His very first commission in 1919 had also been a wedding dress, so it seemed a fitting way to complete the circle of his creative career, especially as the *robe de mariée* is always the high point and grand finale of every couture show. Cristóbal Balenciaga died at the end of March, 1972, of a heart attack.

The lady displays her jewelry
The stand-away collar allowed Balenciaga's clients to show off their jewelry— ideally strands of pearls—to its best advantage. It was equally suitable for coats, like this coarsely woven, beige wool coat, worn by the model Hiroko in London in 1961.

Only half finished?

Many people did not appreciate Balenciaga's "semi-fitted" collection, which only accentuated the waist at the front of the garment. Carmel Snow, however, editor-in-chief of *Harper's Bazaar*, purchased this linen outfit in brilliant poppy red.

They defined their era

Jacques Fath

With his acumen for business and marketing, Jacques Fath (1912–1954) was far ahead of his time. Apart from couture, he also designed reasonably priced ready-to-wear clothes and was the first Frenchman to design a collection for the US market. His popularity with the colorful "movie crowd" led to the serious press dismissing him as a "lightweight." He did not receive due recognition until the mid-1940s. His untimely death from leukemia meant that his great talents never actually achieved their full potential.

Pierre Balmain

Pierre Balmain (1914–1982) trained under Lucien Lelong alongside Dior. The two friends originally planned to launch a couture house together, but Dior hesitated too long and Balmain opened a salon of his own in 1945. The aristocracy, in particular, were drawn to his luxurious elegance and his most famous client was Queen Sirikit of Thailand. Balmain adored extravagant fullness, soft colors, intricate embroidery, and fur.

Hubert de Givenchy

Hubert de Givenchy (born 1927) was the youngest designer ever to open a fashion house of his own, having previously run the string of boutiques owned by Schiaparelli. His amusing designs and fresh colors injected a breath of fresh air into the world of couture, but he soon changed direction and, like his role model Balenciaga, became a champion of classic haute couture, elevating cutting and finishing skills to an art form. He is famous for dressing Hollywood star Audrey Hepburn, both on screen and in her private life.

Charles James

This English couturier, who opened his couture house in New York in 1940, has been described as the sculptor of fashion. An obsessive perfectionist, Charles James (1906–1978) often spent months working on a design. He favored dramatic fabrics, like faille silk or duchesse satin, for his asymmetrical silhouettes and unusual color combinations, such as apricot and aubergine, or pink and gingery brown. He closed down his salon in 1958 after completely losing touch with the reality of the fashion world.

135

Youth culture and
STREET FASHION CONQUERS THE RUNWAY
haute couture

The "Swinging Sixties" were undoubtedly the most colorful decade of the last century, a view borne out by the fact that to this day there is still no general agreement about the merits of this period. Some people consider it the Golden Age of new freedoms, while others regard it as a dark decade that witnessed the breakdown of morals, authority, and discipline. One thing we can be sure of, however, is that the seeds of change sown during that period are still coming to fruition to this day in various areas of society, politics, and culture.

The impetus for change stemmed from the younger generation—traditionally speaking, the most optimistic social group. Thanks to the postwar baby boom, young people accounted for an extremely large section of the population and their influence was greater than ever before. Teenagers, who had first been "discovered" and courted as consumers in the 1950s, had grown into rebellious twenty-somethings, questioning all that their parents held sacred. This was partly due to the fact that nearly everyone was now reaping the benefits of the economic miracle, which had got under way in the 1950s.

However, when measured against what it would cost them in terms of flexibility, subordination, and self-denial, many young people now felt unwilling to pay the price of sustaining it. They rebelled against the authority of their parents, the Church, and the state, exposing the all-too-common double standards that allowed virtually everyone to do the opposite of what was publicly preached.

Generational conflicts of this kind are not a new phenomenon. The difference this time, however, was that young people had not only begun to rebel, but had also developed their own counterculture, which they promoted so forcefully that it did not just simmer away beneath the surface but was evident at every turn. For a time it seemed as if this blueprint for a better world, a world characterized by greater honesty and humanitarianism, might actually work. This, at least, was the common objective which united all young people of that era, whether they were politically minded, part of the pop culture, or simply cherished naive dreams of a peaceful, pleasure-filled life. It was the suffocating constraints of middle-class society, with its empty protocols governing respectability and good manners, which had provoked this

1960

Surprisingly smart

The Swinging Sixties were characterized by bright colors and cheerful patterns. Stripes and circles in bold colors gave mini dresses a fresh, yet innocent look. Colorful plastic Creole earrings and geometric-style haircuts emphasized the impression of graphic design.

Young people throughout the Western world unite in protest

In May 1968, students in Paris marched through the streets with their fists raised, as shown on the above poster, protesting against capitalism and conservatism (left). In August 1968, demonstrations in Prague calling for democracy instead of communism were crushed by Soviet tanks (above right). In 1970, film star Jane Fonda gave an impassioned speech in Washington voicing opposition to the Vietnam War (above left). The same year, Uschi Obermaier (below left and right), "Germany's most beautiful commune dweller," marched with provocative arrogance ahead of Berlin riot police sent to stop the student protesters.

A colorful summer

A year before student unrest erupted on a worldwide scale, all still seemed right with the world. *Vogue* magazine, the world's fashion bible, included a feature on the makeup trends for the summer of '67, featuring a model whose body had been painted in psychedelic patterns.

Joan Baez and Twiggy
Joan Baez, an American folk singer, became the face of young people in revolt, while Twiggy, a skinny model, became a role model for ambitious young girls.

The advent of the Pill prepared the ground for the **sexual revolution**—and freed men from all responsibility

rebellion among the younger generation. In addition, there was the pressure to achieve imposed upon these young people by their hardworking parents of the economic miracle generation: "...You should be better off than we were," coupled with the familiar threat that "while you live in this house, you will do what I say." This frequently led to a refusal to work, as well as a rejection of the family and all the values that go with it, such as marriage, faithfulness, and the conventional division of roles between man and wife. The whole crux of the difficulties seemed to lie in young people's aversion to being put under pressure. And so what if they now refused to be told what to do, or picked partners as randomly and casually as they chose their clothes, which were no longer regarded as a status symbol? It was not long before the younger generation was congratulating itself on its wonderful, newfound liberation. As Uschi Obermaier, a famous German model and commune member, recalls: "Everything was brand new: fashion, music, philosophy and—it goes without saying—our way of life. We did not want the sort of relationships our parents had, and in the commune, one lived with the family of one's choice. Our philosophy was to enjoy life and we experimented with everything."

1961

It was fortunate for these young people that their experimenting coincided with the invention of the Pill, which was introduced in 1961 and offered women, for the first time, simple, reliable protection against unwanted pregnancy. Had it not been for this small, round object, the sexual revolution would never have taken place. Whether it contributed much to the emancipation of women remains a moot point. To begin with, it led men into thinking they could cast off all responsibility, whereas women now found themselves facing the new pressure of having to be ready to have sex all the time. Only very few women can claim, as Uschi Obermaier does, that "I only ever did what I wanted. I never regarded myself as a feminist." However, it was the unexpected consequences of the Pill and the sexual revolution that led to many women joining the ranks of the feminists in the late 1960s.

The sort of freedom Uschi Obermaier enjoyed was also contingent on financial independence. As one of the top models of her time, she could afford virtually anything. Nor was she the only young

person to become rich at an unexpectedly early age. The economic miracle was still in full swing and many young entrepreneurs, who had set up their own businesses—such as clubs, discotheques, porn shops, subversive magazines, boutiques, and, most of all, within the music industry—were now profiting from the economic boom. The emerging youth market was primarily serviced by other young people, who then became rich by selling exactly the sort of items that they liked themselves. And despite their disdain for the wonderful consumer-based society of their parents, these youngsters were certainly not averse to consuming. They merely spent their money on different things—like off-beat fashion, traveling, drugs, and rock 'n' roll.

Music was the element that transcended national, class, racial, and gender boundaries and united the young people of the Western world. In musical terms, Bill Haley and Elvis Presley were precursors of the Sixties' music, which was dominated by the Beatles, followed by the Rolling Stones, The Who, The Kinks, Jimi Hendrix, and Eric Burdon. Models and beautiful little rich girls latched onto these wild musicians like upper-class groupies and helped make sure that this period would go down in history as the decade of "Sex, Drugs & Rock 'n' Roll."

Unlike the Rolling Stones, the Beatles were not content with personal "satisfaction," but aspired to inner enlightenment. By adopting Maharishi Mahesh Yogi as their guru in 1967, they pioneered a movement determined to find the meaning of life in the Far East. The stylish Mods with their "Beatle" haircuts, who admittedly followed new, though recognizable, fashion dictates, very quickly ended up being labeled as hippies, at least by the mass media, which lumped every "long-haired individual" together. But young people themselves were extremely punctilious in discriminating between those who were "hip" (or "hot," "in," or "cool") and genuine hippies, who were, strictly speaking, dropouts with very little interest in anything other than marijuana and LSD trips. Nevertheless, the hippies' aversion to plastic and commitment to the use of natural materials were widely adopted.

By the end of the decade, the plastic flower, with which Mary Quant decorated her clean-cut Lolita-style dresses, had given way to a real flower, which became the symbol of the peace movement. The hippies' "flower power" movement attracted most of the younger generation as well as many adults. Wearing and distributing flowers, they demonstrated against social class differences, intolerance, racism, and war. What began as a protest by the younger generation demanding greater individual freedom became increasingly politically motivated in the USA, as the black population began to oppose racial discrimination. The protests came to a head in anti-Vietnam war demonstrations, with similar student marches being held throughout Europe. One of the issues at stake in this respect included the ideological clash with established authority. Germany and France, in particular, witnessed the emergence of a student opposition movement based on the ideas of Karl Marx and Mao Tse Tung that grew increasingly radical. The students' rejection of what they considered to be an abhorrent political system eventually escalated into the unrest which culminated in the bloody clashes of 1968—the same year that, to the horror of the whole world, Russian tanks rolled through the streets of Prague, crushing the delicate flower of freedom in Czechoslovakia.

In America, meanwhile, the summer of 1968 was once again a "summer of love" with days of open-air concerts in San Francisco, modeled on the 1967 "love-in" pop concerts held in London and Los Angeles. The youth movement celebrated peaceful unity for the last time in August 1969 at the legendary open-air festival in Woodstock, New York—an event which attracted one million visitors and has gone down in history as the biggest such event of all time. After this, Flower Power, pop, and rock seemed to lose their magic. Subsequent concerts degenerated into alcohol, drugs, and violence. The different groups went their separate ways: hippies returned to their communes and Oriental sects, homosexuals became involved in gay rights, women embraced the feminist movement, some became left-wing activists, and a few even turned to terrorism. The dream of "love and peace," which for a time had seemed almost within reach, burst like a bubble. Even so, nothing was the same as before.

This was equally true of fashion. Coco Chanel was soundly rebuffed when she offered to dress Brigitte Bardot, idol of the younger generation, in elegant clothes free of charge. Bardot is said to have dismissed the proposal with the remark "couture is for grannies" and stuck to her unconventional boutique fashion. Elegance was the last thing that young people wanted, because that was exactly what their mothers had aspired to in the 1950s and it was very aging. It was now the younger generation's turn to set the trend and this time it was mothers who were copying their daughters —to an almost embarrassing degree.

It is likely that no one will ever know for sure whether it was Mary Quant or André Courrèges who actually invented the miniskirt. There is, however, considerable evidence to suggest that this groundbreaking creation originated in London, if only because this is where the whole 1960s youth movement first began. The sensational impact caused by the advent of the new fashion, looking as fresh and innocent as a child's pinafore dress, can only be fully appreciated if one remembers that the 1950s were characterized by women with great big busts and spiky stiletto heels. Along came these young girls, all huge eyes and long, thin legs, innocently revealing their budding breasts with the new transparent look—to the delight of all pedophiles, whose only misfortune was that these trendy children preferred to stick to their own kind.

Twiggy, a 16-year old English girl, who weighed a mere 90 pounds yet knew exactly how to make the best of those pounds, was the perfect personification of the new ideal. Three years in the modeling business left her rich enough to retire at the age of 19. Nicknamed "Twiggy" because of her twig-like thinness, she was the first model to be idolized by the masses. Like the Beatles, she was swamped by fans wherever she went.

It was the era of little English girls. The captivating Jean Shrimpton and gangly-limbed Penelope Tree likewise became top fashion models in a way that no one would have believed possible, since neither of them seemed to fit the image of conventional beauty. This in itself was one of the reasons why they inspired photographers such as David Bailey and Richard Avedon.

David Bailey, who was not in the least interested in fashion ("clothes are just clothes"), viewed every photoshoot as the equivalent of a sexual act with

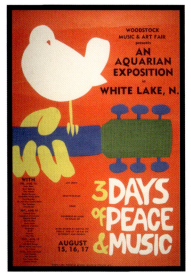

Sex, Drugs, & Rock 'n' Roll

The dove and guitar depicted on the poster (far left) symbolize the themes of "peace and music"—the defining elements of the famous 1969 Woodstock Festival, which featured Janis Joplin (top right) among the artists and where hippie couples (top left) demonstrated just how wonderful life could be. That same summer, Jackie Onassis, formerly Kennedy, took advantage of her newfound freedom as wife of the wealthy Greek shipping magnate, appearing in a mini dress at the Acropolis (left). Three seminal films explored people's attitude to life during this period: *Blow Up*, starring David Hemmings and featuring the model Veruschka (below left), *Breathless*, with Jean-Paul Belmondo and Jean Seberg (below center), and *Barbarella*, starring Jane Fonda (below right). Facing page: Emilio Pucci's psychedelic prints were considered the ultimate design statement of the 1960s—nowadays they are back in demand as retro fashion.

As First Lady, Jackie Kennedy was obliged to renounce *French haute couture* and rely on American designers

the camera representing the penis. It was Bailey on whom the main character (played by David Hemmings) was modeled in Michelangelo Antonioni's notorious film *Blow Up*—made in 1966, in which the German model Veruschka played herself. The film is about a fashion photographer who unwittingly finds himself witness to a murder. When he tries to find out more about the crime, he strays into the moral vacuum of "Swinging London," where everyone is off on a psychedelic trip and not remotely interested in reality. Antonioni's film, with its space-age costumes and vivid fantasy uniforms, was regarded in its day as exceedingly over the top, yet documentary material from London clubs during that period proves irrefutably that the actual fashions were even more fantastic. It was hardly surprising, therefore, that Diana Vreeland, exalted editor-in-chief of *Vogue* magazine, was delighted when David Bailey visited New York with Jean Shrimpton, his current favorite: "Stop—the British have arrived!" she told her staff, presumably meaning: "Stop—everything is going to be different from now on!"

And Paris? The capital of haute couture had certainly not been idle while the rest of the world was worshiping the youth cult. It, too, had discovered a new idol: Jacqueline, the elegant wife of John F. Kennedy, elected in 1960 as president of the USA. The charismatic, young presidential couple awakened hopes for an era of renewal. The Cold War between East and West dragged on, however, and 1961 saw the building of the Berlin Wall, while a year later the Soviet Union tried to turn Cuba into a strategic weapons base, and the USA retaliated by imposing a blockade. The world was a hair's breadth away from nuclear war.

The fact that fashion can play a role in politics was illustrated by the fact that Jackie publicly rejected Paris haute couture and opted for an American designer, Oleg Cassini, who was by no means one of the top names in the fashion world. What counted in his favor, however, was the fact that he had, for a time, been engaged to Grace Kelly, one of the most immaculately presented fashion icons that America had ever produced, and what is more—at least so the story goes—he had no qualms about copying the great Parisian couturiers at Jackie's behest. Some claim that Jackie continued to wear Paris fashions,

but that these had to be ordered by New York fashion houses on her behalf so that she could officially be seen to be buying "American." One thing we do know for certain is that when the Kennedys paid their state visit to France in 1961, she was wearing Givenchy again—as she had in the past—and her appearance at the Elysée Palace was so aristocratic that she was dubbed "Her Elegance" by the press.

Jackie's heyday came to an abrupt end in November 1963 with her husband's assassination. Yet, even during those dark hours, 34-year old Jackie maintained a dignified composure and elegance, still wearing the blood-spattered Chanel suit which she refused to take off, wanting the whole world to see "what they have done to Jack." Jackie remained in first place on the list of the world's most popular women and only dropped to eighth place when she married Greek shipping magnate Aristotle Onassis. Nevertheless, she continued to set the tone in the fashion world. In 1966 she wore a miniskirt in public for the first time, which led the *New York Times* to comment that "the future of the miniskirt is now assured."

Jackie's switch from tasteful little suits, hat, and gloves to T-shirts and a miniskirt, or jeans, inevitably contributed just as much to fashion's new, younger look as the growing influence of the youth cult in London. Another contributing factor was man's conquering of outer space, which, coming on the heels of a period of unlimited growth, now held out the prospect of an unlimited future. In 1961, Yuri Gagarin had made history as the first man in space, but it was the first moon landing in 1969, when American astronauts Neil Armstrong and E. E. "Buzz" Aldrin set foot on the moon for the first time, that really seemed to mark the dawn of a new age, bringing with it changes in our clothes.

The first designer to launch a futurist fashion line was André Courrèges with his Space Age Look, created in 1964. Pierre Cardin was similarly fascinated by futuristic ideas and designed outfits which would not have looked out of place on robots. The most modern designer of all was Yves Saint Laurent, even if his ladies did not resemble female astronauts. He preferred to look to the street for his inspiration and brought the prevailing spirit of the times to the runway, subtly transforming it season by season into haute couture.

1963

1969

Prêt-à-porter (ready-to-wear) and boutique fashions were the main innovation of the decade. All the couturiers became involved in this branch, producing a second, and sometimes even a third, range of fashion lines, which were both cheaper and newer than haute couture. At the same time, boutique owners, like Mary Quant in England, Jil Sander in Germany, and Dorothée Bis in France, were becoming influential fashion trendsetters. This had the additional effect of blurring class differences, not least in matters of fashion, and the decade ended with total freedom in matters of style: the miniskirt existed alongside the maxi, pants were as acceptable as skirts, futuristic designs and patterns coexisted alongside folkloric and psychedelic themes. It was viewed by many people as the death knell of fashion, which could not survive without the kind of fashion dictates imposed by Dior in the 1950s.

Jane Fonda (b. 1937) provided a typical example of women playing experimental roles. Her 1967 role of *Barbarella* portrayed her as sexy and chic in a patent leather outfit worn with boots and carrying pistols—in other words, completely consistent with earthman's fantasy image of women in space. This is hardly surprising considering that the film was directed by Roger Vadim, who ten years earlier had molded Brigitte Bardot into the image he wanted and was now trying to turn Fonda into a space-age sex symbol. Jane Fonda, however, did not prove quite as malleable and she realized quite soon that *Barbarella*, despite the film's huge success, was not a blueprint for a new woman. She left Vadim, returned to the United States, where she protested against the Vietnam War, became involved in environmental protection and women's rights, and, in so doing, became a true idol.

Joan Baez (b. 1941) was another celebrity who used her fame to lend weight to her political work. She was 19 when her first record turned out to be one of the greatest successes ever experienced by an American singer. She worked alongside Martin Luther King within the civil rights movement, joined protests against the Vietnam War, and supported the student revolts. She was a confirmed pacifist and one of the first members of Amnesty International and remains active to this day in the peace movement.

Another supporter of black civil rights in the USA was Jean Seberg (1938–1979), who found herself the target of a CIA persecution campaign. A single film earmarked her for evermore as a symbol of youthful rebellion. *Breathless*, a masterpiece by Jean-Luc Godard, produced in 1960, featured Seberg with her short, cropped hair as a shy, yet spirited American student in Paris, whose fear of love leads her into betraying her lover. Love was after all one of those old-fashioned values, which no one wanted to believe in any more.

Janis Joplin (1943–1970) was considered the best white blues singer in the world, lived life in the fast lane, partied hard, and had just one wish: "not to live to be 70 by sitting in some goddamn chair watching TV." In fact, she died aged 27 in a Hollywood hotel room of an overdose of heroin—one more reason why she became a legend, idolized by young people whose motto was: "Hope I die before I get old"— words taken from the prophetic song by The Who rock band.

Despite all this, the majority of the baby boom generation did survive and have careers, often against their better judgment, eventually bowing to a new genre of middle-class values, and defining—not least because of their numerical superiority—the political, social, and fashion scene for decades to come.

1970

The Shrimp
Nicknamed "The Shrimp," British supermodel Jean Shrimpton was the closest rival to Twiggy, who was considered a little more extreme. She is shown here in a floral-patterned Op Art mini dress posing for her one and only film *Privilege*.

A LEGEND IN HIS OWN LIFETIME:

Yves Saint Laurent

08.01.1936
–
06.01.2008

No one provoked more tears during his career than Yves Saint Laurent. When he unveiled his very first collection, the *New York Herald Tribune* reported that it was "the emotional fashion binge of all time." This was on January 30, 1958, three months after Dior's death. The international fashion community had made the pilgrimage to No. 30, Avenue Montaigne, in fearful anticipation of witnessing either the end or the future of haute couture. Could this 21-year old youngster sustain the splendor and fame of what had become the most prestigious couture house of the century, and, in so doing, rescue the French economy?

He could indeed. What is more, he approached the task with even greater enthusiasm than Dior had when he introduced his New Look. This was probably due in part to the fact that Saint Laurent's Trapeze collection managed to add a youthful casualness to the opulence and skilful cutting techniques employed by the late king of fashion. Saint Laurent's own appearance—so tall, so thin, so young, so shy, and so vulnerable—undoubtedly contributed to the fact that the whole world wanted to hug him.

The Paris press, at least, were ecstatic, rejoicing that: "The great Dior tradition will continue." However, considerable differences soon began to emerge between the late Dior's approach and that of his young heir. Dior had always designed with the image of a mature woman in mind, a woman whose attraction lay in her immaculate elegance. Young Saint Laurent, on the other hand, was determined to design for women in the midst of the turbulent, anarchic days of the 1960s. "Yves the Dauphin," as the French liked to call him, quickly began to blow the dust off couture. "Down with the Ritz, long live the street," was the crown prince's credo and, with this in mind, he rejuvenated fashion by incorporating elements of the youth culture. After three years on the Dior throne, he deliberately outraged his conservative clientele by introducing the Beat Look, which seemed to have burst into his quiet salon straight off the noisy street: black leather jackets, turtleneck sweaters, and short skirts, in homage to the rebellious students of the Left Bank of the

Early signs of genius
At the age of 21, Yves Saint Laurent was taken on as an assistant to the great Christian Dior, demonstrating his skill as a talented design artist. Insiders were quick to realize that this nervous and hypersensitive young man was a creator of genius with a great future ahead of him.

Art and commerce

Yves Saint Laurent first demonstrated his exceptional talent for drawing in 1957 when he started out sketching designs in chalk on a black-board (above right) and later in 1961, as Dior's top designer, on a pane of glass (below left). He had a passionate love of art and in 1965/66 he designed clothes inspired by the work of Mondrian (facing page) as well as mini and maxi dresses inspired by Pop Art (above left). In 1983/84, a retrospective at the Museum of Modern Art in New York exhibited his cocktail dresses decorated with moon motifs (below right).

The shy prince

Beautiful women flocked around Yves Saint Laurent but he only ever developed a close friendship with Catherine Deneuve (left). The most important person in his life was Pierre Bergé, with whom he was romantically involved for many years and who remained his lifelong business partner. Bergé was the one who pulled the strings behind the scenes (below left). During the 1960s, YSL produced a spectacular array of ideas: leather jacket and thigh-high boots for the biker bride in 1963 (above center), three-piece pin-striped power suit in 1967 (facing page), pantsuit with Bermuda shorts and see-through blouse in 1968 (above left), and the perfect safari suit in 1969 (below right). The Russian bride with fur hat and boots in 1976/77 (above right) marked the start of a series of ethnic folklore-inspired fashions.

A princess's dream
Yves Saint Laurent designed this magnificent "infanta evening gown" in 1977. It was made from pink moiré silk with gold embroidery trim and was probably worn as a wedding dress. French photographer Sarah Moon had a unique gift for posing her subjects, portraying them dreamily lost in thought in an intimate and powerfully poetic setting.

Following his first major success,
a pathologically shy Yves Saint Laurent
sought refuge in a cupboard

Seine. This was more than his employer could tolerate. Marcel Boussac, who had financed the Dior empire, split from Saint Laurent and replaced him with the less audacious Marc Bohan.

Although Dior had tended to look to the past for his inspiration, unlike Saint Laurent whose ideas were firmly future-oriented, the two men still had much in common. They both grew up in affluent, upper class families, both became aware of their homosexuality at an early age, and both idolized their mothers. Both men were avid readers and had intellectual leanings. They were both well versed in art and both were excruciatingly shy. They also showed exceptional promise at an early age for sketching fashions—when only 17, Saint Laurent's design won first prize in a competition organized by the International Wool Secretariat (Karl Lagerfeld came second), whereupon Dior, who was himself a gifted sketch artist, hired him as his assistant. And to top it all, both men were extremely superstitious.

Unlike Dior, Saint Laurent was fortunate in love. Soon after his first show, he met Pierre Bergé, who not only came from a cultivated background, but was also an astute businessman. Together they launched a fashion house which would eventually surpass the House of Dior. Most importantly, however, Bergé, who was six years Saint Laurent's senior, adopted the role of protector to his fragile friend. Saint Laurent, who had already fallen from grace as Dior's successor, was conscripted into the army in 1960, where he was so vilified on account of homosexuality that he suffered a physical and mental breakdown after just a few weeks. The medical therapy he received was primitive in the extreme, consisting of electric shock treatment and sedatives, which led to a lifelong drug dependency. It was Pierre Bergé's perspicacity, energy, and devotion which eventually led to his protegé's release. He also helped him obtain a compensation settlement to the tune of 100,000 dollars from the House of Dior on the grounds of breach of contract. Together, the two men launched the fashion house known as Yves Saint Laurent Couture.

It opened in January 1962 and no other show had ever attracted as many people or generated such intense anticipation. The crush of well-wishers, who besieged Saint Laurent afterwards with tearful enthusiasm, alarmed him to such an extent that he sought refuge in a cupboard. From that day on, he suffered the double-edged honor of having to endure the sort of celebrity status normally reserved for sports personalities, film idols, and rock stars. He himself once described this overnight fame as "the trap of my life."

Dior had set himself the task of producing a new style every season and Saint Laurent proceeded to intensify this pressure. He became convinced of the imminent demise of haute couture, regarding it as out of step with the times, commenting: "I am only continuing to run the salon because I do not want to be held morally responsible for putting 150 employees out on the street," and in 1966 he began introducing comparatively cheap *prêt-à-porter* clothes, followed eventually by an even cheaper third "variation" line. This meant that he had to produce not two but several collections each year, a pressure which sometimes drove this somewhat fragile perfectionist to the edge of total exhaustion.

Homage to Cubism
Yves Saint Laurent frequently relied on paintings for his designs. For his 1988 haute couture collection, he used dove and iris motifs to decorate a vivid blue-colored cape, worn with a long, blue evening gown.

Tuxedos forever

Saint Laurent's female version of the tuxedo, like Chanel's little black dress, is a classic outfit that will never go out of fashion. YSL designed several variations of the tuxedo: In 1994 it appeared as a short suit worn with thigh-high crocodile leather boots, in 1988 as a mini dress, in 1995 as a suit worn with fur-trimmed hat, in 1998 as an evening suit worn with a lace top and, in 1996, classically simple for the *prêt-à-porter* market, modeled by Claudia Schiffer (facing page). The formal, masculine two-piece suit was also adopted by Saint Laurent and reinvented for women in sandy beige for the haute couture market in 1971, and in a subtle pinstripe for the *prêt-à-porter* market in 1995.

Ladies, reveal yourselves…

The story goes that YSL almost fainted when he saw the upper part of a naked female body for the first time. The shock must have been good for him as thereafter he was constantly imposing it on his public, for example in 1991 (above right) and in his final collection in January 2002 (facing page). He liked to decorate his risqué styles with bows in pink, his favorite color, which he cleverly combined with mint green and different shades of lilac.

YSL believed that nothing was more erotic than a **well-fitting man's suit** *revealing naked female flesh underneath*

During the 1960s, Saint Laurent introduced various new elements into women's fashion which are now regarded as indispensable features of a woman's wardrobe: pantsuits, safari jackets, transparent garments, and, above all, his female version of the tuxedo, which will always be associated with his name. Like Chanel, who was famous for her practical ideas, many of his designs were based on items from men's wardrobes, yet he somehow always managed to add a suggestion of the erotic to his masculine styles.

His long-time muse and friend, Catherine Deneuve, summed up his achievements perfectly: "Saint Laurent designs clothes for women who live double lives. His clothes for daywear help women to enter a world full of strangers with confidence. However, for the evening, when she may choose her company, he makes her seductive."

Saint Laurent's evening wear reveled in the retro and ethnic looks so beloved of the hippies—he merely made them acceptable to the world of couture. "To my mind," he admitted, "evening is the time for folklore." He led his couture clientele on a series of journeys inspired by ancient China, Peru, Morocco, Central Africa, or the elegant Venice of Casanova's times. His revival of Tsarist Russia with a collection inspired by the Ballets Russes in 1976 was greeted with rapturous acclaim: "A revolution ... it will change the future of fashion worldwide," prophesied the *New York Times*. Others appeared less impressed by Saint Laurent's "Russian revolution," the most expensive couture show ever held in Paris: "too nostalgic," "more fancy dress than fashion" were some of the criticisms leveled at his designs. Saint Laurent himself did not necessarily view it as his best collection, but he did see it as the most beautiful one. His lavish Russian "peasant outfits" unquestionably reaffirmed his reputation as the designer with the best color sense of the 20th century, as did his subsequent "Chinese collection," which displayed even greater theatrical extragavance. No one else would have dared to combine yellow and lilac, or mix orange with pink and red—Saint Laurent had a unique gift for getting the colors right in this respect.

Saint Laurent's "foraging raids" collected inspiration from students (bomber jackets with chiffon skirts!), exotic countries, and past civilizations (Greek toga-style evening gowns, which left one breast exposed), as well as from the world of art. The works of Matisse, Picasso, Mondrian, Tom Wesselmann, and close friend, Andy Warhol all found their way into Saint Laurent's fashion. And none of them could ever feel exploited in any way since Saint Laurent's designs were always a unique homage to the respective artist.

Even a much less vulnerable creator would have suffered because of the mixed reactions of the public, which ranged from effusive praise to crushing criticism. Saint Laurent, who had never fully recovered from his breakdown in the army, fought his recurring bouts of depression and suicidal tendencies with alcohol and drugs. He was never allowed to go anywhere alone and was always surrounded by his entourage of "hippies de luxe." This wild group of people, who often visited the Marrakesh holiday palace belonging to Saint Laurent and Pierre Bergé, included Talitha, the beautiful wife of John Paul Getty Jr., who died of a heroin overdose. Two more were Loulou de la Falaise, Saint Laurent's muse and right hand, who was voted one of the world's best-dressed

Dressed for big game hunting in the big city

The safari look, first introduced in 1968, was one of Yves Saint Laurent's recurring themes. The cotton jacket with its practical pockets was more casual and versatile than the usual blazer, yet still classed as "city wear." It was suitable for all occasions, either for a jaunt into the countryside or for a trip into town. A range of safari-look clothes for men was consequently introduced a year later.

Yves Saint Laurent was adored by the French, who loved the **romantic image of a fragile genius**

women, and who had to renounce alcohol following a stomach operation, and Betty Catroux, Saint Laurent's second slender muse, who is said to have admitted having a problem with drugs.

Saint Laurent himself gave several interviews during his latter years in which he talked frankly about his addiction. Such public admissions failed to damage his image any more than those unforgettable occasions when this once beautiful young man appeared in public bloated, swaying on his feet, and mumbling incomprehensibly. The French, who cherish the romantic idea of tainted genius, simply loved Saint Laurent all the more. In 1983/84, the New York Metropolitan Museum of Art devoted a retrospective to Yves Saint Laurent, the first time a living designer was honored in this way. It was followed by more exhibitions and awards—by the age of 50, Saint Laurent had already been elevated to godlike status, as if he no longer dwelt among the living. Admittedly, many people had long since declared his fashion finished. The truth is that in the mid-1980s, he turned his back on "fashion, which is born of fashion" and concentrated on the sort of continuous evolution that had been usual prior to the war—before Dior introduced his crazy notion of introducing a new look every season. This prophetic decision was vindicated by the *New York Times* when his 1997 collections were shown: "While the public is looking elsewhere on the runway for something new, Saint Laurent is quietly demonstrating what will last..."

There was no holding back the tears at a big gala event held at the Paris Opéra in 1992 to celebrate the couture house's 30th anniversary: Saint Laurent, swaying, but happy, took the salute at the parade of tuxedos he himself had designed. And there were more tears in 1999 when he gave up the *prêt-à-porter* range following the takeover by Gucci. However, he still remained in charge of the haute couture business, of which he had said in 1971: "It might last another five or ten years." Yves Saint Laurent continued beyond his own expectations and did not retire from haute couture until 2002—again to the accompaniment of a veritable ocean of tears.

The world of fashion was to shed its final tears over Yves Saint Laurent when he died of a brain tumor on June 1, 2008 in his Paris apartment. All the fashion experts agreed with Diana Vreeland, the inimitable editor-in-chief of *Vogue* magazine, when she commented that "Coco Chanel and Christian Dior were giants, but Saint Laurent was a genius."

Even after the demise of this sensitive favorite of the gods, Pierre Bergé continued to see that his wishes were carried out: Yves Saint Laurent's ashes were scattered in the rose garden of the Jardin Majorelle at his villa in Marrakesh. His art collection, which included works by Picasso, Matisse, Klee, Mondrian, and Brancusi, was auctioned in Paris early in 2009, commanding the highest price ever paid for a private collection. The grieving widower, Pierre Bergé—who had been Saint Laurent's partner for almost 50 years and became his civil partner at an official ceremony shortly before his death—invested half of this record amount of 373 million euros in the administration of Saint Laurent's estate and the other half in support of AIDS research.

One last look
Every couturier nervously watches his show from the wings. In 1995, a relieved Yves Saint Laurent is seen smiling before going on stage to receive the applause. Seven years later he took his last curtain call before leaving the fashion stage for ever.

AN OUTER SPACE ODYSSEUS:
André Courrèges

b. 1923

Some people believe that fashion can simply be divided into two biblical periods: BC and AC, in other words "before Courrèges" and "after Courrèges." These abbreviations were, of course, coined by space-age fashionistas, who firmly maintain that the advent of André Courrèges launched a new era in fashion history.

Even Yves Saint Laurent, who in retrospect was probably the greatest designer of the 20th century, once admitted: "I had got bogged down in traditional elegance. Courrèges pulled me out of it."

It was four years before André Courrèges, for his part, was able to shake off the influence of his greatly admired mentor, Balenciaga, who resolutely continued to produce designs of conservative elegance. After serving as an air force pilot in World War II, Courrèges, who had studied civil engineering, decided to change direction and join a more appealing world. He applied to work for Balenciaga and started off in his studio as a graphic artist sketching dress patterns, eventually rising to the position of first assistant. Eleven years later he left Balenciaga, saying: "You are like an oak tree—nothing else can grow under such a large tree."

Together with Coqueline Barrière (b. 1935), whom he later married, he analyzed the lifestyle of modern women and projected how they would develop in future. The result was a futuristic, rigidly minimalist style of couture, which was completely divorced from anything that had gone before. Armed with this new concept, he and Coqueline launched their own couture house in 1961, helped by Balenciaga, who supplied them with an interest-free loan.

Instead of "men from Mars," Courrèges' vision involved long-legged "moon girls," who he sent out onto the runway in 1964 wearing white trousers and short skirts, worn with low-heeled goatskin boots. "No one would have dreamed of such a thing before the first space launch," marveled the press, admiring the almost frightening mathematical precision of his simple tailoring. Courrèges favored strong fabrics such as whipcord, gabardine, and double-faced wool, which did not follow the body or its movements: "I wanted to invent clothes that one steps into like entering a house." A civil engineer at heart, he was a proponent of the Bauhaus theory of movement whereby "form follows function": His fashions were designed both to protect and to provide maximum freedom. With this in mind, he approached the task of designing like an architect with regard to cut, and like a sculptor with regard to shape.

Up, up, and away into the future
Technology and futurism were the two main factors which influenced the fashions of André Courrèges. In this photo, he looks like an aircraft mechanic among the stewardesses modeling some of his "Air Fashion" designs in Nice in 1973.

Brave new world

The models who danced their way along the runway showing off Courrèges' 1969 collection in New York were like creatures from another galaxy. The mood was new, young, cheeky, and liberating and inspired many women to follow suit and wear nothing but short little dresses, which fell away from the body, and, above all, flat-heeled shoes. Jumpsuits made from white satin with brass decoration (facing page) or dark blue, transparent fabric embroidered with sequins frequently took the place of the long evening dress.

Short and sinful
These sporty-looking designs allowed an occasional glimpse of what was underneath. This fashion was only recommended for athletic-looking bodies.

A clean future

For snow enthusiasts, Courrèges turned yellow-dyed rabbit fur into a warm outfit. Anyone who wanted to learn more about the car of the future could test his "concept car" at the 2008 Paris motor show.

Enter the snow queen

The *robe nuage* (cloud dress), presented in 1997 and fashioned in organza and cotton, retained its balloon shape like a sculpture.
The wearer was bound to be the focus of attention, either as a bride or the queen of the ball.

Cool, high-tech fabrics, combined with classic, embroidered motifs, created
a new mood of galactic romanticism

"We always inserted lining between two layers of fabric in order to create volume," explained Coqueline, who had also learned her trade in Balenciaga's studio. The starting point of every design was the shoulders, in other words, the only "fixed point of reference," since there were no tucks, gathers, or even draped effects, merely parallel lines, either horizontal or vertical. The austere geometry of his clothes was softened by curved or rounded patch pockets and thick piping. The only decoration consisted of visible topstitched seams, which highlighted the garment's construction like a design sketch.

The proportions had to be redefined for this simple silhouette. The optical balance required a hat or cape with a high hood to create an extended line. The Courrèges duo resolutely avoided high heels or pencil skirts. In their view, as Coqueline once remarked: "Women have been tormented long enough by such things." However, Coqueline, a trained dancer, found she first had to teach most of the models how to walk normally again: "The motion should be a powerful thrust from the thighs and butt rather than working the calves hard."

As a result, the models pranced, danced, and skipped along the runway to modern jazz, turning the show into a kind of dance performance, inspired by "happenings." Courrèges could not have demonstrated more clearly what he—who was a keen athlete, mountain climber, skier, and rugby player—had in mind: "I think the women of the future—morphologically speaking—will have young bodies."

Which is why the mini seemed the appropriate fashion for the modern woman—and it was this sensational innovation which made Courrèges an overnight celebrity. There is still some debate as to whether it was he or Mary Quant who invented the miniskirt, but the British designer is certainly correct in pointing out that there was no possibility of copyright, because so many young London girls began appearing overnight with their skirts cut off six to seven inches above the knee. It is a credit to Courrèges' courage that he was bold enough to introduce the miniskirt into haute couture, transforming this flimsy garment, which owed its existence to a pair of scissors, into a sophisticated piece of clothing, designed down to the last detail. The triangular-shaped mini dress designed by Courrèges gave women the freedom of movement to get into cars, or even climb ladders—there was nothing to get caught, ride up, or cause the wearer any other kind of embarrassing exposure. Courrèges also designed matching shorts and bodystockings to wear with his miniskirts as basic elements of a woman's wardrobe.

Some critics compared his fashions to children's clothes and, admittedly, some Courrèges designs seemed to be taken straight out of *La coupe pour enfants*, a 1946 pattern book: in particular, his baby-doll pinafore dress that had matching hotpants and bloomers to go with the tunic and smart little white ankle- or knee-length socks to complement ankle boots, the latter being as soft as a baby's first pair of shoes. Nevertheless—as all the critics agreed—Courrèges elevated these styles to the level of couture, thereby creating the first consistently modern line.

Only Coco Chanel, the grand old lady of fashion, raged publicly: "This man is trying to destroy women by covering up their figures and turning them into little girls." To which Courrèges coolly replied: "I made women 20 years younger without the use of a scalpel." And he also divulged

---

Cover up
When an icy wind blows through the streets, every urban guerilla will appreciate a protective outfit like this one: knitted jumpsuit, fur-trimmed tunic, flat-heeled boots, and a balaclava-style hood with a slit for the eyes—from Courrèges' 1977 collection

*Courrèges aimed to create **fashion for the year 2000**—in fact, his ideas projected even further into the future*

how: he basically left a three-centimeter (just over an inch) gap between the dress and the skin so that the body could breath and air could circulate. The outer shape gave no clue as to the shape of the figure and there was not even a distinct waistline.

Courrèges' ground-breaking space-age look turned him into the most copied couturier of his time. He blamed the press for this and banned the media for two years. Greatly annoyed, he retreated into his own personal cosmos which consisted of a smart high-tech studio decorated entirely in white and silver. Courrèges was seeking the brilliance, coolness, and purity that were his hallmark.

During the 1960s, synthetic materials swamped the market and Courrèges was the first designer to make them acceptable in haute couture. He was particularly taken with rhodoid, a sturdy, transparent type of plastic. "We cut out typical sections of handworked St. Gallen lace," explains Coqueline "and underlaid them with rhodoid." The effect was galactic romanticism. Courrèges' space-age look made people believe the stars were within reach.

Nor was it only the upper classes who could afford his fashions. In 1968, Courrèges introduced his second couture line, featuring knitted jumpsuits, which resembled playsuits for adults. His firm intention in this respect was to develop the idea of a Chinese-style worker's suit (the "Mao suit"): "In three to four years, every woman will be walking around dressed like this." This particular concept did not, after all, prove to be such an immediate or sweeping success. The notion of underwear as outerwear, on the other hand, did catch on and by the 1980s leggings and leotards had become essential elements of women's wardrobes.

At the start of his career, Courrèges remarked that he "felt inspired by the year 2000." He was wrong. He was probably even further ahead of his time than he realized. When the Japanese arrived in Paris, showing designs that looked as if they had come from another planet, Courrèges was derided as being hopelessly outdated. Four decades later, however, in the midst of the worst financial crisis since World War II, young designers in New York launched their 2009 autumn/winter fashion collection with designs that would have graced a Space Odyssey, featuring minimalist protective-style clothes of monastic simplicity. Although this provoked less excitement and drama than its previous debut in last century's "Swinging Sixties," it nevertheless sparked a similar sense of optimism and confidence.

Courrèges reacted to his belated triumph with a gentle smile. He had long since handed the fashion house over to his wife Coqueline and embarked on other interests. He gained a reputation in the art world as a sculptor and held a major exhibition in Parc André Citröen in 2008. He also retained his former interest in technology and for many years has been working with Coqueline on the design of a car of the future. The first one made its appearance in 1969. In 2002 and 2004 the couple introduced more advanced models and in 2008 their third prototype of the Zooop EV received a positive reception from the experts. Time will tell what achievements the House of Courrèges is remembered for.

Master of geometry

50 years after the girdle was cast off, André Courrèges and his wife Coqueline (below right) finally freed the female body from the last of its clothing constraints. Courrèges, who had studied civil engineering, designed his fashions on a drawing board according to practical criteria and always with a view to the future. His wife, who was a dancer, tested every design on her own body, checking whether it allowed her unrestricted freedom of movement. Even Courrèges' see-through clothes had a quality of kindergarten innocence and freshness.

A new disc

Courrèges created this outfit in 2000 from CDs and artificial leather. It simultaneously reveals and protects the body and was distinctly different from the usual style of disco outfits. This design marks the point when Courrèges turned his back on fashion and switched to sculpture.

They defined their era

Rudi Gernreich

Paco Rabanne

Mary Quant

Pierre Cardin

The concept of going "topless" was as natural to Rudi Gernreich (1922–1985), a dancer born in Vienna, as the high-cut thong, or tanga, which revealed the buttocks. He designed for women with athletic frames, which he wanted to show off to their best advantage.
Some critics were scandalized by his "monokini," the famous swimsuit whose upper portion consisted of two V-shaped stretch straps. Gernreich also invented the "no-bra bra" and the bodystocking of flesh-colored stretch nylon. In California, to where he had emigrated in 1938, he launched his own fashion label, featuring futuristic designs similar to the avant-garde in Paris— for example, clothes with plastic insets, and seethrough blouses.

Paco Rabanne (b. 1934) studied architecture but began his career as an independent fashion designer in 1966 with 12 "experimental dresses" made from plastic rectangles. His next experiment was with dresses made from aluminum decorated with leather and ostrich feathers. His ideas proved a success and his "spage age" outfits became a favorite with the stars. All modern heroines, from French pop idol Françoise Hardy, to Jane Fonda as "Barbarella," to Audrey Hepburn and the James Bond girls, wore Paco Rabanne's chainmail shirts, which were not sewn with cotton or thread, but "tailored" using hooks, eyes, and pliers. He withdrew from the fashion business in 1999 and devoted himself exclusively to more esoteric matters.

At the heart of "Swinging London" was Mary Quant (b.1934), who is to thank for the popularity of the mini, geometric haircuts, and pantyhose in every conceivable shade and pattern. She began her career in 1955 with a small boutique bazaar in the King's Road where she sold simple, handmade pinafore dresses. During the 1960s, this developed into an international empire, for which Mary Quant designed fashions, accessories, and makeup—all uncomplicated, trendy and geared to young people. She was the first to use PVC for coats and boots, invented shoulder bags with long straps, and created her distinctive "Look"—a new word in fashion— specifically with teenagers in mind. She is regarded as the creator of boutique fashion.

Born in Venice in 1922, Pierre Cardin launched his couture house in the 1950s, the golden era of couture. It was modeled on the work of his teachers Schiaparelli and Dior. When he ventured to design a commercial ready-to-wear collection for the Printemps department store, he was expelled from the couturiers' guild, but was soon readmitted when it became clear that modern fashion also needed to be made available to the masses. Cardin joined the avant-garde circle, which was obsessed with the space age, and proved himself a master of modern marketing. He was the first designer to sell to Japan and China and was granted more lucrative licenses than any other fashion designer.

THE JAPANESE
Masters of the imperfect

REI KAWAKUBO

YOHJI
YAMAMOTO

ISSEY MIYAKE

KENZO TAKADA

When Japanese fashion designers Rei Kawakubo and Yohji Yamamoto made their debut in 1981, they rocked the Paris fashion scene. The two of them were in a relationship with each other at the time and together they dethroned the entire designer elite.

"French fashion has found its master in the Japanese," was the headline in *Libération*, a newspaper popular with French intellectuals. Journalist Michel Cressole went on to remark: "What they are proposing in terms of fashion for the next 20 years is far more convincing than what Courrèges and Cardin presented in 1960 for the year 2000 and which now seems so outdated."

It is certainly true to say that although Kawakubo and Yamamoto went their separate ways a long time ago, their influence remains just as strong and trendsetting even now in this new millennium. Their runway models are both ageless and modern, neither Japanese nor European, but as exotic as poetesses from another planet. Female artists, dancers, writers, and eccentrics immediately recognized the potential of these asymmetric and unfinished-looking garments and adopted them as liberating cover-ups. Others needed a little

longer. Suzy Menkes, the *Herald Tribune's* influential fashion critic felt drawn to the Japanese on an intellectual level "but the French can have my body to dress."

In the early 1980s, Western designers veered towards garish tastelessness and ostentatious excess, for example shoulder pads, sequins, and leggings! The austere asceticism of these Far Eastern masters was as refreshing as a thunderstorm. Their designs seemed oversized and sacklike, and deliberately disguised the body instead of focusing attention on it. This was a departure which shocked most people who were not impressed by what was nicknamed "Hiroshima Chic," a style which apparently made them look like vagrants. However, "the Japanese" prevailed and became a success.

REI KAWAKUBO, born 1942 in Tokyo, was the most radical: "As far as I am concerned, women do not need to have long hair or large breasts to feel feminine." And high heels, which she had always abhorred, were definitely taboo. Instead, she concealed the female body under several layers of fabric. Her geometric clothes negated the old-fashioned concepts of Western fashion; they were neither decorative nor flattering to the female figure. Nevertheless, despite being a newcomer to the world of fashion, Kawakubo's innovative designs were truly revolutionary: Her

Lantern cascade
The pleated dresses featured in Miyake's 1994 Flying Saucer collection are reminiscent of the accordion-like Chinese lanterns familiar from kindergarten days.

clothes were for the sort of woman who had not even existed ten years earlier—the sort of woman who wanted to signal her personal and financial independence and did not need a wide-shouldered "power suit" to do so.

Rei Kawakubo, who had studied literature and worked in advertising before becoming a designer, was convinced right from the start that she could succeed as well as any man. It was no coincidence that her own label, launched in Japan in 1969, was called Comme des Garçons (like the boys). One of her most provocative outfits was a black sweater incorporating gaping holes, which she showed as part of her 1982/83 winter collection. To Western eyes, it looked as if it belonged in the rag bag, but was nevertheless perfectly in tune with what Far Eastern philosophy viewed as the ideal. As video artist Nam June Paik, who was born in Korea but studied and taught in Germany, once remarked with great insight: "When too perfect, lieber Gott böse (God gets angry with you)." Rei Kawakubo reacted to European criticism with the ironic comment: "If they only knew how difficult it was to get a machine to drop stitches at irregular intervals..." In 1997 Kawakubo hit upon a spectacular way of challenging the proportions of the human body by placing padded lumps and bumps around her models' bodies, deliberately deforming the silhouette, turning it into something absurd and monstrous and making her models appear misshapen. The padding could, of course, be removed, leaving the sort of perfectly tailored garments that one would expect of Kawakubo—but it left people

thinking about the body and how it should be presented. Kawakubo was good at causing shock waves. No sooner had black been accepted as *the* Japanese color than she exploded that particular unwritten rule in 1994 by launching a collection of brightly colored clothes, while she herself wore neon red. Six months later, she staged her collection without musical accompaniment—a departure which merely served to heighten anticipation in the silent cathedral. Nor does she permit any distractions in her boutiques. Her Comme des Garçons lines are sold in rooms with minimalist interiors, resembling cool, ascetic galleries. They have been used for exhibitions by artists like Cindy Sherman, thereby finally fulfilling all fashion designers' longstanding dream of witnessing art and fashion in a true symbiotic relationship.

YOHJI YAMAMOTO is frequently described as a "conceptionalist." As in the case of concept art in the 1960s and 1970s, his whole thinking revolves around the actual "idea" itself—so much so that its implementation almost becomes unnecessary. In fact, many of his works are left deliberately unfinished. He reduces them down to the essential elements, to his abstract vision. His approach reflects the Japanese concept of *wabi-sabi*, the aesthetics of something that is imperfect. Yamamoto, however, believes that the roots of his work lie somewhere other than in his homeland. "I was born in Japan by an accident of birth. But I have never made use of this label."

Yamamoto was born in 1943 and raised by his mother, a war widow, and became aware early on of the ruthlessness of the system with its

Contrasts
Yamamoto clothes are usually black and severe, but sometimes he surprises his audiences with dazzling reds in fluid styles.

Modern plastron
The inspiration for Rei Kawakubo's TAO collection in 2006 was partly derived from women's traditional costumes featuring a decorated bodice. The plastron shown here is artistic, expensive, and anything but innocent.

Revival
In 2006, in tribute to Miyake's famous plastic bustier, which caused such a stir when worn by Grace Jones in 1980, Naoki Takizawa, his protégé and succcessor, presented a new, softer version in this form-hugging plastic.

programmed objectives and rigid code of honor. He went to university to please his mother, but despite his law degree, instead of a career in law, he opted to help his mother, a seamstress, who was obliged to work a 16-hour day in her studio. She consented to this arrangement on condition that he attended the renowned Bunka fashion college, where he was not only the only male student but also the oldest.

In 1969, Yamamoto won a trip to Paris in a competition. Despite his lack of money, he managed to prolong his stay there for eight months by doing jobs for various young designers. Back in Tokyo, he set up his own firm in 1972 and launched his first collection in 1977. Yamamoto set up a total of eight different firms, including "Y's for Women" and "Y's for Men", his second collections. His collaboration with Adidas proved highly successful and he also launched his own perfume, yet he still does not think of himself as a businessman.

His fashion contemporaries regard him as a poet, artist, and philosopher—and consider him one of the brightest minds in the fashion industry. He has been the subject of books and exhibitions and, in 1989, he collaborated with Wim Wenders in a film entitled *Notebook on Cities and Clothes*. Since then, Wenders has only worn Yamamoto clothes: jackets with narrow, sloping shoulders, small lapels, and three buttons, plus trousers which are wide around the thigh and narrow at the knee. These are set off by a classic white shirt, soft and the very opposite of austere.

Yamamoto's clothes, which are dignified and serious in character and ignore all the usual traditions of feminine seduction technique, integrate elements of the kimono, which literally means "thing to wear." Yamamoto himself, however, describes the source of his inspiration as a collection of photographs by August Sander, taken between the two world wars and depicting anonymous Germans in somber, heavy, everyday workwear in subdued colors. Yamamoto's first designs were made out of similar fabrics—voluminous tents which hid and protected the body. Yamamoto's starting point when constructing a design were two points on the collar bone "from which the fabric hangs best. If it is allowed to live." The beauty of the loosely shrouded figure only becomes evident when it is in motion. Yamamoto has enjoyed cult status for many years and while his designs have become lighter over the years, his message as a designer carries an increasing amount of weight in the fashion industry.

ISSEY MIYAKE has, from the very beginning, tried to establish a link between East and West. He has never forgotten his roots, yet at the same time has always sought something new. By way of illustrating the two cultures, he staged a show in 1979 entitled "East meets West." His philosophy revolves around finding *mâ*, a Japanese word meaning the space or gap between the perfect and the imperfect. This could be the space between the body and clothes. Since everyone has a different shape, the *mâ* is always unique. In Europe, Miyake is regarded by many as a modern-day Fortuny, who became famous in the early 20th century for his sensational pleats set in silk fabrics. Not only did Miyake invent a new method of creating pleats in a range of synthetic fibers and colors, but, like Fortuny, he is a man of many talents and interests, for whom technology plays as important a role as craftsmanship and art—and, like all Japanese, he makes no distinction between fine art and applied art. Nor does he believe in a hierarchy of materials—it makes no difference whether they are synthetic or made of natural fiber. As far as he is concerned, they can both be processed into fine garments. Such impartiality allows him a huge amount of freedom in creating what we must refer to as his "clothes," since he is known to bridle at the label "fashion designer."

Born in Hiroshima in 1938, Miyake trained as a graphic designer in Tokyo before going to Paris where he studied couture under the tutelage of Laroche and Givenchy. In New York he studied the "ready-to-wear" market and it was here that he launched his first collection in 1971. Since 1973, Miyake has been showing his creations at the Paris fashion shows, although his fabrics and clothes are still made in Japan. He refused to get caught up in the Western obsession with creating a "style": "My style is derived from life. And not from style." Which is why he creates light, washable, and interchangeable clothes, which are ideal for a modern, mobile lifestyle. While in Paris he became aware of another significant difference in the way West and East approach fashion: "In Western tailoring the cloth is cut to the shape of the body whereas in Japan the cut is determined by the fabric." It is no wonder that he spends a huge amount of energy on his quest for new fabrics. He has 100 Japanese factories working exclusively for him.

His designs may conceal the body but they allow it complete freedom of movement. This was compellingly demonstrated by the Frankfurt Ballet company, under the direction of William Forsythe, which has frequently appeared in pleated costumes designed by Miyake. Since 1988, when he first began work on what was to become his Pleats Please line, he has continually expanded and perfected the style, and it has become something akin to a uniform for intellectuals and artists, carrying the same sort of kudos as Levi jeans. The individual garments, some in startling colors, can be mixed and matched in a variety of combinations.

Since 1999, Miyake has devoted most of his attention to A-Poc (A Piece Of Cloth), a line which combines state-of-the-art computer technology with traditional knitting techniques. These unsized garments are produced as tubes of fabric with premarked cutting lines from which people can create their own collections—from long dresses to socks. In this way, ready-to-wear items can be turned into custom-made garments. In the tradition of all Japanese designers, Miyake has nurtured the next generation and has already groomed his own successor. In 1999, NAOKI TAKIZAWA, who had been in charge of Miyake's menswear line for six years, also assumed responsibility for women's wear.

Takizawa was born in 1960 in Tokyo and, whilst remaining faithful to Miyake's legacy, has led the label toward the future, trying out experimental materials such as traditional oil-soaked paper, ironed metallic jersey with paper backing,

His Master's mind

Takizawa has remained true to Miyake's legacy and continued Miyake's lines, but, as with this 2008 design, has put his own stamp on them by making the pleats less rigid and more fluid.

Flower power
To celebrate spring, Kenzo had the famous Pont Neuf in Paris (above right) completely decorated with flowers. His farewell collection in 1999 (right) was also dedicated to flowers. Kenzo delighted in colorful folklore (above) and his successor, Antonio Marras, is also proving to be a master of floral prints—and vibrant knits (2008) (below).

wrinkled synthetics, and, naturally, the famous elastic pleats. Eventually, in 2011, women's fashion was placed in the hands of Yoshiyuki Miyamee, who had also worked for Miyake for many years.

KENZO TAKADA, born in 1939, was the first Japanese designer to conquer Paris with his fashions. He came to France in 1965 after being one of the first male students ever to attend the famous Bunka fashion college in Tokyo. In contrast to some later Japanese designers, Takada was an instant hit when he presented his first spectacular show in 1970. His designs were as cheerful and uncomplicated as he himself and met with an enthusiastic reception. They reminded people of the celebrated "summers of love" of 1968 and 1969 when young people all over the world united for peace and freedom. A "flower child" in a Kenzo dress from his very first collection made it onto the front cover of *Elle*, a glossy, modern fashion magazine, turning the Japanese designer into an overnight celebrity. The fact that he had made his early designs from cheap fabrics found at flea markets contributed to the newcomer's success as it was very much in keeping with the philosophy of the time. His boutique Jungle Jap soon became a meeting point for his cosmopolitan clients, who shared the globetrotting designer's love of visiting exotic places and collecting ideas from all over the world. "I am a very visual person," explained Kenzo, wearing his familiar beaming smile. He is only ever called by his first name in the fashion industry. "Traveling is a wonderful source of impressions, I love all cultures and later I wallow in the memories. Then I begin to draw."

Using the basic elements of the kimono from his own native land, he added influences from South America, the Far East, and Scandinavia. He describes his complex mix of prints and styles as "destructured couture." He cites the source of his inspiration as being paintings by Gauguin and Matisse, as well as romantic films. He stages his fashion shows like a film director: His unforgettable 1978 and 1979 shows were held in a giant circus tent, finishing with a horse-woman riding into the arena wearing a transparent uniform and himself on the back of an elephant. In 1993, Kenzo sold his brand to LVMH, a luxury goods company, and six years later, at the age of 60, he retired from the business altogether. This was an unusual step for a fashion designer. Generally speaking, they can no more give up their drawing pencils than a conductor his baton. But as Kenzo put it: "30 years in a career are enough. I want to travel and have time for my friends." In the spring of 2009, Kenzo went one step further and sold his town house near the Bastille, where he had lived for 20 years. With its typical Japanese-style garden, it had been a popular photo background for lifestyle magazines. His extensive collection of Chinese statues, African masks, and Indian dolls, estimated to be worth over 2 million dollars (1.5 million euros), was auctioned off. Kenzo, now aged 70, plans to "start a new chapter" and is moving into a large, 2,200 square foot (200 sq m) apartment in the center of Paris.

Since 2003, Kenzo fashions have been given a fresh lease of life by artistic director ANTONIO MAR-RAS, born in 1961 in Sardinia. Like Kenzo, Marras also has an affinity for traditions and handicrafts, but his particular partiality is for "deconstruction"— in other words expensive materials with holes burnt in them, unfinished seams, and ancient fabrics which are partially darned, patched, stained, or encrusted. The result is different every time, introducing a unique element to the *prêt-à-porter* collection.

JUNYA WATANABE has become the most influential of all the designer protégés. Born in 1961 in Tokyo, he completed his studies at the Bunka fashion college and was taken on by Rei Kawakubo. In 1984, he started as a pattern cutter for Comme des Garçons and just three years later was put in charge of its Tricot knitwear line. He presented his first solo collection in 1992 but still remains part of Comme des Garçons. Despite being strongly influenced by Rei Kawakubo, Watanabe has managed to find a style of his own, characterized by highly advanced cutting techniques and draping effects, and new types of fabric. In his 1999 show, he directed that a continuous shower of rain should fall upon the runway in order to demonstrate that his functional microfiber fabrics were completely waterproof. Not a drop of water penetrated the fabric. At first glance Watanabe's silver-gray evening gown which appeared at his winter 2000/01 show had an almost historical appearance. It consisted of a velvet tube with a broad ivory-colored chiffon ruff, in a style reminiscent of the 16th and

Poetry and geometry
Tao Kurihara is highly acclaimed for her draped effects and prints (above), while her mentor, Junya Watanabe, is regarded as the somber crown prince of Japanese designers (below).

17th centuries. However, the excessively wide ruff, which completely enveloped the shoulders and torso, could only be fabricated from polyster chiffon since silk organza would not have been able to keep its shape. Similarly, the velvet was also polyester but the whole ensemble was—in true couture tradition—stitched together by hand, a typical example of Watanabe's unique talent for turning sculptural designs into light, floating creations. Watanabe's "techno couture" is a great favorite with the avant-gardists.

Continuing the spirit of the master-protégé tradition, from which he himself benefited so much thanks to Rei Kawakubo, Watanabe is in turn mentoring a young female colleague. TAO KURIHARA studied at Central Saint Martin's in London before starting work for Watanabe in 1997 and showed her first collection in Paris in March 2005. She, too, works under the protective umbrella of Comme des Garçons, enjoying all the advantages—from finance to production—that a large company can offer.

JUN TAKAHASHI, born in 1969, is another of Rei Kawakubo's protégés; in 2004 she let him design a collection of blouses which were then sold in Tokyo's Comme des Garçons store. While still a student and member of the Tokyo Sex Pistols, Takahashi launched his own Undercover label, which now comprises several lines. He started out with T-shirts and punk street clothes, of the kind that he and his music friends wore. His designs, which look simple at first glance, are actually a skilful mixture of violence and poetry—for example, fabric which has been slashed and then patched with delicate lace. Takahashi is regarded as a subversive couture talent with a future.

Born in 1957, HIROSHIGE MAKI, a student of Yohji Yamamoto, is also establishing a reputation for himself. His trademarks are rubber clothes, hence his label Gomme. Stretchable bands of rubber enclose the body and adapt to every movement.

ATSURO TAYAMA, born in 1955, is also one of Yamamoto's students and is as shy as his mentor. Away from the main spotlight of the fashion business, he creates extremely elegant clothes which are not noted for their comfort. Like most Japanese, he favors modern materials such as rayon and polyester, and is noted for creating complicated wrapped and ruched dresses, earning him the title of "fashion's Mr Twister." He founded his own Green Label in 1999, a name which has no ecological significance since Tayama often uses fur in addition to synthetic fibers.

KOSUKE TSUMURA was born in 1959 in Japan and trained in Miyake's Design Studio. He is particularly noted for his Final Home project: a nylon coat with over 40 pockets, designed in 1994 as a functional garment in an "end-of-the-world" situation—perfect for travellers who want to carry everything on their person, but also ideal for anyone who is homeless, as the pockets can be stuffed with newspaper as protection against the cold. Once the coat has served its purpose, it can be returned for recycling. The notion of recycling something apart from ideas is new to the world of fashion...

Dinosaurs
Yamamoto's art is simultaneously primeval and forward-looking. His women are from another planet, another time—they are eternal.

Sex, Drugs

THE TRIUMPH OF BAD TASTE

& Rock 'n' Roll

Flowers in their hair, Jesus sandals on their feet, and a smile on their lips: The young idealists of the 60s wafted happily into the seventh decade of the 20th century. Their utopia seemed to be becoming a reality. The future belonged to the young and their "love and peace" mantra. In reality, while this cult of youth lived on, the young people who had sparked the change just got older. Nature, their source of fulfillment and enlightenment, now turned against them. The placid hippies with their beards and long hair soon began to look passé, and before long the watchword was "trust no one over 30." The young people who came after them did not see their lesser years as a blessing, suffering as they did from unemployment, inflation, and boredom; being young did not automatically mean being idealistic and optimistic.

"We wanted to rebel," explains Vivienne Westwood, "as we felt that the hippie movement had run its course, and we had never liked what it had brought with it in the first place." Together with her partner Malcolm McLaren, the former primary school teacher ran the London boutique Let it Rock, where the underground youth culture of the 1950s

lived on, with rock 'n' roll and drainpipe trousers. It later switched to selling leather, latex, and bondage clothing, until Westwood eventually became known as the "mother of grunge." She wore T-shirts emblazoned with radical statements like "Destroy" from the very beginning, years before another British woman, Katherine Hamnett, became famous for her political statements printed on T-shirts. Hamnett's audience with Margaret Thatcher wearing a T-shirt sporting the slogan "58% don't want Pershing" has gone down in fashion history; the prime minister was shocked, but recovered sufficiently to remark, with justification, that Britain had not deployed any Pershing missiles as deterrent weapons in the Cold War between East and West, only cruise missiles.

The women's movement was not invincible either. Feminists were forced to realize that being female was no more a guarantee of a better world than being young. In order to get their political ideas across, many "peace-loving" women resorted to violence, including the journalist Ulrike Meinhof, who was responsible for bank robberies and bomb attacks as a leading member of the Red Army Faction. Alice Schwarzer chose words as her weapons. In 1971 she

Too chic to be a hippie
When the fashion industry requisitioned the clothing of the "flower children," it rid it of any connotations of protest. This couple, the man wearing Indian jewelry and a patchwork waistcoat, and the woman a yellow felt hat with a patterned maxi dress, were perfectly presentable.

Glam rock stirs up the club scene

With his "Ziggy Stardust" persona (opposite page), David Bowie created an "other-worldly" character free of sexual limitations. Bowie helped his friend Iggy Pop (far left) recover from drug addiction, while Gary Glitter (left) was submerged by scandals. John Travolta's dance performance in a white suit in the 1977 film *Saturday Night Fever* unleashed the craze for disco. Stars like Roy Halston, Bianca Jagger, Andy Warhol, and Liza Minnelli all met at Studio 54, along with the younger generation like playmate Bebe Buell (below left) or the actress Jennifer Jason Leigh (below right). Johnny Rotten (below middle), lead singer of the Sex Pistols, eventually settled as a musician and artist in Los Angeles.

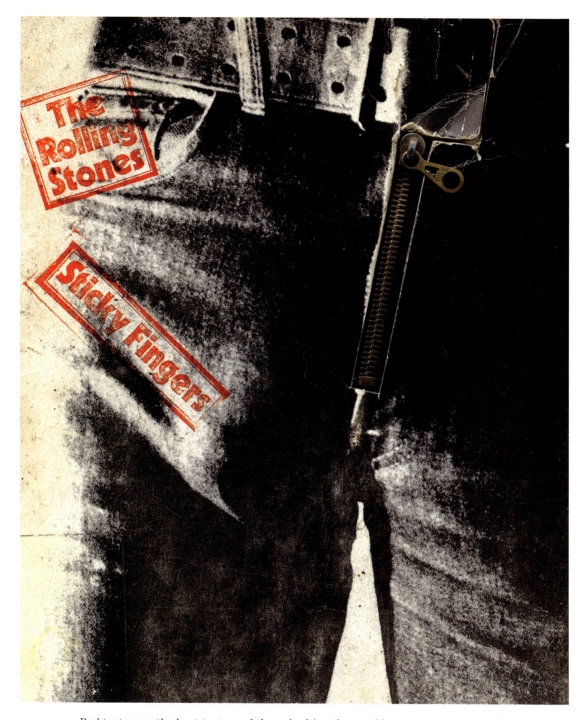

Bad taste was the best taste, and the only thing that could guarantee you attention

The Rolling Stones made an explicit reference to consumer fantasies with the cover of their 1971 *Sticky Fingers* record, designed by Andy Warhol. The original cover featured a real zipper. Equally influential, if not more so, were the costumes of the Swedish pop group ABBA, the epitome of bad taste. Agnetha, Anni-Frid, Benny, and Bjorn wore everything from hippie garb to platform heels, Lurex, silver, acid perms, and knee-high socks to cowboy outfits, making the stage a riot of color. ABBA-mania lasted a whole decade, until the group broke up in 1982. Black funk musicians, on the other hand, favored extreme elegance, as exemplified by the Soul Train Dancers in Los Angeles in 1974. The trend for platform soles among women led to a number of accidents when walking.

incited 374 women to make a public demonstration called "We had an abortion," and her book *Der kleine Unterschied und seine großen Folgen* (The little difference and its huge consequences) kickstarted debate about feminism all over the world. In 1977 she founded her own magazine, *Emma*, the "main organ" of the German women's movement. Many women strove for power, something that had previously been frowned upon. Margaret Thatcher, who won the British general election in 1979, proved herself as the "Iron Lady." She tackled the run-down economy and the "degenerate" youth who had made the United Kingdom a centre of innovation over the past two decades.

While the 1960s are remembered as the great period of the youth revolution, the 70s seem more fragmented, hazier. Yet they were anything but quiet; this was the time when previous upheavals gained traction on a much wider scale. Sexual freedom, conscientious objection to military service, experimental drug use, the call for women's rights—these were no longer minority concerns, but issues that were espoused and accepted by large groups in society. The cannabis-befogged pacifism of the hippies was superseded by a newfound pugnacity among political activists, often exacerbated by hard drugs. The Black Panthers (America), the Red Army Faction (Germany), the IRA (Ireland), and the PLO (the Middle East) were all prepared to use any means necessary to achieve their ends. Terrorist attacks were the order of the day.

Political groups were not the only ones trying to make their ideas a reality. People who had been oppressed—predominantly women—now strove for personal fulfillment, and whole families often fell by the wayside. The old ways of life were declared false; something new needed to be found to fill their place. This led to great uncertainty, as all of a sudden everything revolved around the desires of the individual. The journalist Tom Wolfe aptly dubbed the 1970s the "Me Decade." The celebrity photographer Horst P. Horst thought Wolfe, who had become the star chronicler of American popular culture, "a provincial playboy in a white suit." Yet unlike Horst, a decadent European photographer, that "playboy" knew exactly what was brewing under the shiny American surface of wealth and charity. His essay

Radical Chic was an account of white philanthropists and black freedom fighters in the 1970s, and his later novel *Bonfire of the Vanities* became a bestseller worldwide; far from being sat up in an ivory tower, he knew the contemporary scene inside out.

The end of the Vietnam War was protracted and traumatic, accompanied by the oil crisis in 1972–73 and the subsequent crash of the dollar. The economic boom that had begun in the 1950s was soon over, and the Seventies saw a downturn. The once optimistic youth turned cynical, and showed a different face. This decade has gone down as the era of bad taste for a reason. Platform heels and hot pants, flares and polyester shirts, disco glitter, retro kitsch, and no-future punk; everything was sampled, mixed, rejected, and taken up again. This might be dismissed as a mere expression of protest, but it concealed a liberating, creative instinct whose effects can still be seen today. Those years saw the breakthrough of postmodernism with its electric style, marking a real revolution in fashion.

At first, it all seemed utterly harmless. Even the respectable middle class was won over by hippie styles, and increasingly took to natural materials like wool, cotton, and silk. Loud, psychedelic patterns and colors were replaced by a softer palette of more gentle patterns and smaller prints, inspired by rustic and ethnic clothing. From 1973 the cry of "back to nature" was followed by a beige period; neutral colors like khaki, sand, taupe, olive, or brick-red were great for mixing and matching, and encouraged a whole new way of dressing. Fashion—like life in general—was no longer subject to fixed rules; everyone could dress in what suited them. Putting together a wardrobe of separates, as we do today, is also a legacy of the hippies, who expressed their individuality by dressing as they pleased.

In 1976 Anita Roddick revolutionized the beauty industry. The granddaughter of Italian immigrants, she borrowed £4000 to start The Body Shop in London. Her idea was to use women's traditional beauty secrets to battle against a gargantuan industry that worked with chemical formulas. The concept took off. Within a few years, The Body Shop had become a byword for natural, environmentally friendly cosmetics, made according to traditional methods by women in all corners of the world. Everyone was

The abandonment of good taste
*acted as a **liberating creative force**,*
ushering in individual style

given a share of the profits, in line with the "Fair Trade" ethos. Roddick became a millionaire almost overnight, but she never forgot her original reasons for founding the company: to produce genuine cosmetics that benefited both the user and the producer in equal measure.

While the middle classes diligently took up the cause of environmental awareness, founding Greenpeace, the first international organization for environmental protection, and striving to do everything the "right" way (preparing the ground for the political correctness of the 1990s), haute couture requisitioned the hippies' utopian ideas of a world in which dreams actually come true. If the multicultural, equal, harmonious new world had not yet come about in reality, at least it was there on the runways. Yves Saint Laurent, in particular, gave both the fantastic folk dresses and the black leather blousons of the anti-establishment the blessing of couture, making them wearable for his moneyed clientele, who wanted to have an "anti" edge while still looking good. This trend for shock chic, which gave them the thrilling feeling of youthful unscrupulousness, was also responsible for YSL's Opium, the heavy, sultry perfume that epitomized the decade. Perhaps the Oriental opulence cultivated by the couture salons was also a nod to the petro-dollar princesses, who became their most prolific customers after the oil crisis, and often their saving grace. Without these beautiful creatures from the Orient and the awarding of ever more licenses for all kinds of accessories, many fashion houses would not have survived the recession of the Seventies.

The key idea was anti-fashion. Everything was allowed, from cheap cotton garments to couture outfits, as long as it didn't resemble a "normal" look. The choice of jeans became tricky, as they had become the uniform of non-conformists—and who didn't want to join them? Levi Strauss won the Coty Award, the US fashion industry prize, in 1971 for its blue jeans for a good reason. The blue denim pants were worn everywhere, by men and women, gays and lesbians, rich and poor alike. They could be worn to university classes or the office—not the embroidered, flared version favored in the Sixties, of course, but a faded pair that looked as though they had been much loved for years. Many of those

wearing them looked as though they never changed their clothes, as this was the best way of demonstrating that they cared little about fashion, having more important things to worry about. Yet this wave of androgyny led not to the hoped-for equality of rights, but to equality of behavior. Boys and girls looked equally wretched and miserable; there was no spark of frivolity. And revolution remained elusive. Even when Andy Warhol provocatively adorned the cover of The Rolling Stones' record *Sticky Fingers* with a close-up of a man's jeans-clad crotch, complete with a real zipper, jeans had already become accepted as mainstream clothing, making the idea outmoded.

Only glam rock restored color to the interplay between the sexes, as well as revolutionary potential to fashion. With their elaborate makeup and flamboyant elegance, Gary Glitter, Marc Bolan, and especially David Bowie rebelled against the prevailing slovenliness and cultivated a high-maintenance look. They demonstrated that the unisex look did not have to mean that women should abandon color; men could embrace it instead. If their masculinity was called into question, then this only opened up yet more possibilities: Bisexuals simply had more choice, in their personal life and in fashion. This attitude was enthusiastically adopted by male and female fans alike, and before long London was awash with lurid Ziggy Stardust clones.

In the USA, black funk musicians were having a similar influence on fashion. Coming from the ghettos, they had no interest whatsoever in down-at-heel, drab clothing; they wanted success, and a glitzy appearance could help them stand out. They wore ruched shirts, tight Italian silk jersey pants, black turtlenecks, leather coats, and, like the glam rockers, platform boots. Their platform soles could be over two inches (5 cm) high, and the heels as much as six inches (15 cm). Extreme materials were sought after; clothes made out of a patchwork of different colored squares of snakeskin were seriously cool among the stars of funk. The overall effect was decidedly erotic—the platform shoes and flared pants drew the gaze upwards along the long legs towards the upper body, clad in skimpy silk jersey.

In the evening even respectable professionals who dressed in unassuming gray and beige by day embraced glitz and excess. Bored of their prim

Not everything that came out of the 1970s was atrocious

Hot pants and white go-go boots were an absurd combination, but on the right figure, even this outfit had
a girlish charm. Nonetheless, grown-up women like
Diane von Fürstenberg preferred to go their own route
with fashion. In 1972 she launched her colorful, patterned jersey wrap dress with the slogan "Feel like a
woman, wear a dress!" Within four years she had sold
five million of them, and it remains a staple for women
of all ages who want to be sexy, comfortable, and chic
at the same time. Diane is a former party girl and Studio 54 regular who was painted by Andy Warhol, but
after her divorce from Prince Egon of Fürstenberg, she
worked her way to becoming a designer to be reckoned
with. The British designer Zandra Rhodes also favored
very feminine, albeit dramatic-looking clothing, and
her hand-printed coat made of chrome yellow felt was
first worn by the US actress Natalie Wood (left) in 1970.
Rhodes, who began her career as a punk and retained
her garish appearance, with green or pink hair, drew
inspiration for her striking patterns from nature and
organic shapes.

Whether punk or feminist, women were choosing for themselves

The behavior of many women had more lasting impact than all the excesses of rock groups put together. Punkette Nina Hagen, fitness queen Jane Fonda, leading feminist Alice Schwarzer, black civil rights lawyer Angela Davies, organic cosmetics pioneer Anita Roddick, or Jane Birkin, who breathed erotically in duet with Serge Gainsbourg—all of them saw to it that women were increasingly able to break out of the norm. The ultimate taboo was broken with the Calvin Klein jeans commercial in which the 15-year-old Brooke Shields asked, "Do you know what comes between me and my Calvins? Nothing!" That was a bit too close for comfort…

*Anyone could have their **fifteen minutes of fame**;*
they just needed to believe in Andy Warhol
and the power of disco glamour

business outfits, the disco provided the antidote for good taste. Shrieking polyester shirts, lycra body stockings, halter neck tops paired with silver Lurex hot pants, lace shirts with glitter jeans, artificial silk dresses from the 1940s, cocktail dresses from the 1950s, grandma's twee floor-length flowery gowns, or modern evening dresses, slit to the crotch; everything could be put on show, even the naked body—artfully painted, of course. Disco, once the sole preserve of gays, became the stage for all self-exhibitionists and followers of Andy Warhol's creed that everyone could be famous for fifteen minutes. The Pope of Pop and his acolytes from the Factory were center-stage at Studio 54. The nightclub only remained open for two years before the tax authorities forced it to close, but it became a legend even in that short time, thanks to the "beautiful people" who took coke and danced there to the point of delirium. The disco wave was unleashed and heightened by films like *Saturday Night Fever*, *Grease*, and *Fame*. Even the most remote backwaters saw barns turned into glittering dance halls overnight and people aping the moves of John Travolta and Olivia Newton-John every weekend. As in previous decades, they donned their finery to go out dancing, but now this meant something very different. Crazy proportions and impossible combinations of colors and materials were a hit—"the best taste is bad taste" was the motto of the day.

It was the ironic glitzy kitsch of the disco movement, of all things—only one element in the fashion of that time—that was to be revived shortly before the turn of the century, while Studio 54 was immortalized in the film *The Last Days of Disco*. This was no coincidence. When the prevailing fashion is based on minimalism and basics, there is a distinct longing for baroque extravagance. Back then the American designer Roy Halston was the first to launch a cool, modern line of slinky silk jersey dresses and jumpsuits, pantsuits, and cashmere twin sets; they were pared down, without patterns, mostly in white, beige, or pastel shades. Halston's minimalism was limited to his designs—his lifestyle was utterly excessive, as we might expect from the favorite dandy of Studio 54. He was declared bankrupt in 1984, and died of AIDS in 1990. His brand was resurrected in 1999 as part of the Seventies revival, but Tom Ford had long been drawing on Halston's legacy with his

skintight hipster trousers and jersey shirts for Gucci. The Halston label had another rebirth in 2008 under creative director Marco Zanini, previously Donatella Versace's right-hand man.

The disco generation danced the last ounce of fat off their bodies during the Seventies, not only during "Saturday night fever," but also every day in the fitness studio. The super-slim, skintight fashions pioneered by Halston and seized upon by other designers, made of materials that left nothing to the imagination, required a willowy figure. This became a cult obsession, and often degenerated into diet and fitness fads. And clothing just became tighter. By the end of the decade women had to lie flat on the floor in order to be able to zip their jeans. Yet they often wore their blouses open to the waist so that everyone could see that they didn't have a bra. This was the first time that a plunging neckline came to be worn casually during the day. Women adopted men's blazers as a thrilling addition to their wardrobe, wearing nothing underneath.

Yet these little freedoms were nothing compared to those seized by the punks. They clad their shaved, tattooed, pierced bodies in everything that was considered ugly: garbage bags, ripped T-shirts, black fetish leathers, glittery Lurex, leopardskin, military clothing, Dr. Martens boots... In their deliberate tastelessness they bore some resemblance to the older disco generation, but while the over-30s serenely saw unsightly, ridiculous clothing as amusing and charming, the punks aimed at bitter provocation. They looked ahead in anger, discovered that there was "no future," and nursed a hatred of the previous generation, with its flower-power posturing and back-to-nature babblings. The punks replaced "love & peace" with "sex & violence," and nature worship with jarring artificiality. Out with cotton, in with plastic! Outfits were composed only of elements that did not belong together: red and green Mohawks atop pale, childish faces; toilet chains, tampons, and safety pins as adornment for leather jackets, along with swastikas and skulls, over fluorescent lace underwear from sex shops. With this surprising juxtaposition of incongruous items, their crazy combinations often took on a surreal character, reminiscent of the Dada movement, and all the more so when someone as shrewd as Vivienne Westwood

1977

was behind it, with a brilliant understanding of how to make punk styles fashionable. She also knew when it was time to move on to something else. Unlike others, she did not take part in the punk revival of the 1990s, when designers like Versace and Gaultier gave it unprecedented glamour. The punkettes of the 70s could never have dreamed that their use of safety pins would later inspire couture creations; the previously unknown British actress Liz Hurley bagged a million-dollar advertising contract with Estée Lauder and gained international celebrity status thanks to her appearance in the now-famous "safety-pin dress" by Versace.

In England the stimulus for new trends came from the streets, but in France, Italy, and America more and more designers were setting up their own boutiques and fashion lines. Every stylist who had once worked anonymously for a big fashion house now tried to make it under their own name. Many of these brands disappeared as quickly as they had sprung up, but great designers also emerged from the ranks of these simple stylists, including Claude Montana, Thierry Mugler, and Jean Paul Gaultier in France. In 1973 Pierre Bergé, the partner of Yves Saint Laurent,

and Jacques Mouclier, the president of the Chambre Syndicale de la Haute Couture, ushered in new legislation which allowed young designers to show their collections in public. Unlike the exclusive haute couture lines, which were presented in January and July mostly in private salons to a small, distinguished circle, these designers or *créateurs*, as they are called in French, chose to show their *prêt-à-porter* collections in March and October in front of a larger but still select audience that includes members of the press, buyers and VIPs. Thierry Mugler and Kenzo were the first designers to make their *prêt-à-porter* shows into massive stage extravaganzas that attracted four times as many viewers as the haute couture shows.

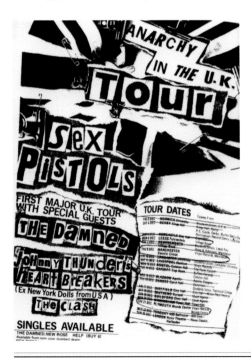

Call to anarchy
On tour in England, the Sex Pistols, managed by Malcolm McLaren and dressed by his then girlfriend Vivienne Westwood, wanted to provoke the kind of unrest sparked by the student revolts in Paris in 1968.

Vivienne Westwood

b. 04.08.1941

If you mention Vivienne Westwood, many people remember her for coming out from a meeting with the British queen and swirling her skirt, showing that she was without knickers, or for being that shrill Englishwoman who wore provocative and tasteless clothing made of latex and leather as a punk. Many more escapades from her three decades in fashion have faded from public memory. Yet Vivienne Westwood is anything other than a scandalmonger. Hers is the classic story of liberation—a fairy tale of someone who raised herself from a punk to a lady.

Vivienne grew up as the eldest of three children in an estate of terraced houses between two villages, a far cry from any kind of glamour. As a teenager she copied Dior's New Look, and her admiration for Dior was always to remain with her. When she was 17 her parents moved to London. Vivienne had the idea of becoming a jewelry designer, but she doubted that a working-class child could ever gain a foothold in the art world. She opted for a local job as a primary school teacher and earned the money for her studies by working in a factory. When she was 21 she met Derek Westwood, who became her first husband, but they separated shortly after the birth of their only son, Ben.

In 1965 her life changed when she met Malcolm McLaren. He was five years younger than she was, but he knew a whole lot more. He had attended drama schools and art colleges, was an expert on rock 'n' roll, and was utterly fascinated by fashion: "He took me by the hand and styled me from head to toe," she says of her longtime companion. Once he had completed the makeover, she sported a peroxide blond "hedgehog" hairstyle, anklet socks with teetering heels, velvet leopard-print trousers or a pencil skirt, and oversized mohair sweaters with stockings. Her appearance alone was enough to entice many people into the Let it Rock boutique that she ran with McLaren in London's King's Road.

The name of the shop was changed many times, and the style of the clothes changed with it. Their greatest immediate success was T-shirts with political or pornographic slogans, and when the boutique was simply called SEX and selling an array of chains, zippers, rubber suits, and other provocative designs, the floodgates really opened. They finally gave the shop the name "Seditionaries," and the punk movement had a home. All year round, it was Westwood who diligently thought up ideas and worked on pieces by hand, yet she did not see herself as a fashion designer.

A timely protest by the former activist
Vivienne Westwood's T-shirts always carried political messages. After the British government passed anti-terror laws in 2005, she protested with the heartfelt plea, "Please don't arrest me."

Back to the future

For fall and winter 2006/7 Vivienne Westwood presented medieval-style dresses worn over tightly bound trousers, but in spring/summer 2009 she sent models down the runway dressed as shiny rock guitarists.

As she likes it

Vivienne Westwood is always good for a surprise. She might dress Carla Bruni in a fur coat and matching G-string, exhibit patent platforms adorned with bullets like a museum piece, or mock the tall helmets worn by British policemen. Her creations include reworked traditional Scottish kilts, cloth printed with riotous drawings by artists (opposite page), and even a picture of a provocatively stuck-out tongue.

*By delving into the **wardrobe** of the 19th century, Vivienne moved fashion forward*

Only at the beginning of the 1980s, when she had turned 40, did Westwood concede that she had developed a unique style. "Until then," she said, "I had never seen myself as a designer; I considered that I had merely collaborated on Malcolm's projects." The couple, who had a son, Joseph Ferdinand Corré, in 1967, lived in separate houses. For Malcolm, music was always the more important thing, while Vivienne concentrated on fashion. The studious former teacher carried out thorough research in the art archives of the Victoria and Albert Museum on the styles, tailoring, shapes, and materials used in the past, resulting in the Pirate Collection, which was the first to be launched under the Vivienne Westwood label on the runway in spring 1981.

Two years later the Victoria and Albert Museum bought one of her neo-romantic pirate costumes, and Vivienne Westwood, previously deemed "not socially acceptable," was proud of the fact. The era of rebellion was over! She had grown tired of drab colors and the underground look; now her pirates swaggered around in gold and ruches galore. A wild element followed with the Savage collection, which featured body painting, mud-smeared hair and Indian prints. The subsequent Buffalo collection also made use of mud and other primitive elements. This was her way of bringing fashion closer to the Third World, as McLaren, her now estranged yet ever-supportive companion, explained.

Westwood made the bold step of going to Paris, where she presented her Punkature spring/summer collection in 1983. This was an extension of her earlier punk styles: Simple squares of material were made into clothes, and rapidly came to be copied on the streets, together with safety pins and bottle-tops as buttons. Only the fabric printed with scenes from *Blade Runner* was out of the reach of poor kids. Unlike other couturiers, Westwood was glad that she was copied so much, even when some people, like her fellow Londoner Zandra Rhodes, adapted her ideas in their own way. The most commonly copied idea was her slinky tube skirt cut from cheap jersey, which clung casually to the hips, leaving the stomach free.

After this, Westwood finally abandoned safety pins and devoted herself to building her business. "Punk is a crucial part of my past," she said in an interview. She also explained why, nevertheless, she wanted to leave this behind: "I was convinced that you just needed to push open the right door, but since then I have learned that no such door exists. There are just more obstacles along the way."

Her biggest obstacle was probably the charismatic Malcolm McLaren, who made himself a jack-of-all-trades as a manager and a soloist on the music scene. For some years after they separated, Westwood remained at his side as a "woman under the influence." She only went her own way in 1985.

She discovered femininity with her Mini-Crini collection, which marked a turning point, with designs dominated by corsets and hoop skirts, those frowned-upon figure-shapers of the previous century. Westwood created a short hoop skirt made of cotton and light tweed, held in place with a frame of artificial fishbone, which ingeniously collapsed when the wearer sat down, allowing it to be worn even in the crowded subway. At that time, when wide-shouldered power suits made every figure look like a Y and women resembled boys, she sent models with pronounced

A fallen angel
In 2009 Vivienne Westwood chose *Baywatch* nymph Pamela Anderson as her muse and model. The ample-bosomed blonde appeared in March on the Paris runway in a red silk dress with a flamboyant tutu and soccer socks.

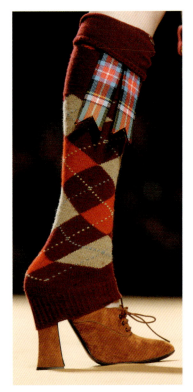

Shoes are important

Vivienne Westwood never set much store by underpants, either in her SEX shop in 1976 (below) or when she appeared before the queen in 1992 (opposite page, above right). But her models wore nothing at all but shoes for the finale of the Paris show in 1994. A year earlier the model Naomi Campbell took a spectacular fall in insanely high platform shoes. The novice at the side of Malcolm McLaren was later to become one of the most influential designers ever, bringing together traditional patterns (above and opposite page, below left) and punk elements (right-hand column) in collaboration with her third husband Andreas Kronthaler (opposite page, above left).

The punk became a lady with Scottish kilts, tweed and twin sets, giving British tradition a new twist

curves down the runway. The "mini-crini" was showcased to real effect with rocking-horse platform shoes. It was like seeing a dancer in a tutu wearing high heels; the viewer never knew what surprising turn would come next.

The Mini-Crini collection was a kind of homage to Dior, who had padded out and corseted women in the same way. His great innovation was to tailor these exaggerated feminine shapes out of a particularly masculine material. This fact did not escape Westwood, who devoted her next winter collection to the quintessentially English Harris Tweed. Her tailored Savile jacket, named after the street that is home to the best men's tailors, became a classic, and new versions are still being made to this day.

Westwood remained loyal to Harris Tweed for the next ten years, in what might be seen as an affectionate parody of the English landed gentry's traditional wardrobe. This includes the red hunting jackets with black velvet inserts, twee twin sets worn by respectable ladies to tea, and, of course, characterful Scottish kilts. "This time I have used the vocabulary of the royal family," declared Westwood, who never shied away from revealing the sources of her inspiration. "I took the conventional and made something unconventional out of it."

Having helped to give durable tweed and English fashion a leg up on the international scene, she was awarded the Queen's Award for Export Achievement in 1988. Everything snowballed after that: In 1989 John Fairchild, the influential publisher of *WWD* (*Women's Wear Daily*) ranked her as the only woman in a list of the six most creative fashion designers in the world; in 1990 and 1991 she was named as the British fashion designer of the year two years in a row; and in 1992 she received the title of Officer of the British Empire, followed by Dame Commander of the Order of the British Empire in 2006, two years after winning the World Fashion Award.

The girl from the English provinces had more than succeeded in turning the establishment on its head: "I have left the dress code of the middle classes and the underground behind. I have come to see the underground as rather suspect... it has no status whatsoever. Quality of life is very important for me, and you can improve it by impressing others with your clothing."

Despite all her prizes and accolades, the rebellious Westwood shows no sign of easing off. Her fashion just gets better and better, and she remains a non-conformist. Now married to her third—much younger—husband, Andreas Kronthaler, whom she met during her professorship in Vienna, she continues to develop her designs, which might take any form at all—except minimalistic.

Vivienne Westwood's aesthetic matches that of haute couture, where exaggerated forms are created by hand. She is firmly convinced that good fashion can only come from a fusion of British craftsmanship and French refinement; nothing else will do.

Like an innocent lamb
Wild women can be made to look angelic. In 1995 Vivienne Westwood dressed the model Kate Moss, no stranger to scandal, in a short tweed kilt, complemented by a silk blouse and a twin-set jacket—and with an angora rabbit in her arms she was the very picture of innocence.

THE PROVOCATEUR:
Jean Paul Gaultier

b. 04.24.1952

What is beautiful? What is ugly? What is elegant, and what vulgar? And finally, what is masculine and what is feminine? Jean Paul Gaultier raised such questions and often provided astounding answers in his shows. While other designers sent the most beautiful women in the world down the runway, he sought out fat, old, pierced, or heavily tattooed women—"real" women, in other words—to present his creations. By doing this Gaultier, who championed women's rights with as much dedication as he did gay issues, did away with the divide between men's and women's fashion, and he now shows both collections together, so that you never know who is going to be wearing a skirt or smoking a Havana. These "mixed doubles" often feature whimsical role-swapping or models stepping out in identical outfits, like twins. In 1985 his iconic men's skirt was the centerpiece of his men's collection, *Et Dieu créa l'homme*, but it did not catch on. Only Gaultier himself continues to show his fondness for the combination of Scottish kilt and sailor's sweater when he comes out at the end of his shows to receive his applause.

And there is plenty of applause, albeit sometimes against all expectations, as his attitude has always been confrontational. His style is an ironic mockery of the French bourgeoisie. Like his British counterpart Vivienne Westwood, his inspiration came from the streets, particularly Paris and London, where he was most impressed by the punks and their razor-sharp outfits. He also aimed to provoke, and most of his shows were the stuff of pure parody; he presented versions of that embodiment of French elegance, the Chanel suit, made out of cheap faux fur, and envisaged the "emancipated woman" as having all the trappings of female seduction—curves, a pronounced waist, stilettos and lingerie. Gay men, who were celebrating coming out in the 1970s, were shown as objects of desire—macho, swaggering musclemen in pantyhose. You need to exaggerate if you want to get your point across. Gaultier has managed to do more for our concept of beauty than many artists, and has promoted tolerance more than most politicians.

Jean Paul Gaultier was born in a Parisian suburb, and his grandmother, a beautician and fortune-teller, had a strong influence on his upbringing. In school the somewhat girlish boy found it difficult to make friends. His constant companion was a teddy bear, which is still his mascot today. He must have been about seven when he saw nightclub dancers in fishnet stockings and

Sackcloth and ashes
Jean Paul Gaultier likes to be seen in a striped sweater and skirt, but for this cheeky 1993 homage to Yves Saint Laurent, who once had himself photographed naked, he wraps himself in rough sacking.

Journey around the world

Jean Paul Gaultier's penchant for ethnic motifs was on display at the retrospective for his 30-year jubilee in 2006. Mantillas from Spain, aboriginal tattoos, Russian Constructivism, the furs and paintings of the Mongols, or a simple striped Breton fisherman's sweater—all these made an appearance in his collections. He used very different materials for his haute couture, such as this fuchsia-colored robe with a fur-trimmed coat and an outfit featuring a short crinoline.

Something wonderful can be made from anything at all—that is the lesson that Gaultier drew from his early experiences

feather headdresses while watching television (still his favorite pastime), and was so fascinated that he sketched them. He made the blunder of taking these sketches to school with him and as a punishment, his teacher pinned one of the drawings to his back and made him go from class to class with it. This really meant running the gauntlet, but to Gaultier's astonishment almost everyone simply smiled when they saw the sketches. It was the first time that he had been shown such appreciation, and he knew that he had found his destiny; his talent for drawing could bring him love and friends.

At 14, Gaultier left school and began sending fashion sketches to all the famous couturiers. Pierre Cardin was impressed by the still naive talent and gave him a chance. Gaultier got his motto, "Everything is allowed; nothing is permanent," from Cardin, and he learned that you can make something wonderful out of rags found on the street; the important thing is the idea, not the material. He has maintained this approach since then. The numerous flea markets scattered over Paris were a rich source of inspiration and treasure trove for him. Collecting, changing, and mixing things anew are the foundation of his style, and he got his eye for it by observing the punks who inspired him on his frequent trips to London in the 1970s.

In 1971 Gaultier went to Jean Patou and stayed three years, learning how to perfect his craft. After that he felt ready to take on the highly competitive fashion market, where young designers had been mushrooming since the introduction of *prêt-à-porter* in 1973. He was 24 when he presented his first solo collection in the Palais de la Découverte in Paris, where he was hailed as the great discovery of the event. Only two years later he was able to found his own company, and he still shows his collections regularly at the Paris shows. The *enfant terrible* label has also stuck with him, with good reason, although he is well over 50.

Like Yves Saint Laurent, whom he deeply admired for his glamour, point-blank eroticism, and shock appeal, Gaultier always succeeded in stirring up a jaded public. He made undergarments key items; corsets and stockings became body-conscious outer clothing. This approach of subverting the original purpose of particular garments might be viewed as postmodern; this is how the Kyoto Costume Institute sees it. This look was possible with new materials that clung elastically to the body. At Gaultier, skintight, multicolored bodies, inspired by the German-American painter Richard Lindner and complemented by old-fashioned laced boots, made an outfit that looked fresh, free, and cheerful, but far from bland. At the same time he made romantic dresses from old-fashioned cotton tulle, with the corset and (purely decorative) garters worn over the skirt. He had created his own take on the innocent yet combative Joan of Arc.

The potential for provocation promised by Gaultier's corsetry was unleashed by the pop star Madonna when she chose his designs for her Blond Ambition tour in 1990. Of all her outfits, the salmon-pink corset with its spiral stitched conical bra cups remains unforgettable. Madonna thought the way a velour-padded atomic bust could completely transform a strict pinstripe jacket was fabulous; it was "the ideal fusion of masculine and feminine power"—the future of fashion.

Breaking cover
Although the model has a military camouflage pattern on her chiffon dress, she is not trying to blend in. Gaultier packaged his perfumes in small bottles modeled on male and female torsos, a reference to Schiaparelli.

The eternal enfant terrible *was*
invited to create haute couture,
and has been **France's greatest talent** *ever since*

The exciting Gaultier costumes were tailored not only to her body, but also to her personality, and she went on to order the outfits for two subsequent world tours from the offbeat Frenchman, including the sadomasochistic riding outfit she wore for her Confessions tour in 2006.

Gaultier's collaboration with Madonna garnered him a lot of press, but it also made him develop a certain stubbornness; today he is known for creating eccentric, almost unwearable designs. The titles of his collections also reveal this attitude: Latin Lover, Women on Their Own, The Concierge is on the Stairs, The Repressed Charm of the Bourgeoisie, or Forbidden Gaultier are all aimed at conjuring up smutty fantasies and blurring any clear way of looking at clothing. The many ethnic influences that Gaultier adopted for his Mongols, The Grand Tour, and Tattoos collections from 1994 to 1995 alienated many people. While the Mongols were dressed in splendid jewelry and sumptuous furs, the "tattooed" models came down the runway apparently naked. Their typical tattoo patterns appeared to be painted directly onto their skin, as the real base layer of nylon bodies and leggings looked just like human skin.

When you extricate the electric outfits from their showy accessories, they remain wittily intelligent and wearable items. In 1997 the Chambre Syndicale de la Couture recognized that his designs were also carefully made according to the rules of couture, inviting the ageless *enfant terrible* to present couture collections. Ever since then, Gaultier has been the great French hope for haute couture, which had been increasingly written off for decades. His artistic spirit and penchant for Dadaesque jokes is strongly reminiscent of Elsa Schiaparelli. He requisitioned her idea of using a human torso as the model for his perfume bottle. The recyclable tin can which it comes in is his one nod to the present day.

Gaultier loves Paris and everything redolent of the turn of the 20th century. He agrees with most tourists that nothing can compare with the folkloric *Bal Musette*; his heroine is the accordion player Yvette Horner. Happily Hermès, one of the oldest traditional Parisian fashion houses, not only bought a 45 percent share of his company, but also offered him the job of overseeing its own collections as the head designer for Hermès' women's collection from 2003 until 2010, before Christophe Lemaire took over the fall/winter collection 2011/2012. The once shrill showman Gaultier had become a *gentilhomme*.

From faraway lands
Like a Mongolian woman from a far-off planet, this model appeared in Gaultier's jubilee show in a shimmering synthetic fiber dress replete with giant zippers and extra-long sleeves. Behind her is a "Japanese woman" wearing a "cage dress" from 1989.

Blond ambition

For her 1990 Blond Ambition Tour, Madonna commissioned Gaultier to create her costumes, and he was so thrilled with his client and her sex-bomb potential that he could not stop drawing her.

They defined their era

| Thierry Mugler | Claude Montana | Franco Moschino | Betsey Johnson |

Woman as fetish—this sums up Thierry Mugler's (b. 1948) fashion designs. His quilted shoulders and corseted waists in leather and vinyl were seen as scandalously misogynistic in the 1970s, but in the 1980s they became avant-garde. In 2003 the former dancer gave up fashion in order to put on big stage shows, creating everything from choreography to costumes and stage effects. As an artistic consultant he was responsible for the world tour costumes of the curvaceous pop diva Beyoncé, among others.

Like Mugler, Claude Montana (b. 1949) put the emphasis on wide shoulders and wasp waists, but his precise geometrical tailoring made his designs more aggressive than those of his colleague. His fans regarded his austere silhouettes as a form of futuristic abstraction; his detractors saw the leather costumes with their large, protruding collars and pencil skirts or pants and high heels as merely vulgar. Lawsuits, bad luck, and a dissolute lifestyle meant that Montana was forced to sell his company along with the name in 1997.

Franco Moschino (1950–1994) set out to debunk the fashion establishment, but he actually ended up being embraced by the very people that he parodied. With the eye of a studied painter and a surreal sense of humor, the Italian transformed conventionally tailored items of clothing into innovative showstoppers, including fried eggs decorating his hemlines or bottle caps adorning a quilted, Chanelesque jacket. His brand was Cheap & Chic. His most famous item of clothing was his "fur coat," made purely from small teddy bears. Moschino died of AIDS in 1994, but his fashion house lives on under the creative directorship of Rossella Jardini.

The American Betsey Johnson (b. 1942) established herself in the 1970s as a specialist in screechingly colorful prints which put people in a good mood even if they found them tasteless. When Julie Christie wore her famous dress with the 12-inch (30-cm)-long extended collar, the former dancer had made her mark as a designer. It took the critics until 1999 to award Johnson a prize for her "Timeless Talent"—one more reason for her to turn cartwheels, as is her custom after every show.

The new era of glamour

1980

I n 1980, 69-year-old Ronald Reagan was elected US president and youth culture became a thing of the past—despite it being the year that Karl Lagerfeld tried to revive the miniskirt. The Western world had become a conservative place once more.

However, Reagan, a former film actor, and his ultra-slender wife, Nancy, injected a shot of glamour into the White House, dazzling the world in their designer clothes. Anyone who could imitated them. Society's latest role models were the "yuppies" (young urban professionals), who had careers in computer-based technology or the media, or else made lots of money playing the stock market and casually spent it all again on conspicuous consumption. Ivana Trump, for example, with her "big boobs," "big lips," and "big hair," was living proof that more is definitely more. She was then the wife of property mogul Donald Trump, and no one epitomized the ideal of the decade better than she did: Rake in large amounts of money and then make a show of it. She resembled one of the characters out of *Dallas* or *Dynasty*, popular television series which glamorized the "good life."

In 1980, 300 million viewers across the world tuned in regularly to watch the TV series *Dallas*, which provided the perfect medium for studying fashion and lifestyle in the 1980s. J.R., Bobby, Pamela, and Sue Ellen Ewing of Dallas demonstrated how pleasant life could be if you were very rich and living on a luxury ranch called Southfork.

Dallas, a city which had grown rich on oil, was one of the best sales markets for Escada, a Munich fashion firm, which was considered the largest in the world. Established in 1976 by Margaretha and Wolfgang Ley, Escada appealed perfectly to the prevailing tastes of the day: If a thing is expensive, it should look expensive! Hence its reputation for elaborate embroidery and gold trimmings. It is hardly surprising, therefore, that Margaretha Ley, a former Swedish top model, was presented with the Dallas Fashion Award in 1987, a major accolade in the fashion business.

It was not long, however, before Escada's extravagantly decorated creations fell out of step with the

Home, sweet home
When Ivana Trump hosted a dinner for friends in 1986, it resembled a state occasion: Elaborate place settings, diplomatic seating order, and formal evening dress were *de rigueur*. It was after all the home of property mogul Donald Trump.

Rise and fall

The 1980s were the best decade of all for the Munich fashion firm Escada, run by Margaretha and Wolfgang Ley (facing page, above left). Even Diana, the "Queen of Hearts," was seen wearing Escada (above). There was a brief revival of interest in this luxury wear toward the end of the last millennium (facing page, below), before Escada, once the world's biggest fashion label, began its downward spiral. The bankrupt company was bought in 2009 by the beautiful Megha Mittal of India (facing page, above right).

The term "fashion victim" refers to anyone who is unable to resist the *many temptations of fashion*

mood of the times. Even the short-lived revival of the glamorous Eighties at the start of the new millennium was not enough to halt the company's decline, and in 2009 Escada went bankrupt. The company was bought by 33-year-old Megha Mittal of India, who plans to restore it to its former glory.

The male counterparts of the elegantly dressed ladies of *Dallas* and Co. could be seen in *Miami Vice*, another TV series. The crumpled linen jackets with rolled up sleeves and sharply creased trousers worn with such casual elegance by Don Johnson and Philip-Michael Thomas were created by Nino Cerrutti. This charismatic Italian was Hollywood's most popular designer during the 1980s. He also dressed Richard Gere in the film *Pretty Woman*. Miami was also a fateful city for another Italian, Gianni Versace, who was gunned down in July 1997 on the steps of his grandiose villa. His death was as puzzling as his life was glamorous. Born the son of a seamstress, Versace rose within a few short years to compete with Armani for the title of Italy's top designer. Unlike his rival, he was not a fan of understatement; Versace chose a golden Medusa head for his signature motif, was not afraid to use vivid colors or unusual material combinations, and was known for exhibiting the body in garments that were so sexy that they only just avoided being considered offensive.

It is hardly surprising, therefore, that Madonna was a great fan of Versace outfits. This pop icon sang the anthem of the decade: "I am a material girl, you know that we are living in a material world." Madonna's fans had a hard time keeping up with her changes of image, which veered from whore to saint and demonstrated to the world that a woman can be anything she wants if she only uses the right label. Madonna must surely bear some of the responsibility for the "fashion victim" syndrome, a term coined in the 1980s for women who blindly buy the latest fashion in the hope that some of the glamour of a Madonna-type superstar will rub off on them. Or perhaps even change their lives.

One of the most popular idols for such daydreamers was Lady Diana Spencer, the shy kindergarten teacher whom Prince Charles, the heir to the British throne, chose as his princess. The fairytale wedding gown, which she wore for her wedding in July 1981, was copied a million times over, and marriage itself, which had been scorned as a middle-class institution during the 1970s, became fashionable again. Anyone who was not getting married could at least wear evening gowns in the new, romantic style. Fantasy and escapism were very much in vogue, and this trend was greatly reinforced by some of the effeminate show business stars, such as Boy George and Prince, who appeared in decadent velvet outfits with ruched shirts. Michael Jackson, megastar of the 80s, withdrew completely into his own realm of fantasy.

Nor were the Paris fashion elite immune to excesses of this kind. Christian Lacroix, the highly acclaimed crown prince of haute couture, was by no means averse to this new fantasy-inspired trend. However, he presented his opulent designs with both wit and sophistication, whereby the richness of the fabric matched the extravagance of the fantasy. "Clothes of such brilliant luxury and defiance," wrote society journalist, Julie Baumgold, after Lacroix's US debut in 1987, "probably have not been seen since eighteenth-century French aristocrats rattled in carts over the cobblestones on their way to the guillotine." But Lacroix did not escape unscathed. His perfume, C'est la vie!, was a flop, and since no couture house can survive without its revenues from perfumes and accessories, his business got into financial difficulties and in 2009 the House of Lacroix filed for bankruptcy.

Bernard Arnault had long since split from Lacroix, whom he had once helped to launch his couture house, and it became impossible for anyone to get anywhere in the fashion industry without Arnault's backing. During the 1980s, Arnault, who was born in France in 1949, bought LVMH (Louis Vuitton Moët & Chandon), the world's largest luxury conglomerate, and since then he has determined which creative designers have the potential to succeed in the global market. Arnault placed John Galliano, a flamboyant English designer, on the throne of Dior and brought in an American designer, Marc Jacobs, to Vuitton. He dropped Lacroix because he refused to bow to international marketing laws.

It would be wrong to imagine that the 1980s were characterized exclusively by the yuppies and their money. Youth culture once again exercised an important influence on contemporary life although this time it was the youth culture of young blacks.

The "black is beautiful" slogan of the sixties' Black Power movement was adopted again and now used primarily to describe the music and fashions of black people. It was in the New York and Los Angeles discos of the 1970s that street fashion and street sounds like hip hop were born. A new style of dancing also emerged, known as breakdancing. And the art of breakdancing required comfortable clothes—sportswear, as well as sneakers. As part of the 1980s' obsession with named brands, hip hoppers simply had to wear Reebok, Nike, or, above all, Adidas. In the words of Run DMC rappers in 1985: "My Adidas and me, close as can be, we make a mean team, my Adidas and me." When Run DMC performed before 20,000 fans at a rap concert in Madison Square Garden and asked the audience how many of them were wearing Adidas sneakers, 20,000 youngsters held up their sneakers. It's now hard to believe that Adidas, a southern German sports firm, had been teetering on the brink of ruin until someone had the brilliant idea of marketing the brand as the number one sneaker for street basketball. This sparked an Adidas renaissance, particularly in the USA, and saved the company.

The homeboy style of young men from the black ghettos comprised baggy pants, sneakers, and baseball caps. These were worn with heavy chains hung with medallions, such as Mercedes symbols, to provide the "bling" factor. White youngsters soon acquired a taste for this style and tried to go one better than the original. By the mid-1980s another black style of music had become popular. It was known as house music, which also had its roots in the disco music of the 70s, but which had also absorbed jazz and Latin influences. House musicians were fond of wearing *Miami Vice*-type suits. The UK had developed its own version of house music, known as acid house music. In fashion, this was reflected in fluorescent tops featuring African designs printed on a mixture of fabrics and worn with Lycra sportswear reminiscent of the Sixties. Although many of these fashion trends never actually reached haute couture status, they, like the Japanese designers, still managed to wield considerable influence in the fashion world. The Eighties' obsession with the stars of dance and sport had bound music and fashion together more strongly than ever before.

However, from 1985 onward, the party spirit became increasingly subdued as AIDS was officially categorized as an epidemic by the World Health Organization. For many young people, this represented a rude awakening, and AIDS effectively put an end to the hedonistic atmosphere of the 1980s. Meanwhile, the next global disaster was already waiting around the corner in the form of the Chernobyl nuclear reactor explosion of 1986. The shock waves reverberated all over the world, bringing home to people for the first time in very real terms the dangers of nuclear energy. Then a number of reports began to appear regarding the hole in the ozone layer, which was said to be widening by the day, and a new level of environmental awareness gradually began to develop among the more clear-sighted members of the public.

The fate of the yuppie cult and its luxury-oriented culture was sealed when the stock market crashed in October 1987. The last stragglers finally put away their aggressively glamorous outfits and decided to merge into the army of discreetly power-suited people who had long since taken over control.

1986

The puppet master
During the 1980s, Bernard Arnault began to buy up one fashion house after another until he had turned LVMH into the biggest luxury group in the world. Arnault, who is also a talented amateur pianist, clearly had a knack for choosing creative individuals to run his brands.

THE FAMILY-ORIENTED PLAYBOY:
Gianni Versace

12.02.1946
–
07.15.1997

Versace's clothes were not for shrinking violets. "I only want to dress celebrities," he admitted with great self-assurance. He welcomed anyone who wanted to stand out—and if they were famous, then so much the better. Most of all, he enjoyed styling stars as glamour-obsessed sex objects. Fashion was, after all, an aphrodisiac to Versace: "We dress ourselves to make someone want to undress us."

In the case of most Versace outfits, however, very little imagination was needed to be able to picture the wearer naked. Versace created deeper *décolletés* and higher slits in skirts than any other designer and for any areas that did need concealing he used fluid fabrics which resembled a second skin. The 1982/1983 season saw the launch of his innovative dresses made from fine metal mesh which turned the body into a shimmering sculpture. Twelve years later, he created fluorescent, high-shine gowns from "ordinary" PVC which were frequently decorated with crystal beads and pearls. His work was reminiscent of Elsa Schiaparelli, who experimented with cellophane during the 1930s. The material was incredibly modern, yet the end product was very classic. This was typical of Versace, who was fanatically keen on classicism, yet had no scruples about mixing it with the colorful splendor of the Renaissance or elaborate Baroque. A fearless colorist, he commissioned the finest silks to be printed with extravagant designs which resembled Byzantine mosaics or tattoos—one outfit was even made from material that had Marilyn Monroe's likeness reproduced 50 times. Restraint was not a word in Versace's vocabulary; instead he came to personify excess in every form.

Many found this vulgar, but Versace's fans loved his way of smashing taboos because this guaranteed them the attention they so craved. For Elton John, for example, he designed a show costume that was studded from top to bottom with diamonds and Swarovski crystal. Thanks to Versace's safety-pin dress, Liz Hurley, at the time an unknown actress, became famous overnight—and also rich, since it brought her a highly paid advertising contract with Estée Lauder. Madonna wore his clothes both in private and professionally and is said to have been paid millions for her appearances in Versace advertisements.

Versace was always very open-handed: He lived like a prince and paid handsomely. During the 1990s, supermodels had become too demanding and too expensive and so were dropped by many of the fashion houses. But not the case of Gianni Versace, who even added a little extra to their fee and booked them all together on an exclusive basis, for he knew that Linda, Christy, Claudia, Cindy, and the rest all had star status—and he enjoyed basking in the glamour of their fame.

The world in his hands
Gianni Versace poses in his library in 1990 like an explorer from a bygone age. His plans for conquering the world, however, were based on an innovative and peaceful campaign of ensuring that the world's most beautiful models and most successful artists wore his fashions.

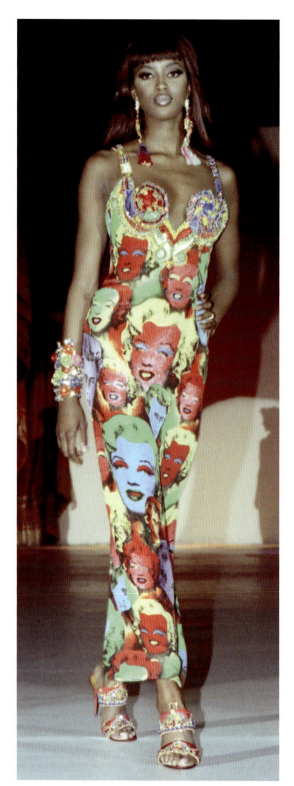

Not afraid of competition

Supermodel Naomi Campbell did not mind being compared with sex idol Marilyn Monroe, whose image was replicated a hundredfold on her gown, while her colleague Helena Christensen trod the runway in a colorful mini dress.

Modern goddesses

Gianni Versace enjoyed experimenting with modern materials such as plastic and metal, which pushed dressmaking techniques to their limit. Wearing these creations, supermodels Karen Mulder and Nadja Auermann resemble goddesses from another world.

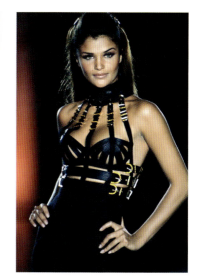

The opulent world of luxury

From 1989 onward, Gianni Versace presented his haute couture lines in Paris under the brand name of Atelier Versace. His designs included gold and silver creations woven from extremely fine metal threads and gossamer thin leather (top row). Even daywear like the three-piece outfit worn by Claudia Schiffer (facing page) was so richly embellished that it represented a valuable work of art in itself. His gold imitations of ordinary punk-style safety pins made Liz Hurley's gown a spectacular success (right, pictured here with Hugh Grant).

Elton John (far right) was a soul mate and close friend. For this pop star with the distinctive voice, Gianni Versace created lavish stage costumes. The contents of Versace's home in Miami were auctioned after his death—from cups with gold-winged handles, to lamps with Medusa motifs, to sofas piled with countless cushions.

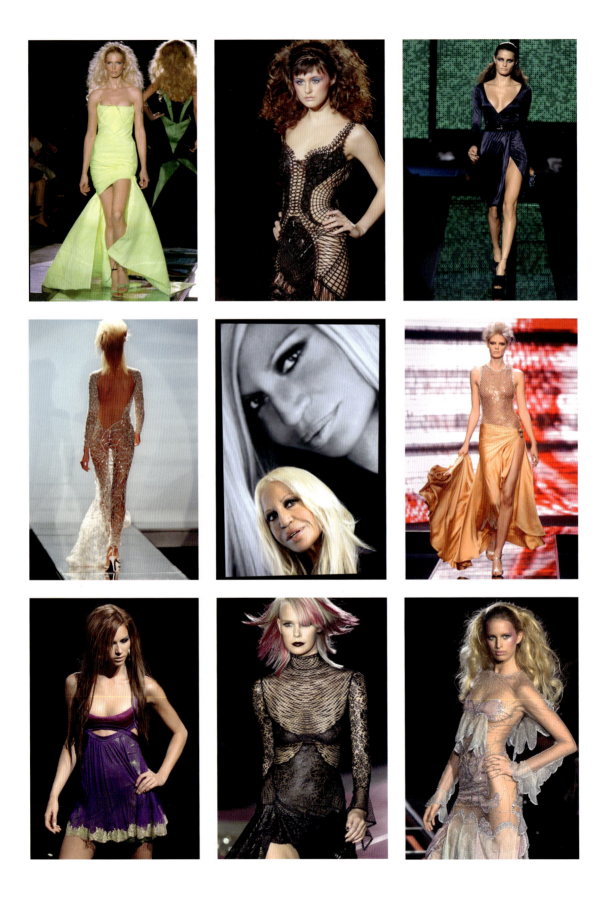

Keeping it in the family—the talent, the business, and, of course, the secret

The only woman who turned down Versace's tempting offer of a publicity role (probably because she was forced to) was Princess Diana. He allegedly offered her one million pounds to appear on the runway. Nevertheless, she provided him with invaluable free publicity: By wearing his clothes, Princess Diana, once pitied as the deceived wife, came to be regarded as an icon of fashion—as well as a seductress who, one could easily imagine, had a string of love affairs. Anna Wintour, head of *Vogue* magazine was probably right when she remarked: "Armani dresses the wife and Versace the mistress." Diana chose Versace.

He had a knack for over-emphasizing the femininity or masculinity of his subjects. He liked to dress both sexes in black leather, with studs and chains, but his clothes never seemed at all aggressive—merely sensual, and even elegant. This was because he knew exactly how to use every fabric correctly, an instinctive skill he had learned back in his mother's dressmaking studio. Instead of completing his architecture course, he chose instead to become a buyer for his mother's dressmaking business before moving soon afterwards to Milan to work as a freelance fashion designer. In the typical southern Italian way, when he launched his own fashion house in 1978, he turned it into a family concern: His brother Santos was put in charge of business decisions while his sister Donatella was made responsible for marketing. An audacious Gianni adopted as his logo a representation of the terrifying head of Medusa, a figure in Greek mythology. It brought him good luck. His label became a spectacular success so quickly that some people questioned whether something fishy was going on. In just one year (1996), "the family" made net profits of 38 million.

When Gianni Versace was gunned down in July 1997 outside his mansion in Miami—his "tropical fever dream," as *The New Yorker* described his ostentatious holiday villa, there was simply no end to the rumors that followed: Was it a lover's revenge, had it something to do with AIDS, or was it linked to a Mafia-type vendetta?

b. 05.02.1955

DONATELLA VERSACE, Gianni's capricious little sister, picked up the reins of her brother's company as its creative director. She was the obvious choice, having been his muse and closest associate, although many feared that she would not be able to live up to the challenge. However, she put up a brave fight and her designs turned out to be just as sexy and glamorous as his. She also introduced a fresh element of modern femininity. Unfortunately, the strain proved too much for her: Donatella, who had always been a free-spending, hard-partying girl, now needed even more alcohol and drugs in order to cope with the pressure of public expectation. In 2004, sales figures fell dramatically and Donatella suffered a breakdown. She retreated to a rehab clinic in the Arizona desert.

After that, things began to improve. Her numerous show business friends, including Courtney Love, Lady Gaga, and many rappers, have been extremely supportive. They all came to Donatella's shows and parties and made a point of wearing her designs. Jennifer Lopez and Madonna, Milla Jovovich and Halle Berry all signed advertising contracts with Versace. And suddenly everyone was praising Donatella's designs. By going to hell and back and openly admitting it, she finally managed to step out of the long, overpowering shadow cast by her brother. The family enterprise is once again free of debt and Donatella is the undisputed creative head of the firm.

Little sister—big talent
Whatever Gianni liked is fine with Donatella: She particularly enjoys working with see-through fabrics, turning them into thigh-high dresses, or gowns with long slits that leave nothing to the imagination. Her haute couture lines consist of floating chiffons and shimmering embroidered fabrics.

THE TOPPLED CROWN PRINCE:
Christian Lacroix

b. 05.16.1951

What is the spirit of the times compared with intellect? There must have been many people who asked themselves this question when Christian Lacroix, a plump-cheeked cherub from the provinces, conquered the Paris fashion scene. This shy, well-mannered young man was like a fish out of water among the frenetic, hysterical crowd of *jeunes créateurs* who were falling over each other in their quest for the latest, most garish, never-seen-before fashions. Christian Lacroix, in contrast, was searching for times past—a dreamer in the mold of Proust, who was always able to tap into his wonderful childhood for creative inspiration.

He grew up in Arles, a town in southern France. Born into a well-to-do family of engineers, Christian Lacroix grew into a thoughtful child, who spent hours up in the attic of the family home, poring over old fashion magazines. At the age of three, he began to draw anything that took his fancy: the gypsies in Saintes-Maries de la Mer, the matadors in the bullring, and even his grandfather, who had his suits lined with green silk and painted his bicycle gold. "He was very arrogant, like an actor," recalls his grandson.

Even as a small child he had a deep fascination for the theater and loved watching the amateur players at the annual fairs or being taken to see children's shows in the theater itself. This early passion had kindled a desire to become a costume designer. While studying art history in Paris, he always rounded off his visits to the theater by sketching all the costumes, and devising new ones as he saw fit. On one occasion, he showed his sketches to his girlfriend, Françoise Rosensthiel, who immediately recognized not only his formidable talent but also their similarity to the latest fashions. The red-haired Françoise—dainty, lively, independent, and extravagant—threw him into total confusion and deflected him from his planned career.

After completing his doctoral dissertation on the subject of dress in 17th century painting, Christian Lacroix was planning a career as a museum curator. However, his girlfriend, who was six years older than him, and their mutual friend, Jean Jacques Picard, both of whom had press-related jobs in the fashion business, urged him to consider a career in fashion. First of all, they managed to get him taken on at Hermès, where he learned all the secrets of the trade. In 1981, Picard succeeded in convincing the prestigious Patou fashion house that no one was more capable of reviving couture than Lacroix, the magician's apprentice. The promised miracle occurred and in 1986 Lacroix won the coveted Golden Thimble award, the highest French couture prize of all, for Patou. Paris fêted him as the new crown prince who, as successor to Dior and Yves Saint Laurent, would bring a fresh sparkle to this, the most French of all arts. On the basis of this success,

Enthroned
After his first two collections, Christian Lacroix appeared in 1988 on the front cover of *Time* magazine surrounded by his favorite models—an honor hitherto shared only by Dior and Giorgio Armani and tantamount to a coronation.

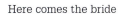

Here comes the bride

The climax and high point of every couture show is the wedding dress and no one possessed more imagination in this respect that Christian Lacroix. Wedding dresses formed the core of his business—on this, the happiest day of her life, even a shy woman can be instilled with confidence to make a grand entrance. Lacroix embellished virginal white, often transparently delicate, with gold and pastel-colored embroidery, adding a touch of blue, or a red bow in a crucial spot—and he always set off the ensemble with a lavish headdress, a dramatic crowning glory securing the veil. His brides could be dressed with nun-like simplicity, or resemble medieval princesses, or even opt for the sophisticated, fashionable look, with a red hat providing the finishing touch. His final bride in his 2009 summer collection wore a gilded headdress resembling a halo—a symbol of hope (facing page).

Dance of the toreadors
Christian Lacroix had every reason to celebrate in 1988: His collection, inspired by the bullfights and vivid colors of southern France, had just won him the Golden Thimble award for the second time. To the right is Marie Seznec, his gray-haired muse.

The pouf, *a short puffball skirt, marked* the **beginning and end of Lacroix couture**

36-year-old Lacroix, together with his partner Picard, launched his own couture house—the first since Saint Laurent had launched his own solo career 25 years earlier.

The necessary funding (eight million dollars) was provided by Bernard Arnault, who had bought up LVMH, building it into the largest luxury conglomerate in France. With such impressive financial backing, Lacroix felt justified in creating designs that were almost scandalous in their lavish excess. These anachronistic collections were greeted all the more enthusiastically for being so out of step with the times. His first haute couture collection in July 1987 was a spectacularly colorful tribute to his beloved Provence: He audaciously combined all manner of vibrant colors, such as orange, scarlet, fuchsia, violet, purple, and bright yellow, augmenting their richness with lace, embroidery, ornate edging, pearls, and gold trim. He also included black velvet waistcoats featuring the cross of the Camargue worked in gold thread and introduced the puffball-style short skirt, known as *le pouf*, which became a classic Lacroix trademark. Waistlines were pulled tight and décolletés plunged low but were draped with a scarf in traditional Arlésienne fashion. The collection ended with the show highlight: the wedding dress, whose short black velvet jacket featured an ex-voto heart on the back embroidered in white and blood red.

Lacroix's creations resembled costumes and therein lay the problem. Only his wedding dresses enjoyed lasting success. He was often commissioned to design the outfits for an entire wedding party, from the flower girls to the mother of the bride, so that the event would be beautifully coordinated.

Lacroix had a reputation for staging spectacular shows. He continued to design costumes for the stage, producing costumes for Mikhail Baryshnikov's American Ballet Theater, for opera companies in Nîmes and Paris, various revue shows, as well as bullfighting spectacles in the Camargue. Architecture was another of his major passions. His premise that "more is more" was clearly evident from the interior design of his couture salon. In contrast to other fashion houses with their nondescript beige color schemes and gilt chairs, Lacroix decorated his salons in rich oranges and reds, with black-painted flames of hell licking up the walls—a tantalizing purgatory. In his latter years, Lacroix turned his attention to redesigning several Paris hotels in similar fashion, his work being warmly applauded by the press and travelers.

His fashion collections were less successful, however. Like many other designers, he had been obliged to produce ready-to-wear lines and sportswear, but neither earned him a huge amount of money. His "second job" as creative director of Emilio Pucci, an Italian label, in which Bernard Arnault's LVMH held a 70-percent share, ended after three years. It was around this time—2005—that Arnault, the luxury goods baron, decided he had had enough of the ailing Lacroix couture house and sold it to the three Falic brothers of Hollywood. They too found it impossible to cope with the debts, which by 2008 amounted to more than 13 million dollars. At the end of May 2009, the House of Lacroix went into administration—in all its 22-year history it had not once made a profit.

Nevertheless, Christian Lacroix is still regarded as one of the last great couturiers. Thanks to his study of history, his vocabulary is far richer than that of his contemporaries, he knows how to utilize every trick and opportunity, draws inspiration from ancient times and exotic cultures, and finds innovative ways of combining them. His is the story of a true individual and perhaps one day it will have a happy end.

A rich color palette
The *pouf*, a short puffball skirt, became a classic Christian Lacroix trademark, as did his choice of exuberant colors in a mix of square and dot designs which were inspired by memories of southern France. In 2007, he redesigned the Le Petit Moulin hotel in Paris.

MASTER OF THE RED ROBES:
Valentino

b. 05.11.1932

Red was always Valentino's favorite color. His frequent visits to the theater had made him realize that it was the color with most dramatic effect. This young Italian, who wanted to conquer Paris, the world capital of fashion, was also keen to attract attention. So he staked everything on red—and won. As far as he was concerned, the only other viable colors were black and white. Throughout his career, spanning almost fifty years, Valentino has stuck to this trio of colors, but it is amazing how much he has managed to do with them! No neo-Baroque, no Oriental fairytale, or psychedelic mix of colors could have produced anything more magnificent.

Valentino owes his name to his mother's infatuation with Rudolph Valentino, star of the silent movies, who in his day was considered the most handsome man in the world. Born in the industrial north of Italy, his real name was Valentino Clemente Ludovico Garavani, but he quickly realized that the megastars of the world are known simply by a single first name. He had a particular gift for drawing and after finishing high school, he moved to nearby Milan were he took a course in fashion illustration, a decision which set the course for his future career. The discovery that no Italian had ever managed to succeed as a couturier in Paris sparked his ambition and at the age of 18, he registered with the Chambre Syndicale de la Couture. His talent soon won him a prize in a competition held by the International Wool Secretariat, an achievement that got his career under way—Karl Lagerfeld and Yves Saint Laurent both started out the same way several years earlier.

Valentino was offered a place in Jean Dessès' studio, where he remained for five years. When Guy Laroche, his colleague in the design department, launched his own business in 1957, Valentino went with him. Not only was he made responsible for creative design but he also took over the running of the business side of the firm. He soon felt ready to launch his own fashion house and with this in mind he returned to Italy. In November 1959, at the age of just 27 and with the financial assistance of his father, he opened his own salon in Rome, which after World War II had become the center of Italian *alta moda*—not to mention the movies! The Cinecittà Studios in Rome were responsible for many of the major European films as well as some of the great Hollywood productions, including *Cleopatra*, starring Elizabeth Taylor in the title role. She was one of Valentino's first clients and has remained a loyal follower of this elegant Italian designer all her life.

Americans loved Rome and they loved Valentino's clothes. Both provided all they could wish for in terms of classic beauty, with a hint of tingling *dolce vita* thrown in for good measure. There were plenty of opportunities for getting dressed up even during the day and it was precisely for such occasions that Valentino created the formal day dress, somewhat shorter than an evening gown but just as expensive, not to mention the wide-legged silk palazzo pants, the most Italian of all glamorous evening wear. In the summer of 1962, Valentino staged his first show at the Pitti Palace in Florence, the Italian fashion capital of the day before this honor eventually shifted to Milan. It was

Valentino sees red
Valentino holds a special place of honor in fashion history for his spectacular red evening gowns. They formed the highpoint of every collection and were particularly popular with celebrities, as they could not fail to draw attention to the wearer.

Elegant severity
Valentino's 1989/90 autumn/winter collection, which was entirely in black and white and featured designs in the Art Nouveau style, was inspired by the work of architect and decorative artist Josef Hoffmann, co-founder of the Wiener Werkstätte.

Timeless luxury

Valentino was much taken with the chic appeal of the *haute bourgeoisie* and it was for this clientele that he created couture of understated elegance using combinations of lace and velvet and featuring very short little jackets, not forgetting the all-important bow.

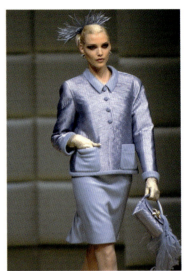

Valentino enjoys a luxurious lifestyle—but renounces real fur out of respect for animals

here that foreign buyers discovered for themselves that this young Italian designer fully deserved the reputation that had gone before him.

Americans, in particular, were delighted to have found an alternative to what they regarded as the excessively expensive French designers and deluged the young couturier with orders. In 1968, Valentino caused a sensation with his Collezione Bianca, a collection of white gowns, all of which bore the magic "V" logo that was to become his trademark. The same year, Jacqueline Kennedy chose Valentino to make her wedding gown for her marriage to Onassis, turning him into a superstar in the USA. He even brought the mini craze to an end in 1970, at least in the couture world, with his calf-length skirts of fine silk and lace. Fashion experts of the day wrote that he was the only designer who could match the French design genius, Yves Saint Laurent.

Valentino was naturally well aware of the current fashion trends. He was greatly impressed by the success of London's young fashion scene and realized that he too needed to introduce a range with a more modest price tag if his fashion house was not to expire along with his limited couture clientele. He was supported in this by Giancarlo Giammetti, a student of architecture, who joined his enterprise in 1960 and became his partner, both in business and in private. Giammetti proved to be an astute commercial director and with his assistance, Valentino launched his ready-to-wear collection in 1970, introducing a range of accessories at the same time. Five years later he took his ready-to-wear collection to Paris and was the first Italian designer to gain acceptance there. In 1989, he showed his haute couture collection in Paris for the first time and was enthusiastically welcomed into the closed ranks of top fashion designers.

Couture was Valentino's natural element—it was a medium in which he could indulge in luxury, allowing himself free rein to decorate his gowns with gold sequins, paste gemstones, feathers, unusual embroidery in silver or mother-of-pearl, and pink imitation mink. It was not surprising, therefore, that the 1980s took the House of Valentino to new heights. The prevailing mood was to display one's wealth on one's sleeve and Valentino's dresses positively radiated affluence, even if the design was quite simple. In 1989, he created a spectacular collection entirely in black and white, intended as a tribute to the Wiener Werkstätte and to Austrian architect and decorative artist, Josef Hoffmann.

In deference to the growing mood of environmental awareness, he stopped using real fur: "We have so many techniques available to us today that there is no further need to massacre animals." He had already invented the fake zebra look in 1962 and he now turned his attention to producing tiger, leopard, and giraffe looks. The addition of a tiny touch of animal to his designs saved his distinctive elegance from becoming boring—just as *rosso valentino*, his special red signature color, injected a touch of passion.

In 1998, HdP, an Italian conglomerate, bought into the Valentino couture house to the tune of around 360 million dollars, and yet despite this injection of capital, the company was still making substantial losses three years later. In October 2007, Valentino, now 75 years of age, and his pugs bid farewell to the fashion runway—through several gala dinners and exhibitions, a lavishly illustrated book, and a documentary film entitled *Valentino: The Last Emperor*.

The splendor of the good old days

Valentino avoided ostentatious glamour, his creations being discreet in their opulence—as with this gold, off-the-shoulder Amazon dress, which Cate Blanchett wore to receive her Oscar in 2005. Be it daywear (top row) or evening wear, "merely" ready-to-wear or haute couture (right-hand column), Valentino always strove for elegance and never left the wearer exposed. He also opposed the use of animal fur; what looks like pink mink is in fact artfully crumpled silk chiffon.

THE FLAMBOYANT BIRD OF PARADISE:
John Galliano

b. 11.28.1960

It was a rusty key that opened the door to John Galliano's success. It unlocked a photogenic but crumbling 18th-century Paris mansion which was to provide a venue for this young, near-bankrupt fashion designer to show his latest collection. John Galliano, who had already been obliged to skip a season due to financial problems, was quick to take advantage of the opportunity. Within two short weeks, he designed and produced 17 outfits, all in black, as he had neither time nor money to spend on expensive fabrics—and in so doing, he assured himself a place in fashion history.

And not for the first time: In 1984, Galliano attracted more publicity than any student before him, causing a sensation with his prize-winning, final-year collection at Central Saint Martins College of Art and Design in London. His collection, entitled Les Incroyables, consisted of eight unisex outfits inspired by post-revolutionary France. The whole effect was both romantic and theatrical at the same time, a style which Galliano never relinquished . His first collection, which was enthusiastically received by the press and the fashion industry, was bought in its entirety and sold by Brown's fashion boutique.

All this may sound like the start of a fairytale career, but our hero first had to get through a number of trials. For a short while London was the fashion capital of the world and home to certain clubs where posers in flamboyant outfits could strut their stuff. One of the most popular venues for these birds of paradise was the Taboo Club, where, contrary to its name, absolutely nothing was taboo and every kind of drug and sexual orientation was accepted. John Galliano, who reinvented himself just about every week, was one of the club's regulars. "Honestly, it took you two days to get ready," he once admitted.

Costume design was in his blood. He was born in Gibraltar and as a young boy went to school in Spain, reaching it via Tangier. The Moroccan souks and markets with their colorful fabrics and carpets, all the different herbs and smells, and the whole Mediterranean way of life obviously had a strong influence on his perception of beauty. In addition, he was immaculately turned out every morning by his Spanish mother in freshly pressed clothes. Consequently, after the family moved to England, where his father got a job as a plumber, he felt like a fish out of water. He also felt like an outsider at school and it was not until he switched to a design college at the age of 16 that he began to meet people who seemed to be a bit more like him. He only felt completely at home, however, at the National Theatre, where he worked part-time as a dresser to earn some money. In this capacity he quickly made a name for himself among the famous actors—as the best clothes presser! Once at Saint Martins, where he eventually registered to study fashion design, he found himself well liked

Not afraid of putting on a show
With most designers it is the bride who takes the starring role, but in Galliano's case it is Galliano himself. The traditional finale of every show involves Galliano strutting the runway in person. He is seen here posing in a multicolored patchwork outfit at his 2006 menswear show.

Fairytale magic

Galliano's modern-day nomad, who is dressed in a trenchcoat, appears wearing ancient facial jewelry while a partygoer is dressed in an outfit inspired both by a fighting Samurai warrior and by the colorful splendor of a Mongolian princess.

It began with transparency

Galliano's first solo show in Paris in 1991 was dominated by lace and open-mesh fabrics (above left and bottom right). In 2002, he invented the urban nomad, self-confidently going about her business like a Tuareg, with an indigo blue-painted face. The 2007/2008 autumn/winter evening wear collection was presented by the skinniest models of the day (middle column from top to bottom). Tulle and ruching characterized the summer of 2000 (above right). The extravagant headgear (center right) which is an integral part of every Galliano show is made by the congenial British designer Stephen Jones, who supplies all his collections, often "lining" them with false hair extensions in fluorescent colors. Since 2008, Galliano has also been designing opulent fashion jewelry, sometimes using it in place of a button on an evening coat, for example (facing page).

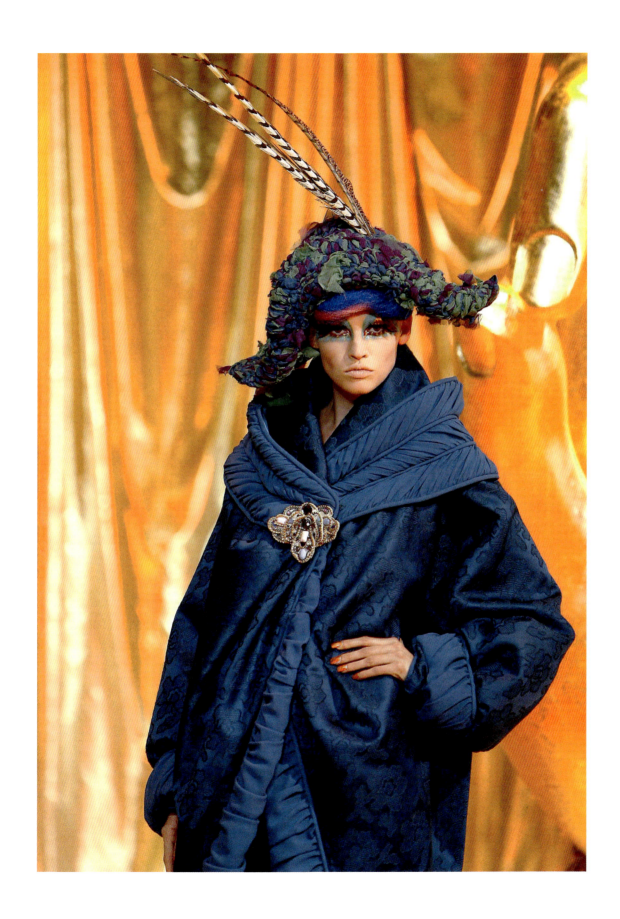

Dior couture—a feast of fantasy

In each of his shows, Galliano takes us on a journey to a different land, or a different era—perhaps to the land of the pharaohs with their masks of Egyptian gods, or to the court of Versailles with its sinfully sumptuous embroideries and sensually plunging *décolletés*, or to a sumptuous, Hollywood-style bordello peopled with Amazonian and dominatrix-style harlots, or to a fantasy world populated by mythical creatures. After traveling to Asia and studying Chinese and Japanese kimonos, he created some of the most voluminous dresses ever to grace the runway, sometimes crowned with marabou feathers as a tribute to Britain's Queen Mother. He often borrows colors and motifs from paintings by the Old Masters—and is not averse to using giant plastic flowers. Each model only appears once, theatrically presented in traditional Galliano style.

Behind the masquerade is a man
who is serious *about moving fashion forward*

by both staff and fellow students, yet he still remained something of a shy outsider despite the fact that people were naturally attracted to him. He was exceptionally good-looking, rather exotic, and had a raffish smile and eyes that dazzled irresistibly. On top of that, he was clearly bursting with ideas. Yet the real reason for his success with others and in the fashion industry was his boundless energy. John Galliano—whose real name was Juan Carlos Antonio Galliano Guillén—was a workaholic who would spend hours on end sketching, sifting through books, and poking around museums and archives. He was very serious about fashion and all those who chose to congregate around him, hoping to share in his magic, had to accept this.

"He was a good team dictator," recalls Lady Amanda Harlech, who gave up her job as fashion editor to become Galliano's Girl Friday. She stayed with him for 12 years and only moved over to Chanel as Karl Lagerfeld's muse because she needed financial security after her divorce. Galliano had no conception of regular working hours or regular income.

Two of his financial backers pulled out within five years of each other. "A genius, but unprofessional," was their verdict. Galliano's cutting patterns were unusual and complicated and not (as yet) suited to mass production. Furthermore, he spent at least twice as much as other contemporary designers on staging his shows, which were a far cry from the normal type of fashion presentation, consisting instead of magnificent sets and the sort of theatrical backdrops one might see on a movie set. They were always designed around a specific theme, as is evident from the various titles of his collections, for example "Fallen Angels," "Forgotten Innocents," and "Napoleon and Josephine." Some critics claimed that by delving into history for his inspiration, Galliano had essentially hit upon an easy method of copying. This was tantamount to accusing a painter of plagiarism for producing a fresh interpretation of the works of Old Masters!

In 1991, Galliano decided to go to Paris, where he continued to work, receiving high praise but insufficient funds. Two years later, his business partner in Paris also pulled out and Galliano was often obliged to sleep on the floor of friends' homes. The turning point came when he was given the opportunity to show his Princess Lucretia collection, which he quickly rustled up at the last minute, the venue for which was a mansion belonging to fashion patron São Schumberger. "This is on a par with haute couture," was the press reaction to the event. Such high praise attracted the attention of Bernard Arnault, chief executive of LVMH, the largest luxury conglomerate in the world, which included the couture houses of Dior, Givenchy, and, the newcomer, Lacroix. In July 1995, Arnault appointed John Galliano chief designer of Givenchy, but soon had even greater things in store for him: In October 1996, he installed Galliano on the throne of French couture, appointing him chief designer of the House of Dior.

His first couture collection for Dior coincided almost exactly with the 50th anniversary of Christian Dior's legendary debut on the fashion scene and caused a similar sensation. Since that day, Galliano has kept on surprising the fashion world, staging one spectacular show after another. He was only able to withstand the pressure of the demands he placed upon himself with the help of drugs and alcohol. This eventually led to a scandal in 2011 when Galliano, heavily under the influence of alcohol, began ranting at some of the other guests in a Paris restaurant and making anti-Semitic remarks. As a result of this incident, the House of Dior sacked him. His successor was appointed in April 2012: Raf Simons, who, prior to this, had successfully continued the minimalist style of Jil Sanders—truly a radical departure for Dior.

Solo for Galliano
The designer's appearance at the end of every show is always an emotional moment, awaited with deep fascination. In the past, it took Galliano two days to get ready to visit a nightclub—nowadays makeup artists, hairdressers, and stylists take care of everything for him.

Oscar de la Renta

Bill Blass

Oscar de la Renta is an aristocrat, born in Santo Domingo in 1932. He was the first American to be made creative director of a French couture house. He spent almost 10 years between 1993 and 2002 restoring Balmain's former reputation for the elegance of the 1950s. This was not his first visit to Paris; Oscar de la Renta had already spent four years working for Lanvin as a young man. Before that, he had served his apprenticeship with one of the great couturiers, Cristóbal Balenciaga, who was then still in Madrid. Faithful to the style of his mentor, de la Renta created elegant clothes using sophisticated cutting techniques and fine fabrics, perfect for prestigious occasions. It is hardly surprising that the First Ladies of US presidents, from Jackie Kennedy to Nancy Reagan, Barbara Bush and Hillary Clinton, chose him to design their clothes. Since 1965, Oscar de la Renta has been an established name in the USA, but has also presented ready-to-wear clothes at the Paris shows, such as the black cocktail dress and the red mini dress and checkered coat ensemble of 1991, shown in the above photos. De la Renta, who is a keen gardener, is married to US millionairess Annette Reed and is generally considered to have succeeded Givenchy as the last true gentleman in an increasingly strident fashion industry.

This American designer, born in Fort Wayne in 1922, still managed to dress his clients glamorously even during the lackluster years of the 1970s. In 1975, he relaunched the cocktail dress, but his greatest moment came in the eighties when he became Nancy Reagan's favorite designer, dressing her in sumptuous, colorful, and decorative clothes which matched the mood of the times. Blass was the son of a dressmaker and even while he was still at school, he used to sketch designs in his schoolbooks, inspired by gowns worn by Hollywood stars. At the age of 15, he began sewing evening gowns, which he then sold for 25 dollars apiece to a New York firm. By the age of 17, he had saved up enough money to study fashion at the Parsons School of Design in Manhattan, where he was an instant success, becoming the first male to win the Mademoiselle award. In 1970, he was in a position to buy the Maurice Rentner company, which he had joined in 1959, renaming it with his own name. Through one of his models, who had good social contacts, Bill Blass gained entry to society's "higher circles" whose members he hoped to dress. Blass developed a reputation for making American sportswear wearable and elegant. At the same time, he designed clothes for "special occasions." In 1999, he sold his fashion house for 50 million dollars. Blass, an inveterate smoker, died in 2002 of throat cancer.

Romeo Gigli

Emanuel Ungaro

Romeo Gigli, born in 1949 in Italy, developed his own individual style of glamour. His designs were created not for aggressive power women or sex goddesses, but with pre-Raphaelite and Byzantine beauties in mind. He designed pear-shaped cocoon coats for quiet, yet self-confident madonnas, seeking the flower of romanticism. They wore gold-threaded blouses with cup-shaped collars and narrow, sloping shoulders over slim, high-waisted pencil pants or skirts, often made from stretch fabric. They adorned themselves with expensive scarves, extravagant ethnic jewelry and long, Oriental-style earrings. Gigli's coats were protective cocoons of lavish velvet, so richly embroidered that it looked as if the treasure chests of an ancient kingdom had been plundered to provide the decoration. He developed his sense for muted, but opulent colors during his travels to remote corners of the world. A former student of architecture, Gigli returned home from his travels with costumes, ornaments, and other objets d'art, having inherited a passion for collecting from his father and grandfather, both of whom dealt in antiques and passed on their knowledge to him. Toward the end of the 1990s, Romeo Gigli was obliged to sell his label; in 2012 he started afresh with a collection for the online shop Joyce.

Having mastered the impeccable cutting techniques learnt during the six years he spent working with his mentor, Cristóbal Balenciaga, Emanuel Ungaro launched his own couture house in 1965. He started out creating strictly modern outfits, which sometimes reflected the style of Courrèges, a fellow designer. It was not long, however, before Ungaro, born in 1933 in southern France to Italian parents, developed a unique style of his own, based on a bold mix of colors and patterns. His creations, which were simultaneously sumptuous and sexy, were bought mainly by American women, many of his clients coming from Dallas. Ungaro, one of the few couturiers who not only liked dressing women but was also sexually attracted to them, created his fashions directly around the female body. With classical music playing in the background, he modeled, tucked, pinned, smoothed, and pleated the fabrics around a mannequin until he was satisfied with the resulting silhouette: tightly gathered at the waist and hips, billowing out in ruches beneath, and often decorated with bows at strategic points. He liked using shiny materials, always in fluorescent colors. Ungaro was able to continue running his couture house independently for longer than most and it was not sold to new owners until 2006. However, none of an ever-changing succession of designers has managed to continue the exuberantly sensual style of his fashions with any conviction.

Dress for Success

1979

The great promise of the Eighties was "Luxury for all", and it seemed to sound the death knell for haute couture. Once-exclusive fashion houses increasingly began to transform themselves into stores that sold everything that might make money, from scent to sunglasses. What had once been the exquisite privilege of the cream of society now became subject to mass consumerism. The brand became more important than style itself, and the hunt for the right logo supplanted good taste. Status symbols were coveted; quality was irrelevant. The magic formula for social climbers was "dress for success."

A bestseller with this title appeared in 1979 and became a bible for those on the up. Career women were gradually gaining ground. Female employees used the new Personal Computer (PC) technology pioneered by Apple just as much as their male colleagues, and the cell phone and Filofax, that ingenious combination of diary and address book, became their favorite accessories, emphasizing a businesswoman's importance more effectively than any feminine adornments. Above all, women learned how to deploy clothing as a means to professional success and the pantsuit became standard work wear for female employees in top positions. Yet women had scarcely broken into the upper echelons of their professions before an even stricter dress code was imposed on them. If they were to play along with the guys, they had to abandon their pants and go back to wearing skirts. Knee-length dark silk dresses that could be worn with the obligatory blazer and dressed up with jewelry in the evening, allowing women to go from the office to evening events, were a hit, and this approach itself was revolutionary. The successful woman generally wore a skirt suit and a silk blouse, nude stockings, low-heeled shoes and subtle gold jewelry, as recommended by *Dress for Success*.

Only Dior's New Look in the Fifties had had such a broad appeal, and that was only designed for "the woman at her man's side," as a symbol of the *man's* success. The career woman, by contrast, was often single and childless. She hid her femininity, wearing sinfully expensive silk lingerie underneath her boxy outfit. Who was she wearing it for? The rigorous body searches at the airport, "the only physical contact that we still have," as a female manager complained.

European women preferred opaque black stockings to nude versions, as this was the only sensuous quirk that was still acceptable as business clothing.

Placed on a pedestal
The career woman of the 1980s, always dressed to perfection, was an object of envy and amazement. She seemed to have it all. Yet only a decade later she was ripe for the museum, eyed anxiously by the next generation, who had different dreams.

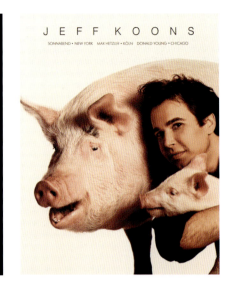

The art of marketing

It was Andy Warhol who taught members of the New York artists' set how to attract public attention. His photo (above) shows Francesco Clemente (top left) with Julian Schnabel next to him, and Jean-Michel Basquiat (bottom left) – three rising stars. Keith Haring (opposite page), whose Pop Shop sold mass-produced merchandise featuring his work, was another member of the inner circle. Jeff Koons demonstrated even greater business acumen by posing with these pink pigs (above right) as part of a successful marketing strategy to promote "trivial art." Working women were trying to boost their incomes by adopting the fashion maxim "dress for success." The first Live Aid concert in 1985, organized by pop star Bob Geldof (right), was a public reminder that there were more pressing issues in life. The proceeds from this concert went to help the starving people of Africa. In Germany, the fall of the Berlin Wall between East and West in 1989 unleashed a sense of euphoria over national brotherhood.

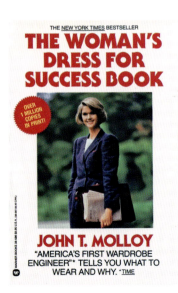

Pure show on the outside, sheer fabulousness underneath

Oscar de la Renta's outfit of a gray flannel skirt and short velvet jacket, finished with a white silk blouse, complied with the strict dress code of the career woman. Under her power suit, things were a little more beguiling—Shu-Ba silk underwear.

Support from the stars

Giorgio Armani understood better than anyone else how to get celebrities excited about fashion. David Beckham posed for his underwear commercial; Cate Blanchett, Michelle Pfeiffer, and Glenn Close all sported his designs at public events; and the maestro took the measurements of his favorite star, Jodie Foster, personally. He provided the clothes for the wedding of his friend Tom Cruise to Katie Holmes in 2006, and in doing so, for the first time he made a foray into haute couture. Ever since, he has shown his Armani Privé collection twice a year in Paris.

Dreaming of a better life

A career woman liked to have elegantly styled cell phones and Filofax organizers (below). Her work clothes came from designers like Ralph Lauren, whose style was made popular by Diane Keaton in the film *Annie Hall* (far left). The pink dress that Gwyneth Paltrow wore to the Oscars was also a Lauren design. Ralph Lauren's all-embracing approach as a designer included interior decoration—glamorous for an apartment; rustic for a log cabin (middle left and right). Armani also designed a complete lifestyle, from fashion to furniture—sometimes elegant and cosmopolitan, sometimes inspired by Asia (bottom left and right).

European designers had to use *American marketing strategies* to make headway in Hollywood and the rest of the US market

Their American counterparts, on the other hand, got into the habit of wearing sneakers to and from work, allowing them to move through the New York crowds more easily. They carried the obligatory pumps in their briefcases.

No one responded to the command to "dress for success" better than the Italian designer Giorgio Armani. He completely revamped dreary business wear, making it suitable not only for the worker ants of this world, but also for women who yearned for a little sophistication. Armani even managed to change Hollywood's concept of glamour, giving the stars the subtle elegance of the bourgeoisie. At first male celebrities like Martin Scorsese, Ben Affleck, and Matt Damon wore his smoking jackets to the Oscars, but later, female stars from Glenn Close to Annette Bening also fell under the spell of Armani's understatement.

Armani's stroke of genius was in taking the lining and stiffener out of the jacket, and thus easing its masculinity. His light, "flowing" suits gave men a softer look and made women look more powerful, making this the first acceptable unisex style. Due to its extra-wide shoulders, which hinted at assertiveness, this type of clothing was regarded as "power dressing," reminiscent of the outfits that Adrian designed for Joan Crawford in the 1940s.

Armani was also massively successful with his suits because he had such a head for marketing. In 1990 and 1991 he landed a singular coup: All the directors, actors, and actresses nominated for the Oscars, as well as the presenters of the awards, wore Armani to the ceremony, having been generously fitted out by a boutique in Beverly Hills, which also supplied the necessary accessories and made alterations. All the stars of the screen leaned in to the microphones and dutifully told the assembled press whom they had to thank for their elegant outfits. At a stroke, this made Armani the most famous designer in America. Of course, other fashion houses subsequently bombarded the stars with offers and presents, but few of them were as shrewd at choosing their "style ambassadors" as Armani, who was very careful in ensuring that the celebrity's image complemented the image of his brand—as he did with Jodie Foster, who was the only one to go on promotional tours wearing Armani clothing.

This cult of celebrity meant that many US journalists no longer made the effort to travel to the once-coveted and mobbed shows in Paris. And why should they? Tomorrow's fashion trends could be better seen on American stars, who received the best and newest designs from Europe for free. Only fashions that had the celebrity "seal of approval" sold. This meant that someone like Armani was able to occupy massive areas in all the major department stores, while almost the only items from French designers that sold were perfumes. Dior's massive Hollywood campaign changed nothing. Nicole Kidman's appearances on the red carpet in John Galliano's eccentric creations were a hit, but she had little impact on sales. The verdict of US consumers on most leading French designers, from Mugler to Gaultier, was scathing: "too fussy, too tight, and unsuitable for modern lifestyles."

Americans, on the other hand, were adept at dressing to suit their way of life. They did not buy clothes, but lifestyles. Ralph Lauren was the best at this: He conjured up an American tradition where there had been none before, celebrating the boots, jeans, and fringed leather jackets worn by the heroes of Westerns to the point where this became the "American look." This had nothing to do with fashion in the classic sense of the word. "I don't like fashion,"

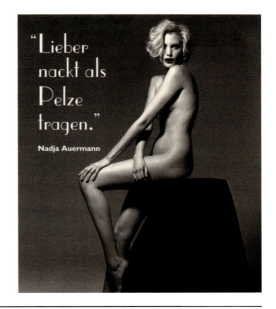

Commitment required
Supermodels like Nadja Auermann proved that they were not just superficial and interested in money when they risked their own skin by appearing on astonishing billboard advertisements on behalf of the animal welfare group PETA, protesting against wearing fur.

said Ralph Lauren; "I just love clothes that never look old-fashioned." His mythical America demonstrated to the nouveau riche just how good money, old or new, can look. The appeal of this aesthetic was its aura of social status. He decorated his boutiques to look like traditional clubs, with leather armchairs, mahogany-paneled walls, and brass fittings. This fed into social climbers' desire for prestige, wealth, and a sophisticated lifestyle. He fulfilled these desires, selling furniture, bed linen, lamps, picture frames, candles, and room fragrance—everything, in other words, that could make life more pleasant.

Ralph Lauren and Giorgio Armani, who expanded his home decoration empire to cover even flowers and chocolates, were the only two designers to create a worldwide brand of their own. Others like LVMH and the Gucci Group bought their respective luxury lines, but Armani and Lauren built theirs up from scratch, with the advantage that every single one of their products matched their personal taste and was easy for customers to identify. Since then, many designers have launched a range of home accessories in a move known as the "candles and cushions trend," but Armani and Lauren are the only ones to have created a complete world, from carpets and bedclothes to silverware.

As the fashion designers were marketing their all-encompassing designs, the artists of the 1980s also began to style themselves as brands so as to sell their work to a wider audience. Post-Pop maestro Jeff Koons, who had worked for six years as a broker on the stock exchange and was well versed in marketing and business practices, even hired an image consultant. This paid off when his 1986 *Rabbit* sculpture, made of mirrored stainless steel, was named as the most iconic work of art of the 20th century. The pinnacle of this self-promotional approach was the *Made in Heaven* series, a set of kitsch, pornographic tableaux based on his marriage to the Italian porn actress Cicciolina. The marriage did not last, but the work catapulted Koons to becoming the highest-paid artist of his time, with sums of up to 23 million dollars changing hands for one of his minor pieces.

The graffiti artist Keith Haring learned how an artist has to market himself in the modern world by watching his friend and role model Andy Warhol. He set himself against the elitist posturing of the galleries in 1986 with his Pop Shop in Lafayette Street, New York, where he sold his works and prints to passers-by. Some of the profit was donated to AIDS charities in 1987, before he himself was diagnosed with the disease. He died in 1990.

HIV/AIDS, which carried off so many artists, awakened an impulse in many circles to make a difference outside one's immediate career. The pop star Bob Geldof organized Live Aid, the biggest ever rock concert, which took place on July 13, 1985 and was televised live all over the world. The proceeds of around 280 million dollars went to those suffering from starvation in Ethiopia and other African countries in need. Since then, a number of big brands, including Armani, have donated a certain percentage of their profits to women and children suffering from AIDS in Africa.

This new awareness was reflected in many areas. In the late 1980s the supermodels Naomi Campbell, Claudia Schiffer, Christy Turlington and other celebrities protested against cruelty to animals and refused to wear fur on the catwalk.

And when the Berlin Wall, the ultimate symbol of the Cold War between East and West, came down in 1989, everyone seemed to be ready to usher in a better world.

AN EMINENCE GRISE:

Giorgio Armani

b. 07.11.1934

Who could have guessed that the men's jacket would be the item of clothing to revolutionize women's wardrobes? The Italian Giorgio Armani boasts that after Paul Poiret and Coco Chanel, he is the fashion designer who has done the most for the emancipation of women, and he might be right. "I envisaged a garment that would fall over the body's contours in a marvelously natural way," he says. To create this garment, Armani "misused" the classic suit jacket, ripping out both the lining and the piping, altering the proportions, rounding off the shoulders, moving the buttons, widening the lapels—and redoing the whole thing from scratch in materials that no tailor would ever have ever considered: coarse linen, Indian cotton, woven hemp, velour, or chamois leather.

The end result was a feather-light jacket, as comfortable and soft as a shirt—one reason why many women also liked to wear Armani's jackets over bare skin. Armani himself recommended delicate tops made of transparent material or silk, with flat sandals or embroidered slippers. He never liked the combination of towering high heels and severe shirts with his suits. As the father of the "power suit," he had actually created a "soft suit" with the express intention of giving career women a suit that they could wear without looking like men in disguise. Clad in Armani, they looked self-assured and urbane, true to his motto: Don't make a spectacle of yourself, but make sure that you are always remembered.

Giorgio Armani, born July 11, 1934 in northern Italy, believes the key to his success to have been the way he never thought about fashion, but rather about people and their lifestyles. After he quit medical school, he worked in the Milanese department store La Rinascente for eight years, first as a photographer, then as a window dresser, and finally in the men's fashion department. He found himself wondering more and more why men bought stiff and boxy ready-made suits when it must have been possible to produce comfortable versions. At the age of thirty he began an apprenticeship at Cerruti, where he immediately began to experiment with jackets. He was soon commissioned as a freelance designer by various different fashion firms. Yet it was only when he met Sergio Galeotti that he came up with the idea of founding his own company. His life partner, who gave up his job in an architect's office, became his business associate, too. Armani and Galeotti set up their own fashion house in 1975 with 10,000 dollars start-up capital.

In July of that year Armani unveiled his new silhouette for men: unstructured suits which discreetly flattered the figure. Three months later he presented similar suits for women. Critics

Sitting comfortably
Giorgio Armani had long reached the pinnacle of his profession as a fashion designer by the time he presented his furniture collection, in Milan in 2006, featuring pieces that were austere in shape, large in size, and bold in color.

Variations on a theme

Giorgio Armani revolutionized the men's jacket and made it into a favorite item in women's wardrobes. Even as part of a pinstripe suit (above, Cruise Collection 2010), it is unmistakably feminine. With each collection Armani has proven the versatility of the jacket—and his own. Whether long or short, strict or asymmetric, his jackets always flatter the female figure. Nowadays they are worn not only with pants, but increasingly with skirts instead.

Armani's private side
In his haute couture line Armani Privé, the Italian maestro often shows off a surprisingly whimsical side.
For Summer 2006 (above) he unveiled a colorful bustier dress with a matching clutch and a cocktail hat made of bright bands.
His classic, high-necked pants outfit was shot in the streets of Naples, playing on the idea that the Armani woman
is desirable yet untouchable.

The **sensuous richness** of Armani's ostensibly restrained designs is revealed when you put them on

were sharply divided: Some hailed Armani as an ingenious innovator, while others dismissed him as a dull bore. Fortunately Fred Pressman, the visionary owner of Barneys in New York, was so impressed that he bought exclusive rights for America. Soon anyone who wanted to be seen as a trendsetter was running around in Armani—especially directors, producers, and advertisers. It was no surprise that the world of film started paying him attention and in 1979 he received a commission to tailor Richard Gere's costumes for *American Gigolo*. This was his breakthrough, and from then on men and women alike felt subtly sexy when wearing Armani.

On seeing the film the fashion press sneered that Armani knew only one color—"greige," that nondescript mixture of gray and beige. Lauren Hutton, a top model and Richard Gere's co-star, looked a little more closely: "Armani uses seven different shades to make one color."

Armani takes the view that luxury should never be ostentatious. This attitude may be as-cribed to his humble childhood in the industrial town of Piacenza. As the middle of three children, the young Giorgio experienced the terror and poverty of the war, yet for all that he always opposed any kind of excess. When his mother laid the table for the Christmas meal with a centerpiece and lots of little vases for flowers, he protested, "Either one or the other!"

This attitude has stuck with him his whole life, but that is not to say that his designs look the same as they did thirty years ago. Take his jacket, the core piece in his fashion, for instance: Sometimes it is waist-length, sometimes knee-length like a riding jacket; sometimes it has lapels, sometimes a shawl collar; or it might even have a peplum or ruffles. Despite all these variations, it is always instantly recognizable as an Armani, due to the muted color palette and the flattering textiles used. At first glance it may appear to be demure, simple, and austere, but on closer in-spection—and even more so on wearing it—it reveals itself to be a real treasure. Armani has been greatly inspired by the Far East, but unlike many of his fellow designers he has never been tempted to create unambiguously ethnically inspired collections. For him, the attraction has more to do with the spiritual quality of the clothing from that part of the world.

When Armani's companion Galeotti died in 1985 after a long illness, he threw himself into his work, taking over the running of the commercial side of the business too. He specifically targeted stars as his style ambassadors, because whatever they wore would be coveted by the large, wealthy middle class. One of the very first Oscar nominees to wear an Armani dress to the award ceremony was Glenn Close, and she has remained loyal to the maestro ever since. "In Armani I feel more beautiful, but not as though I'm wearing a disguise. His designs show off my best features," declared the star, who was accustomed to wearing jeans and T-shirts in private.

It was the stars who spurred Armani on to create an haute couture line. When Tom Cruise married Katie Holmes in 2006 he dressed the couple in Armani Privé, and since then the Italian has shown the most exclusive and sophisticated of his collections in Paris. The stars are personally looked after by Armani's niece Roberta, who has been working for the company since 1997 and is seen as the heir apparent.

The future is beautiful
For his 25-year jubilee in July 2000, Armani's niece Roberta showcased her uncle's fashions (opposite page, middle). Ever since then she has been seen as his heir apparent. It is the designer's relatively new haute couture line (all photos left), more than anything else, that keeps international stars going back to Armani.

THE WOMEN'S REPRESENTATIVE:
Donna Karan

b. 10.02.1948

Seven simple things catapulted Donna Karan to becoming one of the stars of fashion in 1985. Her first collection under her own name was called Seven Essentials, and it also won her the coveted "Designer of the Year" award from the American Council of Fashion.

She was born Donna Faske into a prominent family on Long Island on October 2, 1948. As the daughter of a bespoke tailor and a showroom model, she grew up in the fashion world, and was lucky enough to inherit a talent for it, along with all the necessary knowledge and contacts. She began her training at the Parson's School of Design in Manhattan, but left without graduating, as she received an offer of a job as an associate designer at Anne Klein, having had a summer job for the "Queen of Sportswear." After Klein's death at the age of only 51 in 1974, Karan took over the creative direction of the company with her colleague Louis Dell'Olio. Together they stepped up the performance and turnover of the company, using cashmere, silk satin, and sequins to make a more urbane range of clothing.

Her first marriage to Mark Karan, with whom she had a daughter, Gabrielle (nicknamed Gabby), in 1974, broke down after three years. She took her first steps towards independence with her second husband, the sculptor Stephan Weiss, in 1984. Everything that she had learned from her mentor Anne Klein was poured into her new concept. Her debut collection was an utterly accomplished yet sensuous range of jersey and woolen crepe, opaque tights, and sculptural jewelry by Robert Lee Morris. Donna Karan had dreamed up "seven things" that were perfect for the every-day lifestyle of a professional woman. The basic piece was the black bodysuit, which could be worn with pants or skirts and under jackets, and it was the first of its kind that could be undone with buttons. White body blouses followed the same principle, having the advantage of never coming untucked from the waistband of pants or skirts. Her coats were wide enough to accommodate the broad-shouldered power suits of the 1980s, but also thick sweaters or swishing evening gowns. Her skirts were draped like sarongs, giving business outfits a softer silhouette, but above all else, the "problem zones" around the middle of the body—something that Karan was familiar with—were flatteringly covered up. She sold no-iron stretchy pieces made out of wool crepe, twill, cashmere, and lace, and these proved a blessing for women who had to travel a lot on business. Her aim was to strike "a balance between comfort and luxury, between practicality and desirability."

In her ensembles the sportswear staples of the Forties—wrap tops and skirts, bodysuits, wide leather belts, and the whole concept of a wardrobe made up of versatile pieces that could be

Loud toys
Donna Karan feels like a little girl in fashion paradise in the showroom of her younger, cheaper second line DKNY (Donna Karan New York). She brings countless newspaper extracts together like a puzzle and makes them into highly stylish collections.

286

Among friends

Donna Karan is in her element when surrounded by
other women: whether the iconic "glamour gang"
of the 1980s, including Anna Wintour, the editor-
in-chief of *US Vogue*, and designer Carolyn Roehm
(right), or her close friends, like Hollywood star
Demi Moore (far right), who shares Karan's passion for yoga. Her constant interaction with women
leads to collections that offer freedom of movement,
even when they are extremely form-fitting (like her
stretchy knitwear, above left). Most of Donna's designs are lightly ruffled, sometimes fluttery or floaty
(row of images below). Quintessentially New York:
Karan's giant poster for her DKNY line (above right).
Flattering draping in silk jersey is the highlight of the
Fall 2010 collection (opposite page).

Donna Karan's clothes are women-friendly—
they flatter womanly figures

mixed and matched—were given a new, more aggressive edge. Karan transformed the kind of garments that still looked merely like sportswear when produced by classic American designers such as Claire McCardell and others into the battledress for the fight to the executive's chair, their confident sexiness influenced by Parisian designers such as Thierry Mugler and Azzedine Alaïa, who both favored a streamlined look. She adroitly packaged her designs as part of the feminist success story. As the alter ego of the designer, the grown-up-looking and curvaceous model Rosemary McGrotha acted out the dream of the first female president of the USA in an advertising campaign photographed by Peter Lindbergh. This marked a milestone in marketing, but its vision was (and still is) some way away from becoming a reality.

In 1988 came DKNY, Donna's cheaper line, intended for leisure, weekends, and for younger customers—her daughter Gabby is said to have been the inspiration behind it. Jeans skirts, jumpsuits, T-shirts, casual pants, and jackets were sold in value packs of three. Karan's rule that "only clothes that are practical and that make me look taller and slimmer and more sophisticated, without putting in a lot of effort, appear in the collection," also applied here.

In the late 1990s Karan's designs took a softer turn, being thought-provoking and sensual rather than ostentatiously strong and sexy. The tailoring became looser, and the colors lighter. In doing this she was also responding directly to the needs of women who, like her, felt empowered by their careers. Along with her friends, including Barbra Streisand, whose wedding dress she designed, and Demi Moore, who underwent something of a personality change following her marriage to Bruce Willis, Karan began to follow a spiritual path, often withdrawing to yoga retreats. She described her flagship store in New York as "all about soup and everything warming." Her seasonal advertising booklets not only offered a preview of forthcoming collections, but also seasonal recipes, yoga exercises, travel tips, and other sisterly advice.

A couple of commercial failures undermined Karan's run of success in the 1990s. Her husband Stephan Weiss had been responsible for the perfume Donna Karan New York, launched in 1992, but it flopped. And the men's fashion range, which she designed with him in mind, was perfectly priced, but did not sell well. Then in 1995 Weiss, whom Karan saw not only as her husband, but also as her soul mate, was diagnosed with lung cancer. He quit the fashion company in order to concentrate on his sculpture once more. Going public with the company did not provide a remedy, and Karan was forced to withdraw from the running of the company's operations.

In 2001 she sold the company to Bernard Arnault's French luxury group LVMH for 643 million dollars. Her husband died in the same year, and Donna hid herself away until she felt strong enough to face the world again. Since then she has not designed any more collections herself, but as a top consultant she ensures that the typical Donna Karan style, loved by women all over the world, remains alive.

Family first
The photo middle right shows Donna Karan with her second husband, Stephan Weiss, their daughter, and her daughter Gabby (far left). Since Stephan's death in 2001 Karan has continued to work as an advisor, ensuring that her style lives on.

HOLLYWOOD-STYLE SUCCESS:
Ralph Lauren

b. 10.14.1939

Just like Armani, Ralph Lauren started off in men's fashion. Perhaps that is the reason why neither of them ever indulged in flights of fantasy when designing, but rather concentrated on creating clothes that could be worn for everyday life. And the best place to do it was surely America. "Fashion is moving in our direction," said Ralph Lauren. "Our lifestyle is more modern; we travel and play sport; we move around. We're leading the pack because we have always made practical clothing, and so we're better at it than anyone else."

His observation was accurate. By the end of the 1980s the New York shows were more important than those in Paris, London, or Milan. The sleeping giant had finally awoken, and it had more to offer than sportswear. Ralph Lauren did create a fantasy world, too, but it was one in which Americans felt immediately at home, as though they were returning to a lost paradise. He revived the tradition-conscious lifestyle of the English landed gentry, to which the ruling white classes of America had always aspired—from comfortable tweed jackets to a cultured family life.

His range of suits, photographed by Bruce Weber, remain unforgettable, depicting an obviously well-off and happy family engaged in privileged pursuits on their country estate, complete with dogs and horses. At the same time, he raised the jeans, leather jackets, and cowboy boots worn by the early settlers to the status of classic American clothing. This won over not only his countrymen, but affluent middle-aged, middle-class men all over the world—everywhere that people longed for a defined role in society and a little adventure, Wild West-style.

America's most successful designer was born Ralph Reuben Lifshitz on October 14, 1939, the youngest of four sons of Russian Jewish immigrants in New York. An enthusiastic movie-goer, he imitated the style of stars such as Fred Astaire and Cary Grant, and at high school was seen as an elegant dandy in his cord trousers and tweed jackets, with sweaters casually draped around his shoulders. When asked on graduation what he wanted to be when he grew up, he answered, "a millionaire."

He began his career as a salesman for Brooks Brothers, a company steeped in tradition. In 1967 he bought the rights to the Polo trademark, and went independent a year later with a necktie store called Polo Fashion. Changing his name from Lifshitz to Lauren marked the beginning of his ascent from a poor boy from the Bronx to a market leader on the "fashion mile" of Seventh Avenue. "Ralph Lauren never dreamt of becoming a designer; he simply became one in order to make his dreams come true," wrote his biographer Jeffrey Trachtenberg.

The Great Gatsby

F. Scott Fitzgerald's famous novel was the model and inspiration for Ralph Lauren, and being chosen to design the costumes for the movie version of his favorite book was the high point of his career—the fulfillment of his own American dream.

Borrowed history

Ralph Lauren conjured up an American "tradition" from scratch with his fashion designs and interior decoration. He created an atmosphere of cultivated and confident wealth by using family photos and paintings.

Inherited versus hard-won

The American self-made family has no cause to feel inferior to old European nobility; their taste is just as sophisticated, from classic tweed and other hints at tradition to slightly eccentric elegance. The photo to the right shows (from the left) daughter Dylan, Ralph and Ricky Lauren, and sons Andrew and David. Previously the family generally wore down-to-earth jeans, as proud Americans, but today it is all about velvet and silk, at least for the youngest customers (bottom middle).

Eschewing the Wild West, Ralph Lauren's creative stimulus now comes from New York's moneyed "aristocracy," who want to surround themselves with precious trinkets and wear couture (opposite page and below). Yet he still produces country clothing and casual designs (above).

Each of Ralph Lauren's boutiques
was like an **oasis of refinement**

His success came a lot more quickly than he could ever have anticipated. His neckties, twice as wide and expensive as anything his rivals were selling, sold like hot cakes, and before long he was making shirts and suits to go with them. Only a year later, his manufacturer gave him a loan of over 50,000 dollars to launch a women's collection on the market. Ralph Lauren did this in his own inimitable style, by showcasing his fashions in stylish surroundings, setting up his own boutique inside every department store. This was not the run-of-the-mill "store-within-a-store," but rather an oasis of a cultured lifestyle, which many of his customers liked to imagine themselves living.

Ralph Lauren awakened new desires among the public, and hastened to fulfill them. He supplied everything from carved dressers, leather club armchairs, fur rugs, carpets, and Indian-patterned materials to framed portraits of the "original residents" for the country home whose owners wanted it to look like it had been in the family for generations. Modern lamps, rugs, silver, crystal, delicate porcelain, and silk tassels were designed for the penthouse in town. For each of these different settings, he dressed the whole family, down to the dog, to look the part. His fans espoused the concept enthusiastically, buying their candles, room fragrance, and wall paint—especially popular in later years—only from the all-encompassing Ralph Lauren product range.

This self-made man could confidently say, "I refined American taste." He and his wife Ricky, whom he married in 1964, and their three children were seen as a model American family, like something out of a Hollywood film. It was apt that he was chosen to design the costumes for *The Great Gatsby* movie, all about the nostalgic, elegant feel of the 1920s and the American dream of freedom and self-fulfillment, which was often corrupted into the pursuit of wealth.

"I don't compare myself to designers like Yves Saint Laurent or Ungaro," said Ralph Lauren once. "I'm doing something completely different, and I'm proud of it."

Many consider that his contribution to the history of fashion lay in ingenious marketing rather than the clothes themselves. It is true that his designs were not instantly recognizable as "typically Ralph Lauren." He used the symbol of his polo player logo to link historical inspiration with a vision of escapism that encompassed everything from the country style of Gary Cooper to the androgynous nonchalance of Katharine Hepburn, thus drawing on all the potential for glamour that America's cultural heritage had to offer. By giving wardrobe staples like the polo shirt an urbane look and putting real horn buttons on his tweed jackets he made them more refined. Eveningwear, on the other hand, became more casual, with the standard velour bathrobes trans-

formed into velvet gowns, and cashmere sweaters into floor-length dresses. With their air of clean living, many think his modern classics a little staid. Stylists recommend pairing his elegant satin evening dresses with boots, or his rustic casual pants with high heels. Yet Ralph Lauren's timeless designs really come into their own in a sophisticated setting—and all the better when accessorized with a thoroughbred horse or a beautiful vintage car.

Simply the best
Ralph Lauren borrowed his logo from the prestigious sport of polo, and he also likes to design for exclusive sports, as with his range of impeccable, 1920s-style tennis clothing. Be it sweaters, polo shirts, pet dogs, or evening cocktails, in Ralph Lauren's world everything is presented stylishly.

THE QUEEN OF KNITS:
Sonia Rykiel

b. 05.25.1930

If there is one designer whose work is typically feminine and typically Parisian, it is Sonia Rykiel. A Frenchwoman with translucent skin, flaming red hair and kohl-rimmed eyes, she put her own sense of wellbeing and her own figure at the centre of her fashion in a way that had never been done before. She created her very first designs when pregnant; unable to find any sweaters that would accommodate her growing size and look pretty at the same time, she resorted to knitting her own with needles and wool. Since then, she has amazed the world with "what you can do with a single strand of wool."

Demand for Sonia's flattering sweaters and casual dresses spread among her friends, and then other women. Yet things really took off once she had given birth to her daughter Nathalie in 1962 and was no longer thinking about maternity fashion, but rather about how to create clothing that was as form-fitting and sexy as possible. Her first "poor boy sweater" was a black number that was so tight it looked as though it had been shrunk. She still says that this is her favorite piece of all.

At first Rykiel sold her knitwear collections in the fashion stores owned by her husband, Simon Bernstein. In 1968 she opened her own boutique on the Left Bank of the Seine, in the very year and quarter where the students were rioting against France's bourgeois mores. Sonia, born in Paris on May 25, 1930, actually profited from young women's quest for liberty because, while they wanted to have nothing to do with the many famous couture houses, they found Rykiel's knitwear witty and comfortable, especially as it often had an "unfinished" look. In doing away with seams and linings when manufacturing her pieces and putting the stitching on the outside, she anticipated deconstructivism.

Initially her male rivals made fun of this "knitting Jenny," but Sonia soon proved that she could hold her own. She had soon built a whole empire on her soft knitwear—a family business; Sonia is helped in the firm by her husband Simon and, since 1975, by her daughter Nathalie. In 2012, however, 80 percent of the firm was taken over by the Chinese investment firm Fung Brands. But Sonia remains the heart of the company.

Colorful stripes and coquettish bows have become Rykiel's trademark. Her designs are ideally suited to casual wear, not in the American sense of sportswear, but rather in the French tradition of clothes for simply lounging around. They hang well and are normally narrow—a legacy of the jersey fashions of the 1930s, first devised by Chanel, who like Sonia always used her own needs and preferences as inspiration for her clothing.

Like mother, like daughter
Different generations of a family working in the same company often causes problems, but at Sonia Rykiel it all happened quite naturally; daughter Nathalie has as much of a flair for knitwear fashion as her red-haired mother, and is driving the family business forward.

If there can be such a thing as *sexiness in wool* Sonia Rykiel knows how to create it

Rykiel took no pleasure in designing only practical clothes. "I hope that my creations can bring people a little bit of joy," she declared. Thus vibrant colors were placed on a black background and glittery hearts unexpectedly appeared on chic sweaters. She gave her capes ruffles, and her dresses became ever tighter and shorter. She was an expert at making wool sexy.

Her creations were a particular hit with the career women of the 1980s, who had had enough of sober business wear. On visits to Paris they saw Rykiel's boutique, and realized that comfortable clothing could also have a certain *je ne sais quoi*; to hell with gray formality! Rykiel showed that women could be successful in business while being completely feminine at the same time. But then, anyone who dares to sport a mane of red crimped hair and smoke big cigars can accomplish a lot of things and avoid being dismissed as a "little woman."

Only five years after the launch of her boutique, the untrained designer was appointed the vice-president of the Chambre Syndicale de la Prêt-à-Porter, and in this capacity she looked after the interests of young designers for 20 years. Her own company expanded into perfumes, sunglasses, cosmetics, and men's fashion, but all this was not enough for Rykiel: She also wrote several books and was heavily involved with home decoration. She decorated the venerable Crillon Hotel, one of the most luxurious in Paris, giving it a markedly feminine touch. She also sang, and made a record with Malcolm McLaren. Of course, she was often met with opposition or ridicule, but she learned from her experiences: "What hurts me makes me stronger."

She needs a lot of personal space for her projects, as "they are all solitary activities." This means that it is important for her to have her family and team always close at hand. "I often feel anxious and worried about all the bad things happening in the world. That's why I want to provide a little lightheartedness. In the end it's all about loving and being loved in return."

She describes herself as a thief, wandering the streets with open eyes and ears, soaking up everything and reusing it in her work. This habit means that she is open to discovering new ideas of beauty: "It might be classical, eccentric or intellectual—the main thing is that it must be unusual and surprising!"

When Sonia Rykiel celebrated her 40-year jubilee in 2008, all the greats honored her with a fashion show. Thirty designers, including Giorgio Armani, Vivienne Westwood, Karl Lagerfeld, Christian Lacroix, and Jean Paul Gaultier each designed a "Rykiel" outfit as a homage. Martin Margiela's creation was particularly ingenious—a dress adorned with a mane like Sonia's trademark flame-red locks.

The future of the House of Rykiel seems assured, as daughter Nathalie has given Sonia three granddaughters. The knitting looks set to continue.

A rich palette
At her 40-year jubilee in 2008, Sonia Rykiel showed a cross-section of her colorful, cheerful and inspirational designs. Colleagues like Martin Margiela and Jean Paul Gaultier sent their own witty take on her designs (bottom row, left and far right) down the runway. Like Rykiel herself, they did not shy away from jokes and irony.

Missoni

Gianfranco Ferré

Credit for being the first to free knitwear from a sense of dull conventionality goes to the Italian husband-and-wife team Missoni. In 1966, two years before Sonia Rykiel came on the Paris scene, Ottavio (b. 1921) and Rosita (b. 1931) presented their first collection in Milan. It was a resounding success; an unexpected rush of color grabbed everyone's attention. It was new, young, and more of an art event than a fashion show; the vibrant patterns were reminiscent of Op Art and African prints. The unusual waves or zigzags were made by a complicated combination of many different colored threads.

The individual colors, on the other hand, were themselves made up of a multitude of different colors. The couple also developed new techniques of producing patchwork or making sweaters hang straight. Missoni was extremely popular with sporty types, and it became cool to wear the patterned bikinis on the beach and the jackets in the snow. The designers were fond of sports themselves; Ottavio was once an athlete in the national team, and his first project as a designer was to design woolen training suits for the Italian Olympic athletes in 1948.

Since 1997 the couple's daughter Angela Missoni (bottom right) has been the head designer, and has run the company with her two brothers.

This bearded colossus has a unique place in fashion, as he neither set trends nor has followed them. Gianfranco Ferré (b. 1944) had studied architecture, but he preferred traveling in India to sitting at the drawing board. He acquired his taste for bright colors, sumptuous materials, and timeless elegance there. Upon returning to Milan, he designed first furniture, then fashion for other people. In 1978 he presented his first women's collection, obviously influenced by his experiences in the East. He was most interested in "real women," including famous figures like Nan Kempner and Sophia Loren, and presidents' wives such as Bernadette Chirac and Claude Pompidou. Perhaps this was why Bernard Arnault gave him the job of chief designer at Dior in 1989. This cannot have been an easy decision, as Ferré's structured, elaborate clothes did not correspond to the French liking for chic little outfits. Nevertheless he succeeded in bringing the dusty, traditional house greater sales and prestige. In 1997 he gave up his post at Dior for health reasons and devoted himself once again to his own label. His white blouses with extra-long sleeves and multiple collars became famous. Following his death, creative control of the company became the responsibility of a succession of different designers until it was purchased in 2012 by the Arab-run Paris Group of Dubai.

Norma Kamali

Michael Kors

This former air stewardess, who loved nothing better than to rummage through the stock of boutiques like London's Biba on her trips around Europe, went independent under the name OMO (On My Own) after her divorce in 1978. Ever since then, Norma Kamali (b. 1945) has always been ahead of her time. Even her very first collection, called Parachute, went down in legend. She used parachute silk to conjure up voluminous designs, held in by straps. Her next coup was her sleeping bag coat, modeled on the sleeping bag that she had wrapped around herself to keep out the cold on a camping trip. The feather-light, stitched design is still a bestseller to this day.

In the 1980s she brought sweatshirt material out of the gym and onto the street, giving it shoulder pads and making it into a power suit. She was later to revive and further develop this idea in 2006. Leggings and leotards were also taken out of the fitness center and given a glossy, futuristic look. Even her sneakers with platform heels were something of a hit. Kamali's most successful creations were, and still are, however, her swimwear designs, which range from glamorous and sensual to minimalistic and sexy. Unsurprisingly, she was also the first designer to sell her clothes over the Internet, and intends to do so exclusively in the future.

The native New Yorker (b. 1959) is very much part of the tradition of American sportswear designers, often dismissed by Europeans as purveyors of "boring everyday clothes." Yet this is what is so successful about his creations—they look good from morning to evening, without being complicated. The powerful boss of LVMH, Bernard Arnault, recognized this by appointing the American, previously unknown in Europe, as the chief designer for Céline in Paris, and he remained in this job until 2003. His talent had been spotted much earlier in America; *Vogue* described him as the most influential designer of his generation back in 1996.

This was precisely his aim; "We want to bring our vision of the jet set and luxury lifestyle to men and women all over the world." He did this by creating various different lines, from accessories to swimwear, sunglasses and watches to perfumes, and all with a deliberate sense of understatement. This is amazing, considering that the son of a Revlon model had been brought up to make his career in show business, and had performed in several advertisements as a child. Despite all this, he preferred to study fashion, although he later quit his studies in order to devote himself to practical work in Lothar's, a trendy boutique. He founded his own label in 1981, and immediately began to sell his designs to the big luxury department stores. Today he owns boutiques all over the world.

THE ANTWERP CONTINGENT

Rebel poets from Flanders

DRIES VAN NOTEN

Parisians had scarcely come round to accepting the Japanese fashion invasion when a new revolution took place in London in 1987. The "Antwerp Six," made up of Ann Demeulemeester, Dries van Noten, Dirk Bikkembergs, Walter van Beirendonck, Dirk van Saene, and Marina Yee, presented their collections together, earning themselves a reputation as "wild young things." Martin Margiela, whom many people erroneously counted as one of the Antwerp Six, even though he was already working for Jean Paul Gaultier in Paris, explained that they were, in fact, "the heirs of the Japanese designers, the offspring of Rei Kawakubo and Yohji Yamamoto." With their "unfinished" aesthetic they took the avant-garde baton from the Japanese and ran with it into the 1990s. Apart from the fact that they had all graduated from the demanding Royal Academy of Fine Arts in Antwerp, the only thing that united them was their preference for individual pieces that could be used as a base for whatever outfit the wearer wanted to create. "We're not interested in creating a complete "look"," explained Dries van Noten. Their memorable nickname "The Antwerp Six," was coined by the British press, as they found it too tricky to pronounce or spell the names of the talented young designers. It also echoed the cover names given to criminal groups like The Gang of Four, as well as Enid Blyton's popular children's books from the 1950s, which described the escapades of the Famous Five and the Secret Seven. By all accounts, the unknown designers from Antwerp benefited from this title, which has stuck with them to this day. Before their breakthrough, no one ever associated Belgium with fashion. This meant that the Royal Academy graduates, who had been trained by Linda Loppa, were also forced to club together in order to present themselves with as much impact as possible at the London Fashion Fair. They rented a large delivery truck, parked it at a camping ground, and stirred up as much publicity as possible with the little money they had left. Journalists and fashion mavens lapped up this unconventional approach, and they loved the avant-garde designs of the Antwerp Six, too. Ever since then, Belgium has well and truly made its mark on the fashion map.

WALTER VAN BEIRENDONCK

DIRK VAN SAENE

MARINA YEE

DIRK BIKKEM-BERGS

Beautiful heirlooms
Dries van Noten's clothes never look new; they are pieces that you want to inherit or bequeath, like this combination from 2002.

ANN DEMEULEMEESTER

Sport and sex

Severe tailoring and functionality underpin Dirk Bikkembergs' collections, presented in Milan. For Summer 2005 he added color to sportswear and a hint of sex to his womenswear collection.

DRIES VAN NOTEN (b. 1958) is the most successful of the original Antwerp Six, perhaps for the very reason that he is anything but a revolutionary. In some ways, he was simply following the family tradition: His great-grandfather was a tailor, his grandfather sold menswear, and his father opened the first store selling international fashion in the country. During vacations Dries would accompany his parents to fashion fairs in Germany and France. Yet the sales side of things did not grab him; he was far more interested in creating fashion from scratch, so he enrolled at the Antwerp Fashion Academy. The fame of this institution today is at least partly due to him. Dries van Noten was the first of the infamous gang to set up his own label in Antwerp, in 1985, and is still based in the Flemish city. Many people mistakenly believe Antwerp to be the Belgian capital, much to the chagrin of Brussels, but where fashion is concerned, Antwerp actually has the edge, thanks to the graduates of the Royal Academy.

Unless a collection wins over the critics, it has as good as failed. Dries van Noten ran this risk twice a year in Paris from 1993 onwards, presenting only pieces that would later actually be sold—unlike other designers, who paraded photogenic showstoppers that were dreamed up only for the press, not for the stores. He also refuses to advertise in any way. In spite of this, he has gone from strength to strength. His success may be partly attributed to the fact that his designs never look outmoded. Every one of his pieces gives the impression that it has already had a long history. "I try to create clothes that look like heirlooms," says Van

Noten. This is all part of his concept of "honest fashion," which has a lasting value. The starting point for the designs is always material that he has had specially made in Italy and Spain according to his specifications. This allows him to experiment with very unusual combinations of colors and patterns. He is fascinated by weaving and printing methods, and fashions from other continents. He loves the Middle and Far East, knitting, shawls, wrap skirts over trousers, sheer sarongs under jackets, and, of course, the sari. His designs are often embroidered and decorated with pearls according to traditional techniques from India or Morocco. This results in multicultural marvels that are beloved of modern nomads. His fashions are unconventional, even unique, yet they are the most wearable of the creations designed by the Antwerp Six. "My goal is to create fashion that has a certain neutrality," explains Dries van Noten; "then everyone can put their own stamp on it."

ANN DEMEULEMEESTER (b. 1959), unlike her former classmate Van Noten, permits neither color nor patterns in her work, yet her designs act as a vehicle for the wearer to express her own style. She is also averse to the general press hype. Marketing comes second to the way that the designs feel to the touch, and she puts them to the test by wearing them herself. As a result, she almost exclusively uses natural materials like leather, wool, and flannel. When she made her debut, many thought her style austere and androgynous, but her ingenious wrapping and layering techniques and the combination of delicate and sturdy materials are

Black—what else?

All of Ann Demeulemeester's designs look as though they were made for her idol, the rock poet Patti Smith—always black, yet never monotonous.

A colorful message

Whether his inspiration comes from children's books, movie costumes, or fashion collections, Walter van Beirendonck loves patterns, fantasy, and optimism. In 1998 he paired a skirt with this red shirt emblazoned with a character from science fiction.

No mere cardboard cutout

Dirk van Saene fashioned this dress from paper for Summer 2009. It can be washed and ironed—and all for only 60 euros.

feminine in a completely modern way.

Back then her role model was Patti Smith, and a hint of rock 'n' roll and rebelliousness still lingers in her designs. Demeulemeester is perhaps the most personal of all the Belgian designers, and many of her fans identify with her because of this individualism. "I like simple silhouettes," she says; "I like to dress women in the same way that I would dress a table." She is often described as the founder of the grunge look because she turned her stitches to the outside, left her seams jagged, and generally aimed for an unfinished look, emulating the great Japanese designers. Yet fashion critics soon recognized the fragile poetry behind this martial appearance, and have always given Demeulemeester and her deconstructivist designs rave reviews.

In 1985 she founded her own label in collaboration with her husband, the photographer Patrick Robyn. She has also designed menswear since 1996. Her pieces are now sold in over 30 countries and she has branches in Tokyo, Hong Kong, and Seoul; her aesthetic is more appreciated in Asia than elsewhere. She lives and works in Antwerp, in a house designed by Le Corbusier—it's the only one in Belgium to have been built by the great architect.

WALTER VAN BEIRENDONCK (b. 1957) likes to present himself as an *enfant terrible*, but his eccentric appearance, complete with a Mohawk, full beard and ethnic jewelry, hides a creative thinker who is as reflective as he is witty. Besides fashion, the Belgian is involved in art, music, and literature, has

designed books and costumes for use in theater and film, and makes clothes for bands like U2 and for children. Since 1985 he has been an inspirational teacher at the Royal Academy in Antwerp, where he himself once trained. He encourages his students to grasp every opportunity available to them, despite AIDS and public apathy: "Is it time to abandon Mother Earth? No! We must fight! Fight and believe that there is a future!"

Van Beirendonck likes to emblazon his jaunty knitwear designs, from sweaters to woolen caps, with a graphic "Safer Sex" slogan. He also makes bold use of bizarre patterns and garish colors. From 1993 to 1999 he was responsible for the designs of the provocative Wild & Lethal Trash label, but he also did a lot of very commercial work, such as his collections for Scapa Sport. Thanks to his lectureship, his work as a curator for big shows, and his often ambivalent political statements, his influence on the world of fashion is far greater that his output might suggest. Van Beirendonck sells his eponymous label exclusively in the Antwerp shop Walter, which he has run with his partner Dirk van Saene since 1998.

DIRK VAN SAENE (b. 1959) never intended to design complete collections. Upon graduating from the Royal Academy in 1981, he opened his own little shop, Beauties and Heroes, in Antwerp, where he sold his hand-stitched designs. This meant that he won almost every Golden Spindle prize, awarded to the most promising young designer. He eventually joined the legendary 1987 show in London with his fellow students, and they have gone down in fashion

history together as the Antwerp Six. Yet his path was not obviously destined for success. His collections are too mixed, seeming to jump from one theme to another, making it difficult for the press to classify him. His pieces exhibit the deconstructivism that is typical of both Japanese and Belgian designers, often looking as though the trims and seams have been forgotten altogether. Then all of a sudden he will surprise us with the kind of perfect finish only found in haute couture. He might use traditional materials, or he might resort to latex and kitchen towels. Since 1990 the way he presents his Paris collections has also been fresh and different every time. Sometimes he says, "I want to be hyped too, for once in my life," but sometimes he declares, "Cut the hype! I want to be famous for my good looks!" This irrational behavior might capture the interest of the public, but it prevents him from building a loyal fan base. Not that Van Saene minds. He is inspired by people who unwaveringly pursue their own idea of beauty, even when the world around them is going to pieces.

DIRK BIKKEMBERGS' signature feature is double seams which last forever. At first he used them to embellish shoes, but later they were to form the basis of his career as a designer. Double stitching has become a kind of hallmark for his popular designs, which span menswear and womenswear collections, jeans, and sportswear. The Belgian father and German mother of the 1959-born designer both worked in the army, and the young Dirk was surrounded by uniforms, with their severe tailoring and functionality.

He has adopted these qualities in his own designs, adding an element of eroticism, mostly through leather fetish gear. "Health, sport, and sex" were the three things that interested him, and he has found them to be best embodied in soccer players. While the other original Antwerp Six prefer to show their collections in Paris, Bikkembergs settled in Milan and has dressed an Italian soccer club since 2003, and it now bears his name. Amazingly, he was able to apply his adulation of raw power to sexy women's clothing with great success.

MARINA YEE (b. 1958) is from a Chinese background, but grew up in Belgium and graduated from the Antwerp Royal Academy in the early 1980s. After Martin Margiela withdrew, she took her place among the Antwerp Six and benefited from their joint success. She was able to present her own collection in 1986 with funding from a Japanese investor, but she did not want to bow to commercial pressure, and subsequently went back to the world of fashion. She made a comeback after the birth of her son Tzara in 1992. Ever since then her main focus has been recycling secondhand fashions, combining rough fabrics with delicate materials like brightly colored satin. She also worked on a downright futuristic design for the interior of the Royal Windsor Hotel in Brussels, experimenting with 11 different shades of white, organic shapes, new materials, and light and space, creating "a retreat for people who are always on the go."

Life support
Marina Yee developed a collection of T-shirts artfully embroidered with "bloodstreams" for a charity campaign in 2005.

The Antwerp Six have long become legends, and have prepared the way for a second generation of young designers, who have benefited from the fame of their predecessors. Since their coup in London, Belgium has been associated with exciting fashion, and the doors of the fashion world open more easily to those who come from there or who have trained in Antwerp.

BERNHARD WILLHELM was born in the Swabian town of Ulm in 1972, and was the first German to choose to study at the Royal Academy in Antwerp. While training there he also found time for internships at Vivienne Westwood and Alexander McQueen. After graduating he stayed in Belgium and founded his own label, in association with Jutta Kraus. His very first collection, presented in Paris in 1999, was very much in the still-novel tradition of Flemish design, characterized by cheeky humor and highly personal quirks; in his case, this took the form of prints of monkey hands and kitchen knives, and offbeat updates on the traditional costume of girls from the Black Forest region. Computer games, American football, dinosaurs—absolutely anything can provide the springboard for one of Willhelm's collections, with one proviso: "it must have five skirts." He also believes five things to be essential: soft materials, things that have just been washed, good underwear, boots, and anything masculine; "right now I think that we should go back to wearing skirts." His fashions are a firm favorite of eccentric stars like Björk, as they are not too tight on the body, but looser, with ruffles, drapes, and seams that have

In all weathers

AF Vandevorst manage to make even rain bearable with the metallic sheen on their gumboots, and the lace dress makes them look even more elegant.

been deconstructed and sewn back together, and also because they mix patterns like diamonds, stripes, and plaid with an utter lack of restraint.

RAF SIMONS (b. 1968) did not study fashion, but he was heavily influenced by Linda Loppa, the "mother" of the Antwerp Six. The young Belgian graduated in industrial design, and met Loppa when he was working as a furniture designer and interior decorator. He decided there and then to switch his attention to fashion. Not influenced by teachers or role models, he developed a menswear line in 1995 which featured an extremely narrow silhouette in clothes made out of classic materials. He described it as "couture meets youth culture." Although he met with great success, he took a year off in 1999, only to come back with a radical layered look. In 2000 the amateur was invited to be a lecturer in fashion at the University of Applied Arts in Vienna. In 2005, as Jil Sander's creative director, he took over responsibility not only for men's fashion but also for the women's collections, restoring the label to its former glory. In 2012, he was appointed successor to John Galliano at Dior.

VÉRONIQUE BRANQUINHO (b. 1973) put together her collections like a personal diary, with a few recurring themes: leggings, turtlenecks, blazers, pants, and skirts. Her designs may not have been dazzling, but they were intelligent; sometimes elfin, sometimes somber—just like the ambivalent nature of modern women themselves. At first the graduate of the Royal Academy of Antwerp worked as a designer for some big Belgian brands, but she was able to go independent at the age of only 24, and three years later she also launched a menswear line. Eleven years on, however, the economic downturn of 2008 hit her hard, and her label went under. Branquinho currently works as a designer for the traditional Berlin-based leather company Delvaux.

AF VANDEVORST is the name that the married couple An Vandevorst (b. 1968) and Filip Arickx (b. 1971) chose for their company. The couple met at the Academy in Antwerp. After graduation she worked at Dries van Noten, and he worked for Dirk Bikkembergs as a freelance designer. In 1997 they teamed up to design a womenswear collection together, and presented it the following year in Paris. An is the more thoughtful and intellectual of the pair, while Filip brings a breezy *joie de vivre* to their partnership. Together they inject a new, sexy, cool, and utterly self-assured dimension into fashion for their own generation. Everything is adapted to the *Zeitgeist* "with a sense of humor and leather appliqués," be it riding clothes, kimonos, or bomber jackets. Sometimes they might present clothes in sober hues; at other times the colors run riot. Alternatively, they sometimes base their collections around bizarre themes with titles like "Bees" or "Back to Civilization," and they use their underwear line Nightfall to tell stories. Shoes and accessories are also included in their prolific output.

STEPHAN SCHNEIDER, born in 1969 in Duisburg, he finished top of his class at the Academy in Antwerp, and was allowed to show his graduate

collection in Paris. To his surprise, he received a number of commissions, leaving him with no option but to found his own company. Yet he has never felt that his duties as a businessman impinge on his creativity; a typical German, he feels challenged by such responsibilities: "The clothes are better if you're not thinking solely about the design, but are also forced to bear in mind production and prompt delivery." In his work Schneider grapples with real life; he cares little for escapism or extravagance.

He knows just how difficult it is to make normal clothes for normal people who lead a normal day-to-day life, and he devotes himself to pursuing the ideal type of clothing for such lifestyles. He dresses men and women in the same materials; the tailoring is somewhat severe for women, but slightly softer for men. His unisex designs include classic trousers with elastic waistbands and belted white shirts. Japan is Schneider's biggest market, and he opened his second flagship store after London in Tokyo in 2001.

HAIDER ACKERMANN was lauded as the great hope of Belgian fashion immediately following his debut collection in 2002. His nonchalantly elegant aesthetic of muted colors and clever draping heralded something completely new—and no wonder, since influences from many different cultures were woven into it. Ackermann was born in Colombia in 1971 and adopted by a French family who moved around the world on business, so that he grew up in

Ethiopia, Chad, Algeria, France, and the Netherlands. After high school he chose to study fashion in Antwerp. Financial difficulties meant that he had to leave his four-year course after only three years, although he had always temped alongside his studies, most notably at John Galliano in Paris. In 1998 his former professor Wim Neels took him on as an assistant, and he began to save for his future. He was supported by friends like Raf Simons, and this allowed him to show his first womenswear collection for Fall/Winter 2002 in Paris. Two weeks later he began work as the head designer at Ruffo Research, the Italian leather company which had already given many newcomers, including a fair number of Belgians, a foothold in the fashion business.

At the same time Ackermann was working on his own line, which swathes its wearers in layers of the finest materials, yet shows the figure off to its best advantage with subtle draping and gathers in all the right places. Alternatively, he may add irregular smocking by hand to give everyday pants a more dressy appearance. Asymmetric tailoring, flowing materials and butter-soft leather are the essential components of his silhouettes. Despite their sumptuousness, his designs never look gaudy, but always completely natural, even when Ackermann embellishes them with glitter.

Ackermann designs his clothes for "the woman who sits alone in the shadows of a bar and waits... Her closed-off look just makes her all the more fascinating and beautiful." The press and buyers see him as the biggest talent to come out of the Royal Academy talent pool on the

Everyday wear

Stephan Schneider's only ambition is to dress both men and women in comfortable, everyday clothes. Frippery has no place in his store windows, an approach that has won him many Japanese fans.

Like a piece of her

Véronique Branquinho only designs clothes that she would wear herself, like this sweater and miniskirt combo with over-knee socks and boots.

heels of the famous Antwerp Six. He could well gain as much influence as Martin Margiela, who also trained in Antwerp, yet created a complete fashion universe of his own. Perhaps this is the only truly forward-looking model in an industry that is awash with vanity and insecurity (see Chapter 10, THE MODERNISTS).

Fashion savvy

At Haider Ackermann, zippers are far from boring, while floor-length silk skirts look eminently wearable and surprisingly modern.

Dress
THE MESSAGE IS SEX
to kill

1980

Long live Lycra! Were it not for the invention of this synthetic fiber with its exceptional elasticity, many of the past few decades' most erotic clothes would never have been created—the figure-hugging, clingy fashions by Azzedine Alaïa, for example, which support, flatter, and fit the body perfectly. Lycra was first developed in the late 1950s, originally with support underwear in mind, but it was not until the 1980s that it really began to take off. Lycra is easy to mix with natural and synthetic fibers. Its elasticity makes it possible to produce designs in sizes and shapes that would formerly have required complicated cutting patterns. Anyone who is also a past master at cutting, like Azzedine Alaïa, can produce miraculous results which turn the human figure into a sculptural work of art.

That is why Alaïa is such a favorite with the supermodels. His clothes allow them to flaunt their bodies, demonstrating for all to see exactly why they are classed as "supermodels" rather than just

"models"—and why they can command correspondingly exorbitant fees. "Christy and I don't get out of bed for less than 10 000 dollars a day," as Linda Evangelista famously remarked in 1991, marking the peak of the so-called era of supermodels and simultaneously signaling the beginning of its end. This arrogant remark by a 26-year old model prompted a boycott of the so-called "Trinity," as the three supermodels—Linda Evangelista, Naomi Campbell, and Christy Turlington—were dubbed by the fashion industry. The same business which had helped catapult them to fame and made them three of the highest paid women in the world now turned against them in disgust. The supermodels had become monsters, overshadowing all around them, and they were not so far off the mark in claiming that they were bigger than the product they were supposed to be selling. They had been propelled to megastar status, surpassing even the Hollywood greats, who now suddenly decided it was cool to run around in tracksuits and sneakers

---

A hat, some charm, and not much else
Even if you look like Naomi Campbell, who has maintained her reputation as one of the top supermodels for over 20 years with good reason, you still need a few accessories to look seductive. Here she is seen making good use of a see-through hat trimmed with a garland of flowers and a pair of mules decorated with bows.

Love, sex, and a little playfulness

As times became more permissive, the women who made the headlines were the likes of Sharon Stone, for knowing precisely how (and when) to cross her legs in *Basic Instinct*, or Uma Thurman, who played a dangerous vamp in *Pulp Fiction* (photos left). Flesh-and-blood heroines were eclipsed by a virtual heroine from a video game, superstar Lara Croft, (facing page). Despite the emphasis on sex, love eventually triumphed in box-office hits such as *Pretty Woman* starring Julia Roberts and Richard Gere (above left), *Titanic* with Kate Winslet and Leonardo di Caprio (above center), and *Run Lola Run* with Franka Potente (above right). Anyone who could not find a partner acquired a Tamagotchi (below left) and cultivated the sort of "girlie" image presented by the Spice Girls, who were invited to perform for Prince Charles at the Royal Variety Show.

A virtual superstar and a cloned sheep raised *serious ethical and moral questions:* Just how far should science be allowed to go?

looking like the girl next door. The supermodels meanwhile were sampling all the new opportunities life had to offer, dancing the night away at parties and being feted like goddesses. Not to mention the fact that they were earning a fortune, with the top-earning models commanding fees amounting to millions of dollars a year. These young women under 30 came to symbolize fame, wealth, power, and beauty. They were the very epitome of success. And every man wanted to sleep with them, and every woman wanted to be like them.

Claudia Schiffer, Cindy Crawford, and "The Trinity" were the idols of their day, an era governed by image, power, and glamour. But the term "supermodel" did not gain currency until the end of the 1980s, when the fashion business, like the luxury goods industry as a whole, experienced a serious slump in trade. The supermodels helped to distract attention from the deep crisis within the fashion industry by keeping glamour alive. Fashion designers obviously played a key role in this respect, but they were also helped by photographers like Steven Meisel and Peter Lindbergh, as well as the editors-in-chief and style editors of international fashion magazines, all of whom conspired to turn these models into icons of the outgoing millennium.

Only one Hollywood star was able to compete with the supermodel brigade as a sex symbol and that was Sharon Stone. In 1992, a two-second film sequence catapulted her to fame, turning her within a few weeks into one of the top-earning and most sought-after film actresses. The film clip in question was a scene from **1992** *Basic Instinct*, a psychological thriller, in which the presumed killer Catherine Tramell uncrosses and recrosses her legs during interrogation, revealing that she is wearing nothing underneath her dress. During the years that followed, Sharon Stone tried in vain to cast off this image of murdering vamp, but at the same time enjoyed a reputation of being the cleverest woman in Hollywood—having an IQ of 154. Admired on all sides for her beauty, her elegant fashion sense, and her witty interview appearances, she finally achieved the success she had been seeking as a serious actress when she appeared in Martin Scorsese's 1995 film *Casino*.

But by then another woman had come onto the scene who had a thousand times more sex appeal than all the other living celebrities put together—and was considerably more athletic and enterprising into the bargain. In November 1996, Lara Croft, the first ever virtual idol, was born. No childhood, no awkward puberty, no past, she simply arrived—a power girl **1996** with breathtaking curves, seldom dressed in much more than a crop top and brief hot pants. And carrying a gun, which dangled from a kind of hip holster. She ranged all over the world, from the South Pole right across the globe, searching for magic artifacts which would bring mankind power and riches. All anyone needed to meet this fascinating creature from a distant world was a Sony PlayStation or a PC. The Tomb Raider video game series starring this cyber heroine earned the Eidos company millions of dollars in profits. A study on the world's richest stars, carried out by *Forbes* economic magazine, listed Lara Croft as having a turnover of 425 million dollars, while *Details*, a cult magazine, voted her one of the sexiest women of the year in 1998. The pop group U2 even included her in one of their videos. Streetwear firms developed whole collections imitating the style of Lara Croft, and these were eagerly snapped up by millions of young girls. They flitted around the city on rollerblades and felt as invincible as their heroine. The official Lara Croft website soon spawned numerous—unauthorized—porn sites, where this electronic diva could be seen "topless" or in explicit poses.

Dolly the sheep, the first cloned mammal in the world, was born in the same year that Lara Croft made her first appearance. All of a sudden anything seemed possible: This was a development that not only awakened hopes and desires, but also gave rise to anxieties about a world in which it was no longer possible to tell the difference between what was artificial and what was natural. Ethical questions regarding the cloning of living creatures and genetically modified foodstuffs began to be raised, such as: Should scientists have free rein to go as far as possible or should limits be imposed? And would ordinary people throughout the world even know for sure what was going on? The older generation was already finding it increasingly difficult to keep pace with the rapid development of modern technology. Young people, on the other hand, readily seized every new opportunity that was offered. PlayStations and Nintendo game consoles became the top toy among adolescents, and while the Walkman

---

Separate beds
Placing sex off limits was always a surefire way to increase people's desire for it—as Domenico Dolce knew full well. He wanted the 1987 publicity campaign advertising Dolce&Gabbana's sexy fashions to be photographed amid an old-fashioned setting in Sicily, his strongly Catholic homeland.

Stretch and transparency

While Tunisian designer Azzedine Alaïa clothed the bodies of the world's most beautiful supermodels, such as Linda Evangelista and Naomi Campbell (above), in stretch fabrics, British designer Alexander McQueen opted for see-through materials, lavishly decorated in strategic places.

was replaced by the Discman, sending text messages by cell phone became the main channel of communication. Thanks to the World Wide Web, the Internet grew in popularity, and by the mid-1990s, emails were increasingly taking over from faxes. Internet cafés began to spring up, in which each customer had his own private space to surf the virtual world and chat online—chatting over a cup of coffee and proper conversations were a thing of the past.

The most popular pet of the decade was not a living creature of flesh and blood but an electronic toy from Japan called Tamagotchi. It took the form of an egg-shaped digital pet, which from the moment it hatched, had to be treated like a real animal. Not only did it need feeding, but also it needed to be shown love and affection. If it felt neglected, it died. It was precisely these "human" qualities that contributed to its worldwide success. Young single women, in particular, were delighted to take this electronic creature, measuring just over 2 inches (5.5 cm) by 1 1/2 inches (4 cm), under their wing because it went perfectly with their "girlie look." They wore satin mini skirts which barely covered their bottoms and cropped tops, floral prints, sometimes knee socks, and shoes, as if they were going to their first communion. Sometimes they looked like baby dolls and sometimes like Barbie. They modeled themselves on the Spice Girls. The apparent ingenuousness—and the harmless preoccupation with their Tamagotchi—was extremely deceptive and made it easy to forget that despite their girlish dress they were actually very liberated young women.

When Geri Halliwell, Melanie Brown, Emma Bunton, Victoria Adams, and Melanie Chisholm were chosen in the mid-1990s to form a pop group, no one could have imagined it would be the most successful girl band of all time. As the Spice Girls, these five young women, aged between 19 and 25, stormed the international pop charts with their first single "Wannabe" in 1996 and within a few months they had become as famous as the Beatles. One Number One hit followed another, the path smoothed by a well-oiled PR machine, which made sure that the girls filled hundreds of gossip columns every day and became so popular that Prince Charles even invited them to have tea with his younger son, Harry. Thousands of young girls from San Francisco to Tokyo imitated these five young English girls with their Union Jack miniskirts, pierced tongues, ponytails, tattoos, and Adidas tracksuits, combined with heavy makeup and an attitude of sexual aggressiveness.

In 1996, British designer Alexander McQueen, who was well known for his shock tactics, came up with a design for particularly low-rise pants, aptly named "bumsters," and declared the butt the new *décolleté*. This new style was quickly followed by an innovative wave of tattoos: Virtually every girl now had to have a "tramp stamp," a decorative lower-back tattoo located just above the G-string and, thanks to "bumsters," very much on show.

The Internet also had a dramatic impact on the fashion business: No sooner had a couturier shown his collection on the runway than photos of the models were circulated, seconds later, around the world, enabling copiers to get straight to work. Copies of the outfits came onto the market more quickly— and obviously more cheaply—than the fashion house originals, which were locked into the rigid system of seasonal production. This created a bizarre cycle: Designers would "steal" ideas from the street and transform them into couture, copyists would then turn the designs into "creative" mass-produced clothes—and before you knew it, it would all end up back on the street... Young fashion designers learned a lesson from this and began churning out new designs every six weeks, and in so doing, caused the fashion carousel to spin faster and faster. Established couturiers could not get a look in. On the other hand, individual fashions made from expensive fabrics and involving elaborate cutting techniques, which were less easy to copy, gained additional cachet. The couture in question had to be modern, however, and stretch with the body. After all, it was important for women to be able to flaunt their well-toned bodies, made perfect by means of exercise or cosmetic surgery, without the distraction of any decoration. The message was simple: Dress for sex.

Sex also became the main daily topic of discussion on television: be it the deceived or deceiving Lady Di confiding intimate secrets about royal marriage problems to a sensitive interviewer, or Monica Lewinsky revealing what kind of practices she and President Bill Clinton engaged in, no topic seemed off limits any more. Despite the daily talk shows and their latest sexual revelations—the first erotic TV show in

Germany was called *Tutti Frutti*—movies regained some of their popularity, possibly thanks to the new style of multiplex cinemas, which sprang up in the USA, Great Britain, and Germany during this period. These large movie complexes were sited in the middle of cities, offering a large variety of movie screens under one roof and giving the ailing movie industry of the 1990s a much-needed boost. The biggest box-office hits included *Pretty Woman* and *Titanic*, while Tarantino's *Pulp Fiction*, starring Uma Thurman, and Tom Tykwer's *Run Lola Run*, starring Franka Potente, were also big earners. Red-haired Lola brought in box-office takings that were the second highest returns ever made by a German film in the USA.

Lara Croft, the virtual heroine, arrived on the movie screen in 2001, transformed into flesh and blood in the shape of Angelina Jolie, who was dubbed "the sexiest woman alive." Compared to Angelina's (heavily tattooed) killer body, the waif-like models, who had meanwhile become fashionable, looked rather pathetic, and the abandoned supermodels had to wait a few more years for a triumphant comeback.

The "tramp stamp"
Once Alexander McQueen had redesignated the butt as the new *décolleté*, trouser waistlines dropped lower and lower, exposing an area of the lower back ripe for body decoration. This popular type of tattoo is often referred to—somewhat coarsely—as a "tramp stamp."

THE BRILLIANT BAD BOY:

Alexander McQueen

03.17.1969

–

02.11.2010

The British! They are so determined to shock, be provocative, or push themselves into the limelight that their real talent is often overlooked. Remember Vivienne Westwood not wearing panties in the presence of the Queen and John Galliano with his masquerade-type outfits? But it is Alexander McQueen who takes the cake in this respect. No young designer has been more boorish, more aggressive, or more arrogant in carving out a career for himself. Instead of bowing politely to the audience after his 1995 show, he dropped his trousers on the runway and mooned the audience by way of demonstrating his contempt for the assembled press. He dismissed critics, as a general rule, with a contemptuous "Fuck you," and told the French that couture embroidery resembled "vomit." When he was unexpectedly appointed creative director of haute couture at the House of Givenchy in Paris after showing only a few of his own collections, he acted as if he had a natural right to such a promotion.

It was not surprising that Isabella Blow, an English magazine editor and style icon, who was herself eccentric and sensitive, spotted Alexander McQueen's exceptional talent straightaway. In 1992, she bought his Jack the Ripper final-year collection at Central Saint Martin's in its entirety and, thanks to her position as an influential fashion writer, he quickly made a name for himself in fashion circles. For a short time, he worked as an assistant to Romeo Gigli in Milan, but in 1994 he launched his own label. He himself described his first four collections as non-commercial, claiming that his main aim was to attract attention. His shows were always unique and brimming with emotion and innovation. The theme for his spring/summer 2010 show was entitled "Plato's Atlantis," and was a spectacle which was a dark vision of the end of mankind as a result of climate change—or, at any rate, man's return to the (melt-)water, from where he emerged. In a film made by Nick Knight, Brazilian model Raquel Zimmermann was projected naked onto a vast screen, coiled with snakes and melting in and out of the water before turning back into an ethereal water nymph. The video distracted several of the models who were displaying the collection on the runway: short dresses digitally printed with reptile prints, each one in itself a little work of art in couture quality. And the shoes! As distorting as big, heavy hooves said some, while others found them as poetic as ballet shoes *en pointe*.

Certainly, there can no longer be any doubt that he had talent as a fashion designer. But what about his taste! When *Dazed & Confused* engaged him as guest editor-in-chief, he collaborated with photographer Nick Knight to produce a series of photographs showing people with physical disabilities wearing fashions created specifically for them. Athlete Aimee Mullins, whose

Who's afraid of McQueen?

For years, Alexander McQueen was regarded as the "bad boy" of fashion, always coming across as aggressive, arrogant, and provocative. Success had a calming and civilizing effect upon him and he became more restrained, but his fashions still packed their old punch.

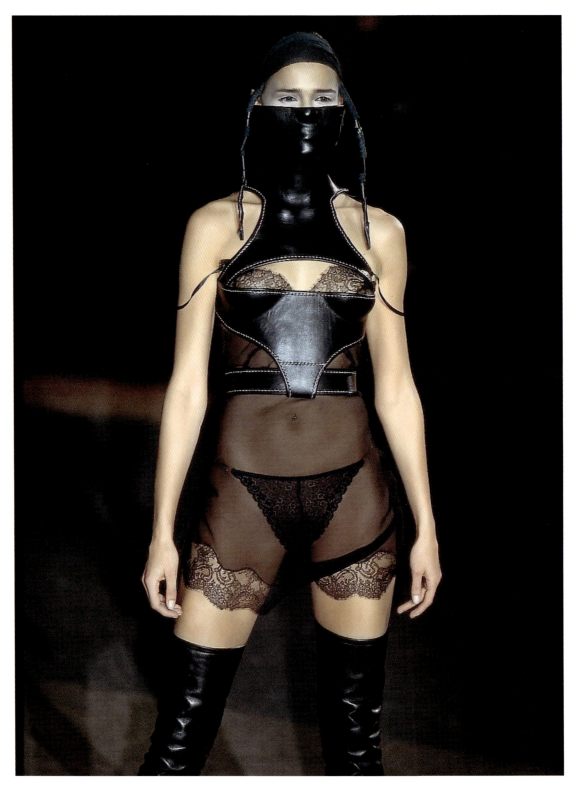

Mummified and tattered

For his 2003 spring/summer collection Alexander McQueen created one of his most spectacular collections, including a black leather breast-plate worn over delicate lingerie and the pale, tattered fronds of his swirling "Medusa dress," one of the designer's favorites.

From head to toe

Modeled by Kate Moss (above), McQueen's "bumsters" were a great success. He inherited a passion for
hats from his patron, Isabella Blow (facing page, below
left, wearing a "Japanese garden" on her head), who
introduced him to Philip Treacy. The latter also designed the hat to go with the McQueen outfit worn by
Sarah Jessica Parker to the world première of *Sex and
the City* in London (below). McQueen wore an original
kilt to the funeral of his Scottish friend, Isabella Blow,
who committed suicide by taking weedkiller.
Although his snake sandals were widely applauded,
his high ankle boots were derisively dubbed "club
feet" (facing page, far right). His strictly geometric
2010 designs (right) were enthusiastically received, as
were his futuristic collections for Givenchy, featuring
reflective patterns, fur, metal helmets, and even LED
lights (facing page, top row).

Show and reality

McQueen's designs often exposed the midriff, one of his favorite parts of the body, as illustrated by this 2006 leather ensemble of leggings and cropped jacket. His outfits were often eminently suitable for everyday wear, as demonstrated by this British couple, pictured above.

McQueen baulked at nothing—
not even *witch-hunts and black magic*

legs were amputated below the knee, was photographed topless for the magazine's front cover with the heading "Fashionable?" superimposed over the photograph. It provoked an outcry on the part of the entire fashion business. McQueen had smashed yet another taboo. But in this case it was more than just another PR stunt. His stylist Katy England recalls that one of his models, who had only one arm, had been moved to tears when she saw the photo of herself: "I never thought I could look so beautiful," she commented.

His full name was Lee Alexander McQueen—but he later dropped "Lee" on the advice of his patron Isabella Blow. He was born on March 17, 1969, in East London, the youngest of six children. His father was a cab driver and at the age of 16, Alexander began an apprenticeship with a Savile Row tailor, whose clients included the Prince of Wales. He is alleged to have scrawled obscenities in the lining of a suit jacket destined for His Royal Highness. However, these and other stories—for example that he had stolen the fabric for his first collection—were set in motion by McQueen himself to bolster his reputation as the bad boy of fashion.

When he showed his first collection for Givenchy in 1996, which featured white goddess dresses and golden antlers, Karl Lagerfeld dismissed him as a "Damien Hirst type of shock artist," but despite this, McQueen remained a full five years with the couture house. During this time, he staged six collections a year, four for Givenchy and two of his own. Each show cost between 200,000 and one million euros—a huge responsibility for a young man, and yet McQueen was equal to the task. His clothes were renowned for their razor-sharp tailored looks. Mr Pearl, a famous corset maker, fashioned lace-up girdles for him which created the sort of wasp waists typical of Dior's New Look and emphasized the shoulders to such an extent that they looked as broad as Adrian's padded power suits. His 1999 autumn/winter collection included a red leather top which looked as if it had been molded from a naked woman's torso and was reminiscent of the plastic red bustier created by Issey Miyake in 1980. Other young designers have often reached back into the past for their inspiration but few succeeded as convincingly as McQueen with his modern interpretations.

His own label will always be associated with "bumsters," those low-rise pants which exposed G-strings and tattoos. His innovation of "skousers" (a hybrid of trousers and skirt) were created according to the same principle and held in place by a chain running straight through the crotch. McQueen was fond of inserting peepholes into his clothes in the most unusual places; his clients loved this kind of *décolleté*, which was ideal for showing off their most intimate tattoos. He had his models wear leather bras over their dresses, decorated shoes all over with spikes, and his computer-generated prints strongly echoed the old art of *trompe l'oeil* effects. As he himself conceded, he was particularly proud of his "jellyfish dress," a swirling creation for the summer of 2003.

In the summer of 2000, McQueen married his partner George Forsyth in Ibiza with Kate Moss as bridesmaid. In 2001, the Gucci group of PPR, a French luxury conglomerate, acquired 51 percent of the alexandermcqueen label.

McQueen once commented that now and again "you have to be allowed to make a mess of things man otherwise you won't get any further." Many people believe that this is what happened in 2007 when he staged a collection based on black magic and witch-hunts. McQueen's runway shows increasingly evoked dark visions, which clearly had their roots in more than a mere desire to be provocative.

On February 11, 2010, Alexander McQueen took his own life.

Pure provocation
Alexander McQueen caused an outcry in the media in 1998 when he and photographer Nick Knight staged a fashion shoot for the magazine *Dazed & Confused*, featuring models with physical disabilities. Athlete Aimee Mullins, who had both legs amputated below the knee, became an idol for many people.

EXCESS AND EXTRAVAGANCE:
Roberto Cavalli

b. 11.15.1940

If Franca Sozzani, longstanding editor-in-chief of *Vogue Italia*, were asked to describe Cavalli's fashion style, she would simply answer: "Sex, sex, and more sex," perhaps adding: "But in recent years, he has been making more evening wear—haute couture for red-carpet events—and that is on a different level." Roberto Cavalli would no doubt appreciate her comments but it would not be enough to satisfy his ambition. He knows that many actresses turn up to pre-Oscar parties wearing his designs, but never, unfortunately, to the Oscar ceremony itself. "I will not be satisfied until the biggest actresses wear my clothes. In that moment I will realize to be the biggest designer in the world," he vows.

He still hankers after this final acknowledgement of his success because it took him a long time to gain recognition. Roberto Cavalli was born in a suburb of Florence. His father was executed along with 91 other civilians in 1944 in retribution for an Italian partisan attack. His mother, a dressmaker by trade, had an extremely difficult time raising him and his sister, and her little Robertino did not make life any easier for her. He was a rebellious child, handicapped by a stutter which made it difficult for him to express himself easily, who refused to do any work at school. Although she regarded him as a hopeless case, he managed to persuade her to send him to art college in 1957. But after three years, he packed it all in, just before his final exams. At the time, other things—such as a Ferrari and a girlfriend—seemed more important to him than a diploma.

He had found the girlfriend all right, but her parents refused to countenance him as husband material since he had no money. Their rejection of him was precisely the incentive he needed! To this day Cavalli is still trying to prove to every mother, every woman, and the fashion industry in general, that he can make money better than anyone else. And that, in his case, all that glitters really is gold!

During his time at art college, he began printing his own designs onto T-shirts and sweaters. His next destination was Como, Italy's textile capital, where he aimed to increase his knowledge of printing techniques. It was not long before he invented a printing procedure for transferring patterns onto an outfit without seams getting in the way. After purchasing a small factory with 16 workers, not to mention a Ferrari, he went to ask for the hand in marriage of his first love—"because I wanted to humiliate her daddy." The marriage lasted ten years and produced two children. In September 1969, Cavalli gatecrashed a party held on the fringes of Florence's biggest shoe fair. He made a bee-line for a beautiful blonde woman, and, during the conversation, claimed

Like a lord
Roberto's house in Florence is furnished with quality and distinction—to the surprise of those who brand his fashions as "riotous." However, no matter how much people try to pigeonhole him, Cavalli is constantly reinventing himself.

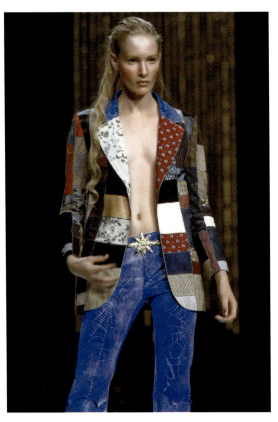

Anything but boring

Be it patchwork stretch jeans (facing page, above), a new outfit for the Playboy bunny, or the Barbie doll (facing page, below), or pecking the cheeks of celebrities, whether Christina Aguilera, the Girls Aloud band, or Carine Roitfeld, the editor-in-chief of France's *Vogue* magazine, and her daughter Lana (facing page, above right)—Roberto Cavalli fulfills everyone's expectations. His self-confidence is kept in check by his wife Eva (above left), a former Miss Austria. Celebrities wear Cavalli at red-carpet events: Jennifer Lopez in black, Scarlett Johansson in gold fringes, Paris Hilton in silver metallic, and Heidi Klum in gold metallic (above). On the runway, wild animals vie with each other—leopards, tigers, and multicolored striped creatures. Only revealing lingerie can hope to compete with them (below).

Zebras rarely turn up singly

Cavalli has always been fascinated by the stripes of the African zebra and has used it in many of his designs. In the summer of 2000, he sent black, gazelle-like Alek Wek down the runway in a black and white catsuit, while blonde Eva Herzigova appeared in a backless, halterneck dress in black with silver stripes.

A mishap and a bit of chutzpah brought about the unknown designer's breakthrough in the fashion world

that his work was in the field of printing leather—the event did, after all, revolve around shoes rather than T-shirts. The woman in question immediately introduced him to her husband, Mario Valentino, who happened to be one of the world's leading shoe designers. He was so interested in this new concept that the very next day, he demanded to see a sample of Cavalli's work.

"Up until that point, no one had printed on leather," admits Cavalli, but by the following day, he had a sample ready, printed with a floral pattern. Mario Valentino was extremely impressed, as were people at Hermès. His brainwave was clearly a stroke of genius, as was his sudden inspiration of using it to create his own fashions rather than handing his invention over to others.

Three years and two fortunate incidents later, he was able to celebrate his breakthrough as a designer. His first lucky break came when he tried to rescue a piece of leather, which had accidentally been dyed blue, by covering it in metallic paint—the result resembled leather gold lamé! His next piece of good luck came when he was offered a container full of used jeans from US prisons, which he purchased, washed, and disinfected. The result this time was washed denim, long before the invention of stone-washed jeans. He began creating patchworks from denim and leather, turning the innovative material into pants, mini dresses, and maxi coats. His collection caused a sensation as well as shockwaves at the 1972 Florence Fashion Fair.

From then on, he received mixed reactions every season. Cavalli has explored every type of animal print, from tiger to leopard—anything in fact that suggested wild or dangerous, whether genuine or as a print, and long before Versace or Dolce & Gabbana hit upon the idea. And whose idea was it to mix lycra with denim to create jeans which pushed the butt upward? Who else but Cavalli, of course! And who was it that printed the image of a snake coiling its way up and around the thigh to a nicely shaped rear? It was these very jeans, modeled by supermodel Naomi Campbell, which led to his spectacular comeback in 1993. Before this, Cavalli had had to cross the arid desert of minimalism, which almost spelled his end as a designer. So much gray and beige, not to mention the sober business suit—Cavalli, who once regarded a zebra pattern as rather plain, still shudders to this day.

If it had not been for his second wife, Eva, 18 years his junior, and now mother of three of his children, as well as his business manager, Cavalli would not have kept going through these periods of minimalism. Eva, a former Miss Austria, who also came second in the Miss Universe contest, at which Cavalli was a member of the jury, managed to convince him that women still wanted to look sexy. And how right she was!

It was now that things really started to happen for Cavalli. Sarah Jessica Parker, fashion icon of *Sex and the City* fame, was dressed in Cavalli clothes, and when the ultimate sex symbol ever, the Playboy bunny, was deemed in need of an image update, it was Cavalli who was called in to redesign the bunny costume. Since then, the Playboy bunny has seemed more Donatella Versace with SM leanings than cute Barbie doll. For their 2007 reunion tour, the Spice Girls commissioned Cavalli to create costumes that would make them look good. Who can recite all the names of celebrities who have worn Cavalli since then? Sharon Stone, Madonna, Beyoncé, Halle Barry, Kate Hudson, Cindy Crawford, Paris Hilton, Megan Fox, Jennifer Lopez... The list goes on and on!

While everyone was grumbling about the recession in 2009, Cavalli launched a new haute couture line, a designer range for dogs, which included ski suits, and opened a new night club in Dubai. "Without excess no success," he remarks, lighting up another Montecristo cigar.

The soft approach
For his 2009 and 2010 summer collections, Roberto Cavalli opted for unusually soft designs, featuring flowing, fluttering, almost demure dresses. Silk and chiffon in pastel colors took the place of leather and denim, gold and glitter. His restraint did not last, however, and by the following season Cavalli had returned to the sexy, riotous designs that have always been his hallmark.

THE JUNGLE DUO:
Dolce & Gabbana

b. 08.13.1958
&
b. 11.14.1962

Dolce&Gabbana are to the fashion runway what Siegfried and Roy are to the variety stage: in other words, celebrated tamers of exotic wild animals. Over the past 20 years, they have, at any rate, successfully unleashed more "animal print looks" than all the other designers put together. They share their passion for flecked and spotted animal fur with all the great designers, from Christian Dior to Yves Saint Laurent, for without it there would be, in their view, "no divas and no goddesses." In 2004 they were finally able to realize their dream of visiting Africa, a journey which reinforced this fascination. Since then, Domenico Dolce is quite certain: "Naomi Campbell is a leopard—bellissima." Fashion editors backstage after a show, meanwhile, are likened to elephants at a watering hole: "They destroy everything and make a lot of noise."

What is more, it is noise for no purpose. Fashion could never wield the sort of influence that would make these two Italians capitulate to its dictates. As they freely admit, they do what they enjoy doing and have no intention of losing either themselves or their freedom in the process, no matter how big their company becomes—and it already has an annual turnover of many millions.

When Sicilian-born Domenico Dolce and Stefano Gabbana of Milan met in 1980 in a Milan studio, there was an instant attraction. This unlikely couple—one small, bald, and provincial, the other tall, elegant, and sophisticated—began creating their own designs in 1982. At that time, they were produced by the textile factory belonging to Domenico's father. It was here that Domenico had learned to tailor a jacket at just seven years of age. Domenico's tailoring skills, combined with Stefano's talent for elegant styling—a skill he had acquired during his training as a graphic artist— led to their first women's collection in 1986, which turned into a resounding success. D&G shows were reminiscent of the great days of Italian film, when stars like Anna Magnani and Sophia Loren portrayed earthy Italian vamps, with some of their lingerie visible. The designs were inspired by the dress and traditions of Sicily where Domenico grew up and where Stefano spent his school holidays: thick, dark stockings worn with wide skirts, decorated with black lace, crosses and garlands. The influence of the Mafia was also in evidence: pinstripe suits and borsalino hats, not just for women, but also for men, for whom D&G have been producing collections since 1990.

Either way, they created movie-style tableaus for their shows and advertising campaigns, which were inspired by neo-realist Italian cinema and were highly rated by everyone, including Madonna, an American with Italian roots. In 1993, this pop icon ordered 1500 costumes from them for her "Girlie Show" world tour, and she is the face of Dolce&Gabbana for their spring/summer

---

Wild at Heart
What may look demure on the surface can actually provoke untamed passions. Domenico Dolce (right) and Stefano Gabbana are specialists in this field. The two designers adore wild animal patterns, both at home and for their fashions.

Wearing a different skin

Dolce&Gabbana have a deep fascination for wild animal patterns in their fashion designs. In 1995, they sent Carla Bruni, now wife of the French president, Nicolas Sarkozy, down the runway in a tiger-skin hooded mini and a bra accessorized with Mongolian lamb skin (above left and below left). Two years later, Carla trod the runway wearing a floppy hat and long patchwork pants with a bikini top (below center). Supermodels Helena Christensen (above center), Naomi Campbell (facing page), and Cindy Crawford (below right) are great fans of Dolce&Gabbana's jungle look and attend most of their shows. The sunglasses with the conspicuous DG initials are a popular status symbol for celebrities.

Deep affection

Up until a few years ago, Domenico Dolce and Stefano Gabbana were a couple; now they remain business partners and good friends. They both love the traditions of their native Italy, from the black dress to highly visible lingerie—we need only recall the film appearances by Anna Magnani and Sophia Loren. In 1987, model Marpessa modeled their latest collection between Sicilian housewives, and stars like burlesque dancer Dita von Teese (above left), Liz Hurley (above center), and Madonna (below right) also appeared in D&G lingerie. Singer Kylie Minogue trod the runway modeling D&G clothes in 2006 (below left), while Lauren Hutton, supermodel, film star, and businesswoman appeared in an animal print trenchcoat to mark the 20th anniversary of these two Italian designers (above right).

Spectacular shows

The Dolce&Gabbana duo have a reputation for staging spectacular shows with unexpected surprises. As part of their 2007 summer show, Domenico and Stefano had a model carried onstage in a cage. The outfit being "guarded" in this way was a metallic gleaming mini outfit, resembling a corset with exaggeratedly broad hips, which looked as if it could have been worn under extravagant dresses at the end of the 19th century. One year later, they produced the corresponding over-garments: skimpy bodices above lavishly billowing skirts made from pretty, printed fabrics. The dark red velour shoes with killer high heels and platform soles guarantee a stately entrance.

While Domenico is *constantly seeking to explore new territory*, Stefano prefers to stick to his roots

2010 collection. "She is a strong woman," says Domenico, admiringly—as are Jennifer Lopez and Kylie Minogue, two other celebrities who are known for favoring D&G designs. Nevertheless, the duo agrees that the days of muses are a thing of the past. "Nowadays, one should be inspired by 'real' women. Absolutely real," remarks Domenico.

Strangely enough, it is Domenico, who came to the northern Italian city of Milan from Taormina in Sicily, who wants to project fashion into the future: "I love the new. I'm a very curious person." Stefano, on the other hand, prefers to stick to what is tried and tested, which in D&G's case includes bustier-style dresses, broderie anglaise, the white shirt, and sharply tailored pant-suits. "We argue about every collection," they readily admit. But they always have and this has nothing to do with the fact they still continue to design together despite separating as a couple in 2003. They start by producing a set of designs each so that every collection begins with two lists "Yes" and "No." And always it's "No brocade, no animal prints!" Both of them feel they have already done too many of those. And yet... Domenico wants to inject 80 percent new material into the collection, while Stefano wants to retain 80 percent and introduce a mere 20 percent in new designs. In the end, the collection will inevitably include animal prints, brocade, and bustiers—but all in new combinations.

It is precisely this that appears to be the secret of their success. When the entire fashion industry began harping on about volume rather than form, D&G likewise tried to focus more on the possibilities of the fabric rather than shape. And what was the reaction of their clients? A resounding "No!" "All men and women want to be sexy," concludes Stefano Gabbana. "For three seasons we worked on volume, not shape, and in the end, you know what the customer said? No! Our clients stopped buying our clothes until they fitted as snugly as they had in the past." They prefer to follow the example of their role model Azzedine Alaïa, who has been consistently producing the same body-hugging style for the past three decades. "I love his work," enthuses Stefano, "but I would love to do it before he does, you know? But we're not jealous."

Both admit to being ambitious, not in terms of making money but of doing better. "I am my own greatest competitor," says Domenico. And the best advice comes from the clients, who no longer buy because they need something (everyone already has too much), but because they want something special. The bestsellers are the cruise and pre-spring collections, which do not appear in any fashion magazine. "The client can find something in the boutique that no one else has and that is what she likes," says Stefano. D&G clients prefer to be seen to be independent of what fashion magazines recommend and like to regard themselves as trend setters—like Victoria Beckham, for example.

Domenico and Stefano are always on the look out for something new and are not content with producing 14 collections a year, including ones for children. They also produce accessories such as sunglasses, fashion jewelry, perfumes, and, most recently, makeup. Apart from Armani and Versace, no other Italian fashion house has managed to build up such an empire. And what else might Domenico Dolce and Stefano Gabbana do? Well, in 2006, they opened a restaurant in Milan, and the Metropol, where theater performances and other events are held.

Homage to a sex idol
One of the women whom Dolce and Gabbana would have dearly loved to dress was Marilyn Monroe—in 2009, they paid tribute to the Hollywood star in the form of an elegant evening gown in black and white, with images of Monroe printed on it.

THE KING OF CLING:
Azzedine Alaïa

b. 06.07.1940

He refused to accept the top award from the French government because he does not like Nicolas Sarkozy—even though the latter's wife, Carla Bruni once modeled his designs and still wears his clothes to this day. He also regards the practice of most fashion houses of putting on four or five shows a year as an "inferno of commercialism." He himself creates two collections at most, if that. Nor does he keep to a specific deadline for showing them, but presents them whenever he feels they are ready. Azzedine Alaïa is unique in every sense, which is why his followers are prepared to wait patiently until he invites them to a private showing at his home over coffee or tea and cookies. What they see is unlikely to cause a sensation, as Alaïa's basic fashion style has not changed for over 30 years. He simply produces variations and refinements.

"If you have found the right way," explains Tunisian-born Azzedine Alaïa, a very short man who is nevertheless regarded as the greatest living couturier, "you do not need to look for any other." He nearly became a midwife's assistant. As a young boy, he used to help the local midwife, who had brought him and his twin sister into the world in Tunisia on June 7, 1940. Madame Pineau owned a collection of copies of high-end fashion journals, which she stored in her midwife's case. In between heating up water, passing towels, and looking after screaming newborn babies, there was always time to pore over the photos of beautiful models in the magazines.

Little Azzedine's appreciation of the female body, the softness of which he loves and respects to this day, prompted Madame Pineau, the midwife, to enroll him at art college to study sculpture. After graduation, Azzedine's first job was working as an assistant to a dressmaker who made copies of Dior designs. In 1957, he moved to Paris where he got a job with the House of Dior. This promising start only lasted five days, however: "It was the time of the Algerian war and as a North African I became a *persona non grata*."

He could not even find anyone to rent him a small room. Luckily, Alaïa, with his passion for fashion, had a series of encounters with women who took him under their wing like a little mascot and took an interest in furthering his career: The Comtesse de Blégiers offered him a place to stay, in return for which he looked after her children and her clothes. During the five years he spent with the Comtesse, he began creating his own designs for former acquaintances in Tunisia and new friends in Paris. In order to develop a thorough grasp of his trade, he went to Guy Laroche, in whose haute couture studio he worked for two years until Simone Zehrfuss, the wife of a prominent

---

A faithful soul
When Azzedine Alaïa feels he has found something good, he sticks to it. This diminutive Tunisian designer dresses predominantly in Chinese-style workman's clothes with Mao-style jackets and is always surrounded by a pack of friendly Yorkshire terriers, which he takes with him on his travels.

Fans and friends

Singers Grace Jones (facing page) and Tina Turner (left) are close friends of Alaïa, and he knows how to dress each of them to their best advantage. Another long-term friend is the painter and director Julian Schnabel, shown above right with musician Lenny Kravitz and models in Alaïa's studio during the making of *The Diving Bell and the Butterfly.* Naomi Campbell (below right) is one of the supermodels who stay with Alaïa in his home, where he cooks for them and they affectionately call him "Papa." Singer Victoria Beckham (below left) illustrates how sexy Alaïa's fashions can look on the red carpet—while Michelle Obama (below center) demonstrates that his couture is equally suitable for diplomatic occasions.

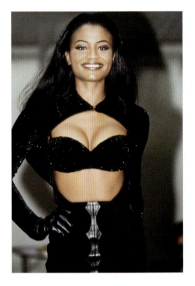

The human body as a piece of art

Alaïa, who originally intended becoming a sculptor, molds his figure-hugging clothes—and sometimes the heels of his shoes—like sculptures. Models like Helena Christensen (above) and Naomi Campbell (right) love what he does. Singer Farida, like Alaïa, comes from Tunisia and models for him out of friendship (below left). Alaïa not only knows how to make the best bustiers (above right), but he can also make skirts swing and accentuate small waists (right). Even now, he still pins every pleat and fold by hand himself, unrolling the fabric straight off the bolt (facing page, with model Veronica Webb). Only very few couturiers still work in this time-consuming manner. It is no wonder that Alaïa is never ready to show in time for the traditional collection deadlines and only holds private viewings.

Private viewings

Azzedine Alaïa ignores the usual dictates of the fashion business and shows his collections outside the traditional seasons and then, as a matter of principle, only in his private rooms in the Marais. Clients and buyers eagerly anticipate his masterpieces in black stretch fabric—be they long or short, his designs are sure to please. In Alaïa's hands, leather can end up looking like lace, not only thanks to the perforations, but also because it is so soft that it drapes as well as any fabric, as illustrated by this backless design in 2009.

Influential women *take this hard-working little Tunisian immigrant under their wing*

architect, persuaded him to set up in business on his own, having supplied him with the necessary funding to get started.

He opened his first studio in his apartment, the small rooms of which he filled with sewing machines—even the kitchen, bathroom, and hallway were not spared. The apartment became a hive of activity as word quickly spread that Azzedine Alaïa was a promising new designer. His patron, Simone Zehrfuss, introduced him to poet and novelist Louise de Vilmorin, whose partner was André Malraux. They were the most influential couple of the Parisian intellectual scene and it was in her salon that Alaïa made the acquaintance of elegant women such as Cécile de Rothschild and her female relatives, and the actresses Arletty and Greta Garbo. All his clients visited his private studio incognito to have their clothes fitted directly onto the body in such a way that they emphasized the strong points and concealed any weaknesses. He was just as gifted in this respect as Adrian, Hollywood's top costume designer of the 1930s, whom he greatly admired and whose client, Greta Garbo, he "inherited." "She had a nice shape," he recalls, "but she was not skinny. It was her face, though, that was most impressive: those eyes, the nose!"

Alaïa's first ready-to-wear collection was shown in 1981. Four years later, he was voted best designer of the year and his collection, the best of the season. The award ceremony in the Paris Opéra was a memorable event, where singer Grace Jones carried the diminutive designer onto the stage in her arms.

He has always been drawn to tall, strong women and has enjoyed dressing them: Jessye Norman, Farida, Michelle Obama... His closest friendships, however, have been with top international models like Naomi Campbell and Stephanie Seymour, who have often stayed with him and call him "Papa" for the way in which he fusses over them and cooks for them. Helena Christensen, Tatjana Patitz, Claudia Reiter—all models with "feminine" shapes—also prefer Alaïa designs in their private lives. Most of the models would have exchanged their entire fees for his clothes but "Papa" is generous and gives them all away.

His secret is his intimate knowledge of the female body and how to make it look sexy. When other designers rejected young Stephanie Seymour as a model because her rear was too rounded, Alaïa worked out a cut which made a virtue of it. He made the most of flat chests by pushing up the breasts with wide, leather corsets, transforming them into *décolleté*-filling focal points. His favorite materials include Lycra, soft glove leather, and viscose, a largely forgotten fabric. He learned his technique by taking apart and reconstructing clothes made by the Old Masters of fashion. Since 1968, he has been collecting originals by Cristóbal Balenciaga, Paul Poiret, Madeleine Vionnet, Adrian, and others. It was Vionnet's bias cut, in particular, that Alaïa took a stage further using the latest stretch fabrics. His spiral seams circle the body, both supporting and accentuating it.

Alaïa, who wears nothing but Mao-style jackets like a Chinese workman, albeit of silk or satin, prefers to work late at night in his vast studio-cum-apartment in the Marais which he moved into in 1990. Julian Schnabel, a well-known American artist, was given the job of designing it. The two men had become good friends over the years, as Schnabel's various wives were such frequent clients of Alaïa.

In 2000, Alaïa went into partnership with the Italian Prada group, but in 2007 he bought his label back again, although Prada still continues to produce and market his much-coveted shoes and other leather goods.

A regal entrance
Even Azzedine Alaïa's grand evening gowns have no need of color, pattern, lace, or any other type of decoration. He relies solely on the sculptural impact of his tailoring techniques, as illustrated by this gown consisting of a molded leather bodice and skirt with Godet pleats.

Rick Owens

Hervé Léger/ Leroux

His favorite color is "dust," a nondescript beige-gray in a range of shades from light to very dark. Consequently, his famous leather jackets, asymmetrical wraparound skirts, and even his organza blouses all look as if they have been rescued from some attic or somewhere. Twenty years ago, Rick Owens decided he wanted to make his clothes look worn and faded, so he began washing and drying fine leather and transparent crepe fabrics in the machine before making them into short jackets, transparent T-shirts, and bias-cut skirts à la Madeleine Vionnet. Rick Owens, born in 1962 in California, was first tipped as an up-and-coming designer among rock stars and models—Kate Moss wore one of his distressed leather jackets—before his discovery by *Vogue* magazine enabled him to stage his first runway collection in New York. In 2001, he moved to Paris, where he was appointed artistic director of the Parisian fur house Revillon; he now holds the patent for all Revillon products. At the same time, he has continued to develop his own label without compromising his individual style: His sensuous goddesses still resemble high priestesses from a dangerous sect, full of dark secrets. His style has been described as "glamour meets grunge" and he is credited, along with Alexander McQueen, with having invented the morbid Goth look.

A single dress, created out of sheer desperation in 1989 late at night, transformed him into a celebrity. The show was almost upon him and he needed something special. Hervé Léger reached in desperation for a roll of edging fabric, wrapping it round and round a tailor's dummy until it resembled a dress. And what a dress! It was like a second skin, elastic and firm, both revealing and shaping at the same time! The bandage dress—the suggestion of the word "bondage" is no accident—turned Hervé Léger, who was born in 1957 and who had designed everything from hats to furs, into a star of the Paris fashion scene. It is true that he owes much of his inspiration to Madeleine Vionnet and Azzedine Alaïa but neither of them had pushed the idea of bias wrap to the extremes that he did. Regardless of whether he was working in wool or silk, he mixed everything with Lurex, Lycra, or Elastane, turning the resulting fabric into multicolored bandage dresses. In 1998, Hervé Léger sold his label to the US group BCBG-MaxAzria, which dropped him as their designer just a year later. Since then, he has been marketing his sharply tailored clothes with their fantastic *décolletés* under the name of Hervé L. Leroux—with increasing success to such stars as Halle Berry, Keira Knightley, and Kate Winslet.

Roland Mouret

Antonio Berardi

How similiar their stories are! It was a single design which also saved Roland Mouret and catapulted him to success in the fashion world: The Galaxy dress of 2005 became the most photographed hit of the season. It was coveted by all the stars, with Scarlett Johansson and Dita von Teese leading the way. For good reason: both women are very well endowed and are therefore never without a bra. Roland Mouret's Galaxy cocktail dress was perfect for their hourglass figures, enabling them to show off their assets in the best possible light. Women quickly realized the potential of this ingenious but simple cut, which accentuated the bust and other curves, flattened the stomach and narrowed the hips, flattered the upper arms, and broadened the shoulders to make the waist appear narrower. Despite the design's overwhelming success, Roland Mouret split from his financial backers and was obliged to find another name for his label. He left New York and returned home to France (where he was born in 1962) and in 2007 he launched a new label under the name of RM with a new business partner and a new collection. His latest silhouette is narrow and exotic, with over-the-knee skirts and slimming wraparound skirts and pleats. With Roland Mouret's help, one of his fans, Victoria Beckham, has had considerable success.

Despite being born in England in 1968, Antonio Berardi's aesthetics are wholly influenced by his Sicilian family roots: "I love curves. I find women like Monica Bellucci wonderful." Sometimes, he wraps them in a coat, decorated with dozens of tiny light bulbs which form the shape of a crucifix. What is underneath, however, is unashamedly sexy, shows a good deal of skin and reveals every curve. He celebrates hourglass figures with skin-tight leather suits, sharply tailored corseted dresses, and sparkling off-the-shoulder mini dresses. Even his silk boyfriend blazers cling to the figure so tightly that "heroic seduction"—a description on the press release for his spring/summer 2010 collection—is guaranteed. Like most successful British designers, Berardi studied at Central Saint Martins and worked for three years under Galliano. In 1999 he went to Milan and then to Paris, an environment which did not suit a designer of his temperament; he is inspired by Italian morality and a British propensity for breaking taboos. He came back into the spotlight when he returned to London—in a very emphatic way: No sooner was Victoria Beckham seen wearing his spectacularly high, heel-free boots than celebrities were lining up to get their hands on them.

CHALLENGING LEGACY

Old houses—new names

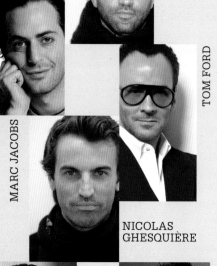

RICARDO TISCI

MARC JACOBS

TOM FORD

NICOLAS GHESQUIÈRE

CHRISTOPHER BAILEY

STEFANO PILATI

OLIVIER THEYSKENS

ALBER ELBAZ

TOMAS MAIER

There is an old saying to the effect that tradition is not kept alive by hanging onto the ashes but by passing on the flame. These words have particular relevance in the fast-paced world of fashion, where tradition, at least as far as individual fashion houses are concerned, is not a deep-rooted concept. It was not until the latter half of the 20th century that a couturier had any expectations of his house surviving him. His "legacy" was generally carried on by a former protégé, who a few years later would launch his own fashion house and continue, broadly speaking, following the style he had first learned in the trade, evolving and stamping it with his personal signature. During the past 25 years, as customers have become increasingly obsessed with the name on a label, the situation has changed dramatically: Now, all of a sudden—and provided the design was right—an old, established name seemed a surer guarantee of a higher turnover than a new line, however cleverly it was launched. Designers, meanwhile, found themselves facing an unprecedented challenge: Anyone who was newly appointed at the helm of one of these fashion house dinosaurs not only had to anticipate trends and evolve a strong, personal signature but also had to balance these factors against any vague expectations which potential clients might have of an already established brand. If they were successful, then even faltering firms like Gucci, Balenciaga, or Bottega Veneta could rise phoenix-like from the ashes in a shimmering vision promising dream turnovers, while established fashion houses like Louis Vuitton and Burberry could prepare to hit new heights.

This is the stuff of which fashion fairytales were made during the 1990s and 2000s. The scene was set by an American designer, who was relatively unknown at the time and joined Gucci in 1990 to gain experience, contacts, and money to launch his own label. By this time, this world-famous Florence label was a mere shadow of its former self: Gone were the days when the jet set were falling over each other to get their hands on purses with a bamboo handle, moccasins with a metal snaffle, or floral print scarves. Gucci was hitting the headlines, not so much because of its products, which had become rather stuffy but, more often than not, as a result of increasingly outrageous scandals, culminating in 1995 when the wife of Maurizio Gucci, grandson of the firm's founder Guccio Gucci, had her husband murdered. It was around

Sinful in white

Tom Ford chose white, the color of innocence, for Gucci's erotic evening gowns in the style of former screen goddesses like Jean Harlow.

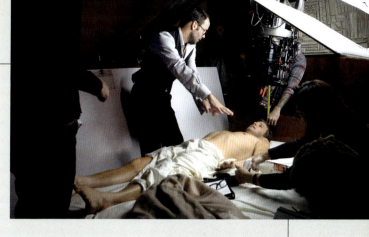

this time, however, that the firm's luck began to change. An American designer, who had been promoted to creative director within just four years, presented his ready-to-wear collection. The fashion industry gave a collective gasp: brief hipsters in shimmering velvet, ultra skinny blouses of gleaming satin silk, luminously bright colors, and *décolletés* plunging to the navel or below. A new star by the name of Tom Ford was in the ascendant. He had pulled off the astonishing feat of catapulting a fashion house, which was only surviving by virtue of its past reputation, back into the present without saddling it with an image that did not reflect its roots. Although, in his opinion, the writing had always been on the wall, Ford later elucidated what he saw as the reasons for the years of decline: "What was missing was a strong personality." And this had clearly been rectified. He recognized the firm's potential and he built on it to develop a completely new and distinctive style. No other designer produced such narrow silhouettes or created more provocative *décolletés*, which, however revealing, were always stylish rather than sleazy—the concept of "safer sex" transferred to fashion. Ford's criteria with regard to fabrics likewise reflect his objective of cultivating an image of glamour, and luxury. He generally opts for "rich" materials, such as satin, velvet, leather, and fur, and where patterns do occur, they generally reflect some kind of leather—his spring 2000 python print dresses, for example, or his autumn 2001 cocktail dresses. The latter are now regarded as fashion icons: they were created from small,

overlapping squares of fabric, which bobbed gently up and down with every movement and not only resembled 1920s flapper dresses but also put one in mind of crocodile skin. Ford's designs are mostly straight and lack any ornamentation. If he does include decorative elements, they are often associated with leather goods, for example, rivets, buckles, clasps, and zippers... Fashionistas all over the world find it very hard to resist the sex appeal of Tom Ford's creations and his style was soon adopted by some of the world's greatest celebrities. Madonna was the first to be seen wearing Gucci at an awards ceremony. She was soon followed by Hollywood divas like Gwyneth Paltrow, Halle Berry, and Jennifer Lopez. Purses and little clutch bags had likewise cast off all trace of their staid image, and became even more coveted than in Gucci's heyday in the Fifties and Sixties. The glamorous and extremely prosperous era of Tom Ford lasted ten years, after which it ended just as suddenly as it had begun. In 2004, Ford's contract was not renewed and he and the Gucci group parted ways. His final autumn collection recalled some of his most famous designs during what had been for Gucci a momentous decade: There were blue velvet jackets, similar to those in his very first 1995 collection; a new version of the crystal-studded, flesh-colored goddess robe, which Nicole Kidman

Setting the scene
After a creative break of four years, Tom Ford re-emerged in 2009 to direct his first film, entitled *A Single Man* (above). He is as talented a director as he was a designer for Gucci, where he positioned the company logo in places that it could never be overlooked, whether it was on a G-string or a crocodile purse.

Dress or pants
As far as Tom Ford is concerned, fashion has only one goal—seduction. In this respect, it is irrelevant where the *"décollétes"* are sited. Color is also used to send out signals.

Handbags—the main event

Marc Jacobs carved a career for himself in the field of young fashion. He is equally successful with Louis Vuitton, but now his focus is on purses, whether as accessories to a summer mini dress with a wide belt (and pockets) for 2010 (above), or to a transparent trenchcoat (below). The Alma Graffiti became a coveted It bag.

wore to New York's Metropolitan Opera; and a revival of those 1996 spectacular white jersey dresses inspired by Roy Halston. But this collection is only part of his legacy: Ford's less tangible, but even more consequential creation for the couture house was the newly invented Gucci girl, a woman exuding sexual self-confidence, highly polished, brimming with the barely controlled energy of a wild animal about to pounce—an image so strong that it would sustain a whole generation of successors. It was not only Ford's boldness in terms of fashion but also his financial success that created a stir: Within a single decade, the company's value increased from 200 million to 2.5 billion dollars, a more than twelve-fold increase—although the trend had already begun to show signs of slowing down after one or two years. It was no wonder that Ford's example seemed worth following. From 1997, several other old-established Paris houses attempted to reinvent themselves using the same formula as Gucci. However, the top name in luxury accessories was about to spring a big surprise: Louis Vuitton appointed Marc Jacobs, the so-called king of grunge, as its chief designer. Jacobs, whose name had been linked with the anti-fashion movement of the 1990s, had had his own label for eleven years. Since his appointment in Paris, he has managed extremely successfully to keep both balls in the air. While his own New York line is characterized by undemanding flea market aesthetics and the avant-garde, his work for Louis Vuitton reflects the demands of one of the largest luxury houses in the world. What both lines do have in common

is a tendency toward deconstruction, and toward a mix of retro elements, which not only hark back to the Forties, Fifties, Sixties, and Eighties, but also reflect the influence of modern-day street chic. His more feminine collections for Louis Vuitton echo the glittering past of haute couture and cultivate grand, sophisticated gestures—elegant flounces edging the collar of a short black coat, voluminous puff sleeves on a cocktail dress—as well as deliberate breaches of style, such as slinky herringbone skirts and white, rabbit-fur bomber jackets. As Sarah Mower, an American fashion journalist once remarked, the secret of Jacobs' success lies in his ability to tap into the long neglected gray area between glamour and the everyday—his fashions are fascinating because they combine aspects of both worlds. Occasionally, the LV monogram, which is commonly associated with this luxury brand, appears on dresses and jackets: The logo, introduced in 1896, with the LV monogram and the four-leaf flower motif, was inspired by the *fin-de-siècle* passion for Japanese and Oriental graphics. Jacobs has always pursued his own, punchy agenda with this logo, the hallmark of Louis Vuitton: For his spring 2000 collection, he asked artist Stephen Sprouse to create a graffiti version of the monogram which "defaced" the original Louis Vuitton logo. People were soon clamoring to get their hands on this must-have combination of super luxury and subculture and the purses were snapped up in no time at all. In 2003, a Japanese designer, Takashi Murakami, created yet another version of the monogram design, this time featuring the LV logo in a

Artfully ruched

Marc Jacobs helped get Louis Vuitton's fashion range off to a good start with dresses like this figure-molding, ruched design.

rainbow of colors against a white background. Finally, in 2007, Richard Prince, the US multimedia artist, collaborated with Louis Vuitton and Marc Jacobs, spraying images and texts over the LV monogram. Nor did Jacobs tire of altering the classic logo in other areas, thereby creating a succession of new "It bags." He had it embossed in black leather and silver vinyl, pressed in mohair, woven into denim, painted onto white fur, or sewn onto Capri pants, money pouches, backpacks, and duffel bags, and decorated with tassels, or fur trim. The brilliant creativity of Jacobs and his team is evident in the breathtaking diversity of variations on a simple, familiar old theme. If one considers the wide selection of purses which accompany every fashion collection—and sometimes it even seems as if the fashion collections are just an accompaniment to the handbag collections—the choice is almost dizzying: The range of materials comprises a wide variety of fine leathers, fabrics woven and embroidered by complex techniques, ostrich feathers, and semiprecious gemstones. Then there is his ingenuity with the "hardware"—the handles and straps, the inside of the bag, and the lining, the fabric of which must coordinate exactly with the outside of the purse. Despite the huge turnover in clothes, sunglasses, and jewelry, Marc Jacobs' "target" each season is to win the "purse war." For no matter how much the ready-to-wear collections contribute to Louis Vuitton's international fame, their primary importance is as ammunition for helping to keep the company's core business going. And it is precisely in this area that Jacobs, over the past 12

years, has redefined the term "luxury" thanks to his extravagant creations, his fabrics, and his cleverly conceived designs. It is not without reason that the prototypes shown in the fashion shows are the best-kept treasures of the collection, and are only presented to the press after the show on a separate table under the watchful eyes of numerous bodyguards. "Sometimes I feel like the purse police," groans Marc Jacobs in an interview with *Vogue* magazine, not without a certain impishness. "I personally love making *prêt-à-porter*, but I can also well understand Louis Vuitton from a business point of view." The unfailingly striking originality of LV's purses and its larger bags is such that people are almost ready to snatch them out of the models' hands during a show and it would seem that this pressure, this sort of tension, is not just a burden but also acts as a driving force for Marc Jacobs' creativity.

In 1997, in addition to his coup with Louis Vuitton, the LVMH president, Bernard Arnault, was holding another ace up his sleeve in the form of a designer to boost another old-established fashion house within his luxury conglomerate. This designer's profile was not dissimilar to that of Marc Jacobs: Although not yet associated with any brand names, he already had an established label of his own, despite his relatively young age. His name was Alexander McQueen, and after John Galliano was poached by Dior, he took over as chief designer for Givenchy. However, McQueen, who was branded the "hooligan of British fashion," lacked sensitivity with regard to the predicament and requirements of a

Showstopper
With clients like Madonna and couture dresses in bright red, Givenchy is once again the focus of attention.

A new approach
Givenchy was once a traditional couture house that dressed the nobility. Creative director Ricardo Tisci of Italy completely revitalized it with his passion for leather, lace, fur, drapes, and asymmetrical lines—extremely elegant but with a modern sharpness.

traditional fashion house of such distinguished stature, and which found itself struggling under enormous financial difficulties. Although he remained until March 2001, McQueen himself admitted he was relieved when his contract expired, remarking that it had stifled his creativity.

The search for a suitable successor lasted four years. Eventually, in 2005, Ricardo Tisci was appointed—an Italian with a weakness for "gothic touches" on the one hand, and for space age aesthetics on the other. Not only did Tisci succeed in providing Givenchy with a range that was in tune with the prevailing mood of the times without destroying the brand's identity, but he also attempted to revitalize the faltering haute couture business. "When I started, we only had five clients; we now have 29," remembers Tisci with satisfaction. The most famous of these is Madonna, for whom he created her 2008 "Sticky and Sweet Tour" costumes.

In the fall of 1997, when Alexander McQueen showed his first collection for Givenchy, Paris Fashion Week was in the grip of some dramatic changes—John Galliano presented his first show for Dior, Stella McCartney was showing for Chloé, while Marc Jacobs was presenting for Louis Vuitton, so much so that the debut of a new chief designer almost went unnoticed. The couture house in question—Balenciaga—had become too insignificant to matter, even though it had dictated fashion history during the Fifties and Sixties. Despite efforts by designer Michel Goma toward the end of the Eighties to develop collections that tied in with the brilliant designs of Cristóbal

Like one of his own
Creative genius Balenciaga introduced stand-away collars and short sleeves; his young successor Nicolas Ghesquière gives them a new interpretation.

Balenciaga, while at the same time incorporated contemporary elements, this once great house was slipping into inglorious oblivion. It was sustained mainly by its illustrious name and a fairly successful range of perfumes. In 1995, 24-year-old Nicolas Ghesquière, who had previously worked for Jean Paul Gaultier, was taken on to run Balenciaga's licenses department and put in charge of golf wear, and also window dressings for the Far East market. However, when the acting chief designer Josephus Thimister was fired for having bombarded an audience at a show with a cacophony of ear-splitting music, the gifted Ghesquière was promoted within the house to take his place. The legacy he inherited is not an easy one. Even now, the clothes of Cristóbal Balenciaga remain icons of fashion history: costumes and coats in skinny tunic form, box- or barrel-shaped and designed to flatter and envelop the body instead of mercilessly drawing attention to any weak points, like thick waists, for example. The Spanish genius, Balenciaga, favored deep black, gray, or brown tones, especially for his daywear, while in the evening, he preferred bright colors, such as red, pink, or violet. His color palette, like his design patterns, was often influenced by his homeland, by traditional costumes or paintings by a range of artists from El Greco to Goya.

Right from the start, Ghesquière's collections reflect the influence of this fashion genius. His first shows were dominated by the color black and two famous Balenciaga silhouettes: the cape-style jacket and the loose sack dress. Ghesquière combined these with narrow skirts and trousers. The latter, in particular, especially when worn with a blouson jacket, soon became his personal signature—the influence of the Eighties, that is to say, the period in which he was growing up, is clearly evident in his designs. Ghesquière did not always have access to Balenciaga's extensive archives; it was only after his promotion to chief designer that he could begin examining the collections.

He has so far presented 25 collections and the way these have evolved reflects how he has delved deeper and deeper into the material, taken possession of it, analyzed the component parts and used these as a basis for creating remarkable new designs which still embody the spirit of Balenciaga. Ghesquière initially devoted himself to muted colors and outlines, followed by balloon skirts, cocktail dresses, and then Balenciaga's Air France uniforms of 1968. These he propelled straight into the 21st century by means of a combination of flying jacket, a cummerbund of crocodile leather, high gladiator sandals, and a pleated skirt with a deep, riveted waistband. One of the highpoints in Ghesquière's study of Balenciaga was his 2006 autumn collection: High hats and platform-soled boots make the models look toweringly tall and there was also a speeded-up version of the changes in silhouette which Cristóbal Balenciaga wrought over a period of 30 years—evolving from stiff peplum jackets, to simple tunics and shift dresses, to Jacquard evening gowns with skirts that stood out like three-dimensional bubbles. Many of them were made in the same fabrics that Balenciaga himself used and that were, in some cases, difficult to

A love of geometry
Creative director Ghesquière launches his clients into the 2010 summer season with slits, wrap-arounds, and stripes.

Following in the footsteps of Yves Saint Laurent
Be it a discreetly transparent creation, or an elegant tuxedo, Italian designer Stefano Pilati has proved himself a worthy successor to Saint Laurent, the most brilliant designer of the century.

obtain. This Spanish genius only created haute couture—ready-to-wear clothes made in such high-quality fabric are an absolute rarity. This review of the highpoints of Balenciaga's fashions was inspired by a major retrospective of the work of the great designer, organized the same year by the Musée de la Mode et du Textile—Ghesquière was invited to be co-curator. After this, the influence of Balenciaga's creations was no longer quite so prominent, but was nevertheless still present—for example, in the floral prints of the 2008 spring collection, the Goya-inspired tops of draped velvet and taffeta in the 2009 spring collection, and the artfully pleated wraparound skirts of fall 2009. Occasionally, Ghesquière merges Balenciaga's heritage with his own penchant for techno materials, sometimes in a single design—for example, the sack dress with its inserts of shantung silk and plastic. "My relationship with Cristóbal Balenciaga has nothing to do with building up a legacy," says Ghesquière, "it is a study of his creative work, whereby the priority is to research this work. He observed a fascinating strictness in design, and never compromised. If someone wanted a dress from him, she had to enter his world. I like that." And because projecting forward is just as important and inspirational to Ghesquière as looking backward, his collection for spring 2010 does not contain any references to the past, but is focused on street chic—albeit with impeccable cuts and an air of formal severity.

In November 2012, Ghesquière left the House of Balenciaga which nevertheless continues to adhere to its image of the woman for whom this fashion was designed. Cristóbal Balenciaga himself created haute couture for the prosperous working woman who cannot be too extravagant in her daytime wardrobe. To this day, the "Balenciaga client" is still a professional woman, affluent and aged between 20 and her mid-forties. The fact that such women buy ready-to-wear clothes signals a general move away from custom-made couture to high-quality, expensive alternatives, which can be bought both in the fashion house's flagship stores, as well as in high-end department stores.

For established fashion houses, this means a shift from haute couture to ready-to-wear, not least because of financial considerations. Admittedly, Yves Saint Laurent was still producing haute couture up until 2002, but he had sold his prestigious Yves Saint Laurent Rive Gauche ready-to-wear line to the Gucci group in 1999, where it was managed initially by Tom Ford. Within two years, he had increased turnover by 200 percent, but the blatantly sex-oriented image of his clothes was not really compatible with the sophisticated Saint Laurent house. However, when this great couture house closed its doors in 2002, it was the ready-to-wear collections which saved the world famous label. And after Ford's departure in 2004, Stefano Pilati proved to be a designer whose elegant, French style suited the Yves Saint Laurent image far better than Ford's sex offensive.

Timeless elegance and a dramatic improvement of the ready-to-wear lines were two of the main aspects of Olivier Theyskens' contribution to the Maison Nina Ricci, founded in 1932. Theyskens, a Belgian designer

Severe but naughty
For his summer 2010 collection, Stefano Pilati mixes a richly decorated white blouse with a pair of brief shorts—a contrast Saint Laurent would have liked.

who rocketed to fame overnight at the age of 21 when Madonna wore one of his designs to the 1998 Oscars, had worked for Rochas between 2002 and 2006, developing a line which was somewhere between ready-to-wear and haute couture. This "demi-couture," as it was known, focused on pieces which were too expensive to mass-produce, but did not meet the strict couture rules about hand-stitching and numbers of fittings. Not only was it enthusiastically received by fashionistas, but it was also considered a viable business strategy by many businessmen. Theyskens' acclaimed ready-to-wear collections for Nina Ricci—Victorian-style evening dresses with flounces and high collars, or crumpled, tight-fitting pantsuits—bear comparison with haute couture in terms of their lavish design. Theyskens seemed perfect for the job of chief designer: His sensitivity toward the attitude of women of his time, his graceful silhouettes, and timeless romanticism were completely in tune with Nina Ricci's philosophy and he was duly celebrated by the press. Despite this, however, the Belgian designer left Nina Ricci in spring 2009, apparently as a result of differences with its owners, the Puig Fashion Group. His successor was British designer Peter Copping, who had been in charge of Louis Vuitton's womenswear collection under Marc Jacobs.

Yet another *grande dame* of the Paris fashion world was given a new face in 2006: Lanvin, founded by Jeanne Lanvin in 1909 and therefore one of the oldest fashion houses of the world still in existence. Alber Elbaz was born in Morocco but grew up in Israel and previously worked for Yves Saint Laurent. He was appointed Lanvin's chief designer in 2001, since when he has produced collections characterized by stunning, expressive, feminine elegance. Widely acclaimed by the press, his fans include Nicole Kidman, Chloë Sevigny, and Sofia Coppola. In 2006, he gave the corporate identity of the fashion house a new face, one unmistakably associated with Jeanne Lanvin, since its dominant color is a light, forget-me-not blue, a favorite color of hers after discovering it in a Fra Angelico fresco. And the packaging for the clients' purchases has printed on it the 1907 Paul Iribes illustration of Jeanne Lanvin and her daughter.

The distinctive characteristics which make a label famous are often the best starting point for breathing new life into a company. In the case of Bottega Veneta, a luxury leather goods house founded in 1966, the firm was renowned above all for the high quality of its exclusively Italian-made products; for its ethos of understatement, whereby the firm's logo did not appear on the item, or at least only inside the label; and finally, for a unique leather-weaving technique developed by the company called *intrecciato*. These features made Bottega Veneta's purses and luggage a favorite of the international jet set in the 1970s, but during the 1990s, Bottega Veneta's prestige

Romantic silhouette
Olivier Theyskens' farewell collection for the House of Nina Ricci included a series of elegant designs with wide shoulders and cascading ruches.

dwindled and its popularity dropped far behind brands like Gucci and Prada. Losses were offset by using less expensive materials like nylon—a step which risked compromising an image that had always stood for absolute top quality. Admittedly, the appointment of designers from the British underground scene, such as Giles Deacon, and Katie Grand, did make the company an international name once more, but the excessively visible logos on its products lost the company its last remaining regular clients. In 2001, faced with bankruptcy, the company was taken over by the Gucci group. The appointment of a new chief designer was another brilliant move on the part of Gucci's creative director, Tom Ford. He suggested Tomas Maier, who came from Pforzheim in Germany. He restored the label's original, simple and elegant style, removed the all-too-visible logos and adopted the *intrecciato* weave as a prominent leitmotif which from now on would characterize not only many of the brand's purses, but also other items of the ever-expanding fashion collections—for instance as a decorative element on leather jackets and motorcycle helmets, or as the basis of a design for a Fifties-style dress fabric. His first collection in 2002 consisted exclusively of sports sweaters and jackets. By March 2004, Maier's show in Milan involved 60 models. Each of his fashion shows is now frenetically celebrated and his work is vindicated by the label's commercial success. He has increased turnover several times over and according to a poll commissioned by the New York Luxury Institute, Bottega is regarded as the most prestigious luxury label of

all—even ahead of Armani, Chanel, Hermès, or Gucci.

Christopher Bailey, who was just 30 in 2001, was, like many of his fellow designers, relatively young when he was appointed chief designer of an international label: Burberry. He recognized how important a label's roots were for it to survive as a great couture name, having previously worked at Gucci alongside Tom Ford, designing womenswear collections. His move away from the blatantly sexy image and riotous colors for which he was known to muted trenchcoats and the hallmark Burberry check represented a dramatic change of direction, yet English-born Bailey proved to be the perfect choice for this traditional, 150-year-old London firm. His unique style was perfect for the image he created for Burberry in the 2000s: impeccable tailoring and choice of fabric, yet not too elegant, and with a hint of cool casualness, although without any suggestion of slovenliness. When Bailey joined the firm, Burberry was desperately in need of revitalization: The famous hallmark check, which had been the firm's signature and used to line all its coats since the 1920s, had been adopted by louts as their latest craze. This led to such a spate of cheap copies that the prestigious status of the original was seriously compromised. It was Bailey's task to make "the real thing" a coveted item once more—a task he devoted himself to with enthusiasm: "I sometimes describe Burberry as a diamond that's been trodden into the ground a little and all I had to do was shine it and polish up all those facets." Bailey accomplished this by introducing a

Ideal appointment
Alber Elbaz, Jeanne Lanvin's chief designer, creates a young and very classy mixture which is as popular in faraway Taiwan (below left) as it is in Paris.

Mixed patterns

German-born Tomas Maier is extremely clever at incorporating the typical *intrecciato* weave, Bottega Veneta's signature pattern, in a modern yet discreet way (below). His ambitious designs helped lift this established house out of the doldrums (above).

new line. The word "Prorsum" ("forward") originally featured as part of the symbol of an equestrian knight in armor, the Burberry logo since 1901. One hundred years later, Bailey adopted this logo to launch a successful new line in Milan. He chose "Burberry Prorsum" as the signature for a small, exclusive collection in soft, muted tones, ranging from khaki to smoky blues and grays. The collection also included some flamboyantly extravagant garments, such as handmade jackets made from feathers, silk organza, and fox fur. Even the much abused Burberry check was prominent again, proudly proclaiming its roots, both as a pattern on purses and clutch bags, or—greatly enlarged—on an extra long scarf. Every Prorsum collection since then has created a huge demand, but these show specimens are virtually unobtainable: They are prestige items, coveted by fashionistas and frenzied journalists, and not for copyists, louts, or quiet provincial types.

The Prorsum range with its prestigious reputation has more than served its purpose. The company is raking in money from its classic Burberry London collection, from the Thomas Burberry outdoor sportswear range, from accessories and perfumes, and even children's toys—and how! In the very first quarter of 2008, turnover rose by 26 percent, even though the luxury goods market was in crisis. It is precisely such situations that highlight the difference between ostentatious stylishness and real quality: The latter may be expensive, yet it represents value for money—in the truest sense of the word—in terms of design and workmanship. "In difficult economic times especially," explains Christopher Bailey, "people do not go for mass-produced goods but for things which are worth the investment, because of their individual character." Generally speaking, this is where old-established houses have the advantage, as no one doubts their quality or charisma, provided they are in the hands of a designer who understands not only how to interpret their DNA but also how to revitalize them.

Claudia Teibler

The miracle of London

The way in which Christopher Bailey was able to brush the dust off the Burberry trenchcoat and restore it to popularity was a heartening achievement for the whole fashion industry.

The
BACK TO BASICS
Modernists

The exaggerated glamour and aggressive sex appeal of the 1970s and 80s gave way to a new period of relative calm. In many respects, the years in the run-up to the third millennium were rather like the *fin de siècle* at the end of the 19th century. Many people were unsettled by the sweeping changes, and vacillated between restraint and wild enthusiasm for abstraction. "Cocooning" was the watchword for the new desire to retreat behind one's own front door—after all, you could remain in constant contact with the world via the Internet and cell phone. The flood of information was overwhelming and mostly negative: wars and famines in Africa, futile peace efforts in the Middle East, the flash point of the Balkans, environmental and political scandals all over the world, violence in the cities, genetically modified food... People were expected to know about everything, but soon they simply wanted to switch off, or seek out more emotive, safer fare. The response to declining consumption, record unemployment and the economic crisis was basic denial.

Many people lost their interest in fashion. They saw their wardrobes as already full to overflowing. Bargains were deemed chic, while basics, as American retailers dubbed any failsafe garment, were worn everywhere, as they were practical, subtle, and demure, like the era itself. These basics included blazers with classic tailoring, pantsuits, pencil skirts, and that staple of existentialists in the 1950s, celebrated for its minimalist look: turtleneck sweaters, preferably in black. Basics soon filled the rails in the shops and dominated the runways, where even the simplest pieces had a luxurious touch. Only the best materials were used, the tailoring became ever more sophisticated, and there was an almost fetishistic attention to detail. Designs that looked simple were, in fact, extremely complex and expensive to produce, but wealthy customers allowed themselves a little hidden extravagance. As always, Karl Lagerfeld had a *mot juste* to sum up the situation: "Luxury is when what is invisible is as exquisite as what is visible. The real luxury is in the lining."

People rediscovered "good taste," and while the wealthy rejoiced in it, many others basked in the good conscience that came from opting for a politically correct "eco" look in natural colors, following the "less is more" mantra. Grunge, the "anti-fashion" inspired by American underground bands, who only wore thrift store finds, was briefly a hot trend. A combination of shabby items, like plaid shirts and army boots, and romantic pieces, like flowery

Closed off yet interconnected
This "brave new world" with its technological advances fascinates modernists, who are adept at dressing tastefully yet unobtrusively, and use virtual means to communicate with others all over the world. They feel most at home with like-minded people.

Looking for new heroes

The New York designer Marc Jacobs' artfully disheveled grunge look (opposite page) earned him a role at Louis Vuitton in Paris. Many European women look to Alberta Ferretti, Alessandro Dell'Acqua, and Anna Molinari for an alternative to grunge and minimalism. All three designers focus on feminine clothing made of delicate, transparent materials (above, left to right). Nan Goldin's photorealism, in which she records even her own black eye, had as much of an impact as installations like Christo and Jeanne-Claude's draping of the Berlin Reichstag. The young magician Harry Potter is now a hero for the whole family, having cast a spell over millions of readers.

386

An exotic sylph

Devon Aoki was considered too young (only 13) and too short (only 5 feet 6 inches (1.68 m)) when she was discovered in 1995, yet this American with a Japanese, German, and English background became a supermodel and film star almost overnight.

"Intelligent materials" warm you up when it is cold and cool you down when it is too hot—they open up a **whole new world** *of possibilities for fashion*

dresses and crochet vests, became the uniform of protest against the global crisis. When, in 1993, Marc Jacobs, the "guru of grunge" distressed expensive silk to the point that it looked like flannel, and sent it down the runway on models with dreadlocks, grunge had finally become an upscale look, thus heralding its demise. Marc Jacobs' career, on the other hand, really took off from this point on.

In the mid-Nineties this reserved style, founded on basics, turned into a veritable cult fashion that came to be known as minimalism. Its strict yet sensual aesthetic was achieved with chic, elegant designs in black, and later gray. Other colors and patterns were frowned upon, with the exception of the pure white classic shirt. The Austrian designer Helmut Lang was the most uncompromising and avant-garde of the minimalists. A review in 1997 in *Artform* magazine marveled at his "respect for elegant convention and an incredible nose for the Zeitgeist." Lang really propelled fashion forwards, both with his designs and by experimenting with new materials. His winter 1999 collection, for example, featured pure silver tissue on silk. Although it was the last word in exclusivity, it formed part of a simple design. This was the very essence of luxurious minimalism.

Lang was one of the first designers to use "intelligent" materials that were primarily intended for other purposes. He knew that technological innovations would play as significant a part in the future of fashion as creative processes. In fact, many of these promising new textiles had been developed by the US Ministry of Defense and NASA as protective clothing or armor for extremely specialized high-tech operations. Gore-Tex, Kevlar, and Velcro had originally been invented for the US Space Program, but now they are taken for granted as a component of our everyday wear. These new materials afforded the wearer comfort and freedom; they may be no-iron, microbe-free, breathable, thermal, resistant to UV rays, made of anti-stress fibers, scented, or even moisturizing. Whereas previously several layers of clothing had been necessary to ward off heat and cold, wind and rain, now all of a sudden a single thin layer of "techno" material did the same job, and it was no longer the sole preserve of sports outfitters, but also designers. "The combination of sports clothing and street clothing is a contemporary phenomenon,

borne of necessity. It radiates modernity, cool, and dynamism," said Jil Sander at the end of the Nineties. The German designer's fashions were über hip, and in demand all over the world. Her success essentially paved the way for future German designers. The true heirs to her aesthetic are Strenesse by Gabriele Strehle and Boss Woman.

Expensive, minimalist design became a byword for utter exclusivity. The more pared down the outfit, the better; if there is nothing superfluous, then nothing can go wrong. An aversion to traditional affluence was especially typical of the super-rich. The perfect showcase for the designs was the cult concept store Colette in Paris, where the clothes were not presented all together, but rather separately, as rare pieces. It soon became a Mecca for fashionistas. The Spartan designs were a refuge in a vast, tumultuous world where the array of options was dazzling. Jewelry fell out of fashion, and only the subtlest accessories were permitted. Any self-respecting minimalist would kit out her wardrobe with handbags, sunglasses, and shoes by well-known labels, provided that her wallet could stretch to it. Toward the end of the Nineties attention shifted to deluxe pieces that were brilliantly designed and beautifully made; they did not necessarily have to carry a well-known label. At the same time, a new generation of young designers began to gain recognition. They shunned celebrity status and mistrusted the media. Despite this, or perhaps precisely *because* of it, Martin Margiela became a star, having refined the has-been dirty grunge look so that it now became a kind of intellectual deconstructivism. Margiela categorically refused to give interviews, and the label in his clothes was white, without a name. A 22-year-old Belgian designer Olivier Theyskens, a shooting star on the fashion scene, followed in his compatriot's footsteps, but he could well afford to decline interviews without suffering any ill effects; ever since Madonna had appeared at the Oscars wearing one of his designs, a black satin coatdress, his name had been on the lips of all the fashion insiders. Madonna had done it again! What on earth would fashion have done without her as a driving force in recent decades?

The new ranks of models were pale and delicate. Being super-young and super-skinny was vital to their success. The runways were awash with doll-

388

like young girls and dreamy sylphs no older than 16, embodying the yearning for innocence. Devon Aoki, a very young Eurasian girl with a baby-doll face and a perfect pout, became a top model. Yet hollow-eyed models were also paraded on the runway, hinting at damaged youth; those that did not look sufficiently marred by drugs were made up to look like they were. The photographer Nan Goldin became the chronicler of real "Heroin Chic;" her documentary images were published in glossy magazines, which all of a sudden wanted to show the raw truth. All this sparked protests against the wasted-looking models, the prime example being Kate Moss.

Yet in some places, especially in southern Europe, women were not satisfied with basics and minimalism. With this market in mind, designers re-released a number of pieces that referred back to earlier fashions. There was a Sixties and Seventies revival, with flares and fringing, the Courrèges look, and stylized daisy prints. Jackie Kennedy's sleek shift dress was a big hit once again, and copies of Pucci's psychedelic prints were to be seen everywhere. Individual designers could gain a foothold simply by concentrating on discreet, flattering designs. The Italian designer Alberta Ferretti (b. 1950), who was influenced by the films of Fellini, was a past master at this. She set up her own label at the age of 24 and made her name with her romantic, frothy creations. She has not put a foot wrong with her line, Philosophy by Alberta Ferretti, and continues to be successful into the 21st century.

The northern Italian designer Anna Molinari (b. 1949) also had a hit with her feminine pieces, including delicate chiffon dresses and fine knitwear, presented under the Blumarine label, based in Milan, since 1981.

"Every woman should be an object of desire," says the Italian designer Alessandro Dell'Acqua (b. 1962). His voluptuous, sexy designs certainly fit the bill, but they manage to make the wearer look elegant at the same time. His legion of fans has been steadily growing since his first womenswear collection was shown in 1996.

Yet despite the great commercial success of these three Italians, the real attention went to designers who were increasingly crossing the boundaries between fashion and art. After his label was sold to the Prada group and he retired from fashion design in spring 2005, Helmut Lang took a break, only to return in 2008 with his first big exhibition as an artist, held in Hanover, Germany. On the 20th anniversary of the launch of Martin Margiela's label, the Antwerp Fashion Museum held an exhibition in honor of the Belgian's "surrealist tradition," as the director Chris Dercon called it. Many people mistakenly saw the designs by the Cyprus-born Hussein Chalayan as so unwearable that they would be better as museum pieces. In years to come fashion may well start to look like Chalayan's "monuments," as he calls his clothes, including the dress embedded with 15,000 LEDs which he showed in his Airborne collection in 2007. Perhaps *haute technologie* is the fashion of the future?

Artists like Christo and Jeanne-Claude may also have influenced fashion and allowed it to restore its sense of mystery. They were the talk of Berlin for two whole weeks when they swathed the Reichstag in fabric in June 1995. If only the poetic sense of lightness that they evoked could have lasted forever. Instead, it was as fleeting as the rise in the stock market at the beginning of the 21st century. The economy of many of the 15 EU member states picked up after the introduction of the single currency, the euro. With more than 370 million people, this is the largest economic region in the world. The German share index, the DAX, reached its peak in March 2000, but the hope of imminent riches faded fast.

Yet there were also grounds for hope. A new hero had appeared on the scene, who, much to the delight of teachers, succeeded in tempting children to leave the television, computer games, and cartoons, and concentrate instead on reading. He was none other than that famous wizard-in-training, Harry Potter.

THE MASTER OF DESIGN:
Martin Margiela

b. 04.09.1957

Martin Margiela knows better than anyone that a blank canvas makes the ideal background for any kind of work. He distances himself from any analysis of his designs and is fundamentally opposed to philosophizing about fashion. But there are others who are more than willing to do it for him. Why does he have no logo, not even a signature on his labels? Why does he refuse to appear in person, pose for photographs, or be interviewed? Is it contrariness or coquetry?

Margiela set up his company in 1988, at a time when brand mania was at its greatest pitch, and when many designers were prancing around like princes, embracing everything that screamed glamour. He called his label "Maison Margiela," and shunned the kind of personality cult that was *de rigueur* at the time. When answering questions—something he would only do by fax—he refused to use the word "I": He would always say "we," meaning Maison Margiela and all its employees. They all wore anonymous white lab coats, as was the custom in the couture studios of yesteryear. For Margiela, everything revolved around his work—creating fashion.

Many people saw this as a clever marketing ploy. Indeed, Margiela, born in the Belgian town of Limbourg to a family of wigmakers and perfumers, was the first designer to really intrigue others with his secretiveness. He is often erroneously cited as one of the Antwerp Six along with Ann Demeulemeester and Dries van Noten, but he had actually graduated from the Antwerp Royal Academy a year earlier and was already working as an assistant at Jean Paul Gaultier in Paris by the time that his six compatriots made a name for themselves in London. Unlike most designers, Margiela did not choose prestigious premises in the Rue de Faubourg Saint-Honoré as his head-quarters, but rather a former railroad workshop in the northern suburbs of Paris. This was all the more apt given his approach to design; he would break fashion down to its basic components, as if he were carrying out repairs, and put them back together in a completely different way. For his first collection he put the stitching on the outside of the garments. Shoulders were rough and unfinished, adorned with only a "cigarette" of rolled material. Margiela believed that the wearer should "interact" with the design, so the final shape was determined by the body of the wearer. The end result was the complete opposite of the wide-shouldered power suits of the 1980s. Margiela created long apron-like skirts made out of outsize suit trousers or men's jeans, picked apart at the seams and reconstructed as skirts. These shapes were to be a constant feature of his next ten collections; unlike other designers, he sets great store by continuity.

Good workmanship was always vital to Margiela. Old items of clothing, materials and accessories were taken apart and reworked to create surprising new pieces. In 1991 he brought out

---

The great enigma

"Ah! Lucky 'tis that not a soul doth know. That Rumpelstiltskin is my name, Ho! Ho!"—this might well be Martin Margiela's favorite rhyme. He has always refused to have his photograph taken, and he likes to style his models to the point where they are unrecognizable.

Exhilarating and menacing
This jacket made out of recycled white sneakers has a lighthearted feel to it and is a good example of Margiela's belief in sustainability. He also recycles old gloves and pants in a similar way. At the other end of the spectrum, this cloak, made of severe woolen nooses and a black hood that masks the face, which was part of his Winter 2009 collection, looks threatening enough to be the ideal garb for an executioner.

Seduction by a stranger

You always have to look twice at Margiela's designs to
make out what they are, or simply to understand his approach to fashion. Faces hidden behind stocking masks
and hair divert attention away from the clothing, but the
designs themselves are jarring: epaulettes made of wigs
(below), ripped seams (right), a cape made of angel hair,
blouses with built-in hangers, pants that only seem to
have one leg, laces and threads wrapped around everything from boots to leggings, and lustrous jackets with
slashed sleeves (opposite page, from top left). Who would
ever wear such clothes? Amazingly, Margiela's designs
have always made a rapid transition to everyday fashion.

Fashion fit for the museum

The 20th anniversary of Maison Margiela was celebrated with an exhibition held in its honor at the Antwerp Fashion Museum. Visitors could see that even trench coats deviated from the norm in their complexity. There is a long tradition of surrealism in Belgium; Margiela, playing his part, laces women up like packages, unravels clothing, makes boots out of gold foil, and designs circular leather vests.

*Margiela takes the view that **if something is truly good, it will always be good**, and he is always using old things in a new way*

a sweater made of unpicked old army socks, like strips of skin that had been pieced back together with rough stitches. In 1994 he enlarged the kind of dolls' clothing worn by Barbie and Ken to human dimensions, without adjusting the proportions; it would be hard to imagine a less flattering fit. Other ideas, on the other hand, were a marked success. In 1996 he had photographs of heavy winter coats printed on feather-light summer fabrics like transparent artificial silk, a roguish trick that provoked winks and nudges while at the same time feeling exquisite on the skin.

One season Margiela showed no new designs at all, but simply all his favorite pieces from past collections dyed gray. He was proving that something that is really good will always be good. In October 1998 he sent life-size puppets down the runway wearing sweaters, their empty sleeves dangling limply, and dresses with plastic jackets clearly ironed onto them. All the designs could be folded as flat as shopping bags. They were presented by men in white lab coats, who carried them out on clothes hangers or the puppets. What was Margiela trying to say? Perhaps he wanted to demonstrate that we should not throw everything away; even plastic bags can be put to further use.

Margiela's fashion provides food for thought, at least where other designers are concerned. He is often seen as a "designer's designer." Not only do they imitate him—the visible stitching and uneven seams have long been adopted as a standard technique—but they also discuss the meaning and intention of his work endlessly. His style is most often described as deconstructivism, although he dislikes this term. His principal aim is to reveal something that is normally hidden in fashion: the way an item of clothing is constructed. The resulting designs have included blazers made of toile—the material used to make samples—tacked together with rough stitches and presented as a finished piece, and a woman's jacket designed by turning the back of a man's jacket round to the front.

This emphasis on technical prowess also led to the venerable French house of Hermès appointing him as their head designer in 1998. In 2003 he handed over this position to Jean Paul Gaultier, with whom he had started his career in Paris.

The label of "conceptual art" does not really fit with Margiela either, as it implies that his designs are purely fantastical creations, without being wearable. He has, in fact, taken part in countless exhibitions, beginning with the Art and Fashion Fair in Florence in 1996. Only a year later he was given a solo show in Rotterdam, where he showed designs covered with a lurid mold; Margiela had cultivated the bacteria himself. One exhibition followed another, including Radical Fashion at London's Victoria and Albert Museum. The 20-year anniversary of his label was the occasion of a big retrospective at the Antwerp Museum of Fashion, which transferred to the Munich Kunsthalle in 2009 at about the same time as Margiela's first Munich store opened. This is supervised by Renzo Russo, the owner of the jeans company Diesel, which took a majority share in Maison Margiela in 2002. Rumour has it that Martin Margiela left Maison Margiela at the latest in 2010. Perhaps the elusive designer simply made himself superfluous—an ability that is practically an art form in its own right.

Against disposable society

Margiela strongly believes that everything around us can be of use, and that we should not differentiate between "good" and "bad" materials—as proven by his body blouse, which is made of plastic shopping bags.

THE PURIST:
Jil Sander

b. 11.27.1943

Even as a shy child, Heidemarie Jiline Sander set great store by order and beauty. She really cared about the appearance of the bread she ate. If it was not cut into equal pieces and nicely served and arranged, she would refuse her meal; her eye was hungrier than her stomach. What's more, her will was just as strong as her way of seeing things, so she started trying to make her aesthetic vision a reality from an early age.

She grew up in postwar Germany, with all the hardships of that period. Then came the economic miracle, which brought a lot of kitsch with it; taste and a sense of refinement had to be developed from scratch. Jil Sander was miles ahead of most others in this respect, as she was never seduced by frippery. She studied textile design at the engineering college in Krefeld and later went to Los Angeles as an exchange student. She returned to Hamburg in 1965 and worked as a fashion editor at *Constanze*, a women's magazine, and later *Petra*. It soon became clear to her that she had to be the one pulling the strings if she was to be satisfied with the end results. She had received a fee from the chemicals company Hoechst for producing a trend collection for the new synthetic fiber Trevira, and she now invested this into her own debut collection, which consisted of 150 simple jackets, skirts, and pants.

She chose to set up her own boutique—the only way she could ensure that her designs were presented and sold to her exacting standards. Sander rented a former lamp shop in Hamburg-Pöseldorf, a Hamburg suburb, and painted it snow white on the inside and a deep black on the outside. She christened it with her own name, which she had changed to Jil Sander, "as Heidi sounds too cute and too German." Her debut collection sold out within a week, and she began to import French designer fashions from Chloé, Sonia Rykiel, and Thierry Mugler. This was as novel for Germany as her whole boutique. Up until then, people had only bought stiff, bourgeois designs off the peg in sterile stores. It was 1968, the year of the student riots; Sander was 25 and stirring up her own revolution. Her aim was to change Germany's whole fashion landscape.

She was a great success. The black store soon became a Mecca for "women with class," as Sander called them. She deplored decorated "dolls" and jewelry-bespangled "madames." Her aim was instead to dress self-confident women with the finest materials and the kind of precision tailoring previously seen only in menswear. At first she concentrated on making pantsuits which liberated women from worrying about what to wear. Endless deliberation, faux pas, and rumpled clothes were a thing of the past; in these suits women were taken seriously and treated with respect. This was also partly down to the designs, which did not allow them to slouch; the suits were so

---

The fragrance for women
To Americans, Jil Sander looked the quintessential blue-eyed, blonde-haired German woman. She was in Los Angeles in 1992 to present her perfume, called "Pure for Women"—a clean-smelling scent in a simple bottle, for women, by a woman.

Fast track to success

1968, the year of the student riots, was also the year that Jil Sander founded her own company. She single-handedly painted the outside of her boutique black, schlepped around mannequins for the store windows, worked in the office, and designed clothing for professional women (opposite page). In later years she was never seen in a skirt, but her collections featured ever more dresses, in a comfortable shirt style, in flowing silk, or often with a high neck, ideal for business meetings. Sanders' pants outfits never looked masculine; the material was too fine and slinky (above, on the model Helena Christensen). The trench coat modeled by Claudia Schiffer was also a hit with its silky material and its classy pale hue. This kind of look was designed for successful women—women like Jil Sander herself, who bought a magnificent villa near Alster in Hamburg.

Flying high
The greater Jil Sander's success, the bolder she became. In the late 1980s she surprised the fashion world by presenting the widest skirts since the 50s, made of crushed pleats. Here the design is modeled by Tatjana Patitz, and photographed by Nick Knight.

The *"Queen of Less"* never skimped on the discreet luxury afforded by the very best materials

narrow that the sleeves were only just roomy enough not to become shapeless, while the smart white blouses had just the right amount of stretch to make the wearer feel comfortable while sitting perfectly upright.

Yet this was not enough for a lot of people. Jil Sander's debut collection in 1977 in Paris was a flop. She only dared to do another fashion show 11 years later, in Milan. It was a resounding success. Fashion had outgrown the heavy designs of the Seventies and the frivolities of the Eighties, with their sequins and puffball skirts. Jil Sander really came into her own in the Nineties. Her return to Paris with her own flagship store on the Avenue Montaigne, symbolically taking over the former headquarters of Vionnet, was a triumph. When she declared at its opening in 1993 that, "a dress is perfect when there remains nothing more to remove from it," her statement was no longer misunderstood as a creed of frugality and dreariness. The assembled fashionistas, including Marella Agnelli, Marie-Hélène de Rothschild, Jeanne Moreau, Fanny Ardant, and Isabella Adjani, knew that the minimalism championed by the "Queen of Less" was the height of luxury. Cashmere and wool were always double-faced and sometimes mixed together so that the material would not look too costly, or it was treated so that it looked like common felt, when in fact it was feather-light and as soft as down.

But Jil Sander wanted more, saying that it bothered her that she was only ever praised for the "quality" of her clothes. She had long given up the cold and uncompromising silhouette of her early years in favor of a complex palette. Her collections became softer, more artistic, and full of emotion. She experimented boldly with little drapes, soft lines, variety, and playfulness. More and more dresses appeared. In the mid-1990s the woman who had worn a dress for the very last time on her 30th birthday designed a whole array of delicate gowns with pleats, slits, and trains, ethereal in their incredible simplicity. She did "not want Jil Sander to feel so deadly serious."

This meant that she always had a difficult task in front of her. Her creed was that "ethics and aesthetics cannot be separated." She refined and pared down every trend until it no longer looked "trendy," as she was all too aware that "true simplicity is difficult to achieve; it has to look effortless."

While most designers were cashing in with second or third lines and innumerable licenses, Jil Sander remained incorruptible and stood staunchly by her concept: "We are not going to trumpet our name everywhere."

Only in 2009 did she launch a low-priced collection for the Japanese fashion chain Uniqlo. In the intervening years she went through a very difficult time. In 1999 she sold 75 percent of her common shares in Jil Sander AG to the Italian Prada group. A year later she fell out with the head of Prada, Patrizio Bertelli, and left the company. She returned as a designer in May 2003, only to throw in the towel again in November 2004. To the surprise of the fashion world, five years later, working for the Japanese fashion chain Uniqlo, she tried her hand—successfully—at designing modestly priced fashion for the masses. February 2012 saw her spectacular return to the firm she had established 44 years earlier and which had meanwhile been sold by Prada to a Japanese textile concern. Eventually, in fall 2013, Jil Sander decided to withdraw from her company for personal reasons.

A new chapter
When her collaboration with Prada broke down in spite of successful collections (see photos above), Jil Sander took a break. She returned in 2009 with the +J collection for the Japanese fashion chain Uniqlo (below right with company president Tadashi Yanali).

A MAN OF HIS TIME:
Helmut Lang

b. 03.10.1956

From the very beginning Helmut Lang wanted to be an artist, "but I had too much respect for artists." Today his experiences have taught him that "everything is equally difficult"—as he said at his first solo exhibition as an artist, in 2008 at the Kestner Gesellschaft in Hanover. Prior to that, he had had a meteoric, 20-year-long career as a fashion designer. This exhibition marked Lang's coming full circle as someone who had set out to understand the world and himself.

He grew up in a remote high mountain valley in Styria, the green heart of Austria. After his parents separated, this son of a Viennese truck driver went to live with his maternal grandparents, who had immigrated to Austria from Slovenia. His father's parents came from Poland and Czechoslovakia. Had he lived in Vienna, this might have been a run-of-the-mill Eastern European mixture, but in the countryside he was an outsider, a role that was to stick with him all his life. He was a good pupil, and his teachers made sure that he got into business college, from which he graduated in 1976. After an extremely frugal and strict childhood, Lang simply wanted to let off steam. He dabbled with writing and painting while working as a waiter in a trendy bar. He noticed that his clothes were not really upscale enough for his surroundings, so he designed a couple of pieces for himself. He had his first T-shirt made by a company which mass-produced clothing—either he did not know any better, or he may have deliberately opted for a mass-produced look. His friends noticed his new clothes and soon started asking him to make things for them. As time went on, he began to get commissions from society ladies.

He knew that he would have to rise above this playful amateurism at some point, if only because his bills were mounting up. Although self-taught, he resolved to become a professional designer, and made the bold move to Paris in 1986. His very first show there was a remarkable success, and Lang soon became "one to watch" for fashion journalists in the know. After only a couple of collections he made it to number two on the list of the most influential designers, quite an achievement in the boom years of the 1980s. "Back then fashion was showbiz," he later said of this time. "There was no longer any difference between fashion, parody, and costume making." Setting himself apart from this approach, Lang reminded those who came to see his shows that clothing should be something that people can wear. The more designers in Paris and Milan were hyped and awarded prizes, and the crazier the runway extravaganzas, the more simple Lang's designs became, and the more austere his shows. This simplicity caused astonishment. How could he wring so much style from such simple designs? It all looked so pure and so new.

A reluctant star
The newcomer Helmut Lang makes a shy appearance at his show in Paris in 1997; here the model Marie-Sophie Wilson playfully encourages him to take a bow. Yet he was soon to become the darling of the press, lauded as the crown prince of the avant-garde.

Discreet modern charm

Helmut Lang had men and women walk down the runway together, both dressed in beautifully finished, understated evening wear. Often it is hard to tell what material is being used (below right). Naomi Campbell looks uncharacteristically demure in the perfect coat (left).

From restraint to perfection

Few designers have championed pared-down fashion quite like Helmut Lang, who knows exactly what is important: skillful tailoring, the finest materials…˙ and true friendship. His designs are always worn on the runway by the same models, including Cordula Reyer (right).

Glamour for modern times

Collections are no good without some kind of showmanship, and Helmut Lang knows how to create the right effect. The sandals (top) feature luxuriant ponytails; this tank dress has green and pink underskirts; and the cotton undershirt (opposite) has risqué peepholes.

Lang was not interested in *being a rebel*, but he has brought long-lasting changes to fashion

Lang's designs were uncompromisingly modern and yet utterly timeless. Classic garments like the waiter's white shirt were thoroughly updated with beautiful materials and a narrower fit. The waiter's long apron evolved into daring dresses which gaped where the aprons did. His repertoire also featured a radically pared down version of the dirndl bodice. By looking back at the past, he managed to see the way forward. Lang was the first to make dresses out of latex. Paper and polyester were readily deployed, and he was particularly keen on using "intelligent" textiles that responded to temperature, even though they showed all too clearly where the warmest parts of the body were.

Lang's designs demonstrated a new kind of honesty; instead of bombarding the individual with fashion diktats, they blended into the background, enhancing the wearer's personality. His flattering designs could be integrated into anyone's wardrobe, as they looked different on each person who wore them. He based his suit designs on wide-shouldered versions, making them wearable for men and women. Unlike other designers, he presented his menswear and womenswear collections together, so it was especially important that the slim fit would look sexy on both. Fashionistas and artists soon became avid followers of Lang, and he came to be one of the most copied designers of the 1990s.

With a brilliant sense of timing, in 1998 he decided that the future of fashion lay in New York. His arrival there was met with so much hype that he canceled his show at the very last moment, provocatively presenting his new collection on the Internet instead. A few months later he broke another tradition of the fashion world. New York fashion week had always come after Milan, London, and Paris, but Lang felt that this was too late for it to make a real mark on the new season, so he announced that instead of November, his collection would be shown in September, along with a live Internet broadcast. This caused a major upset, especially when two of the biggest US designers, Calvin Klein and Donna Karan, decided to follow suit.

Lang was not interested in acting the rebel; he simply followed his own instinct stubbornly and unwaveringly, and was invariably right. He felt at home in America from the very beginning. He and his customers had been raised on the trusted American basics, including parkas, jeans, and T-shirts, and cargo pants with multiple pockets. In New York he made a luxury collection out of his own basic elements—everything that he loved, but in the very best quality. It featured fur jackets in the style of parkas, jeans made of ivory-colored moleskin, ripped cashmere, and the good old camelhair coat in a sleek new shape. He even revamped the satin cocktail dress of the 1950s, giving it a long train that could be carried over the arm. Elegant dresses were paired with downy stoles that were tacked to the shoulders to look like wings. The press were effusive in their praise: "Helmut Lang is already in the 21st century."

Despite his resounding success, Lang was not quite satisfied. In 1999 he sold 51 percent of his company to the Prada group. In 2004 he signed over the rest of his shares, and in spring 2005 he broke away completely from his label, Helmut Lang. Prada sold the label to the Japanese conglomerate Fast Retailing in 2006.

As ever, Lang took a little time to work out what his next step should be. In 2008 he made his debut as an artist with an exhibition of sculptures and installations in Hanover. He was simply returning to his first love, art.

Think pink in the evening
At Helmut Lang, a pink sash is enough to take an outfit from day to evening. The color of the pants and the soft material of the layered T-shirt go one step further, and the cool attitude of supermodel Kate Moss only adds to the look.

THE PHILOSOPHER:

Hussein Chalayan

b. 03.14.1970

The runway was set up to look like a living room, with a suite of chairs and a round coffee table. Then came the models. They pulled off the chair covers and transformed them into dresses by pulling them on. At the very end, the model Natalia stood in the middle of the low table, slowly pulled it upwards, secured it at her waist and walked off wearing it as a wooden hooped skirt. Appropriately enough, the exhibition was called "After Words"; the spectators were certainly speechless by the end, hanging around in a daze.

Was this fashion?

Hussein Chalayan has never asked this question of himself; fashion does not interest him. He simply says that he makes clothes, along with art, performance, and film—often simultaneously. His autumn/winter 2000/2001 collection was based on the theme of flight and exile, asking, "what do people take with them, and what do they leave behind?" Chalayan himself comes from a half-Turkish, half-Cypriot family which had to leave the capital, Nicosia, when it was split into two parts. He was 12 years old when he came to London and became a British citizen. This experience means that he knows how it feels to have no particular place where he belongs, and a sense of uprooted wandering is the hallmark of his collections. Many of his projects question everything that is normally taken for granted. When, for instance, he covers only the face of the model with a Muslim veil, leaving the rest of her body naked, onlookers feel the greatest pity for the girl's "dehumanization," rather than her nudity. "The veil," says Chalayan, "gives every women who wears it an aura of death."

His great passion is the human body. This led him to study design at university, rather than architecture. He wants to create a space around the body, an environment that could protect it no matter where the person went. For bad weather he designed a cocoon with a hood that would automatically cover the head and switch on a light if it became dark.

At the age of only 23, he proved that clothes could be more than just fashion with his graduate collection at the prestigious Central Saint Martins College, London in 1993. Entitled "Buried," for this collection he buried the clothes in his garden for three weeks to see what changes the silk dresses riddled with metal shavings would undergo in such an unsuitable environment. They managed to survive the process in an immaculate condition, and the London designer store Browns purchased the whole collection. This honor had previously been conferred only on John Galliano, exactly 10 years earlier.

Mystical aura
Hussein Chalayan often evokes memories of his childhood on the divided island of Cyprus in his designs and in installations. A young olive tree and a statue with an enveloping cloak are enough to transport him back there.

The future vs. the past
A dress that appears to be made of soap bubbles and a skirt that rises and falls of its own accord—this is how Chalayan sees the fashion of the future. He finds women who are denied their faces by the traditional Islamic veil more disturbing than nudity.

On the point of fleeing
Hussein Chalayan's experience of emigration inspired this installation in 2000; it turned out also to be a show for his collection.
At the end, the models put on the chair covers—ultimately people can only take away what they can carry.

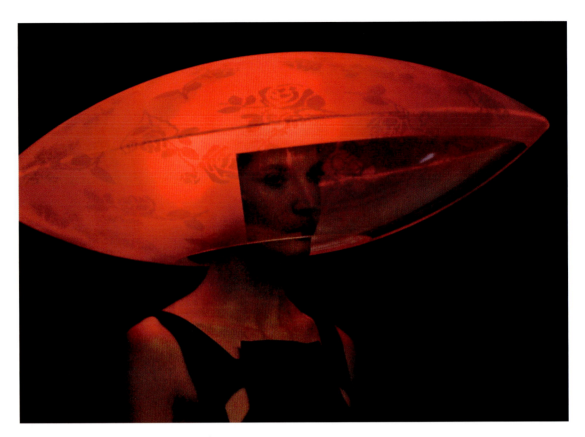

All lit up

Hussein Chalayan works with all kinds of technological innovations in order to challenge age-old
preconceptions. To help us see and be seen better,
he lights up helmet-style hats from the inside and
embellishes dresses with radiant Swarovski crystals (opposite page). In his world, flat coffee tables
become skirts as women get ready to leave—as his
family did when they emigrated to London. Laser-
shredded nylon tulle can look remarkably like mink,
while hard rubber inserts might be bulletproof vests.
Protective clothing is hip, hats become helmets, and
leggings are made of thick latex. And when summer
comes around, everyone can waft around in sleeve-
less, fluttering dresses, which lift up all of their own
accord, as though blown by the wind.

*Chalayan is convinced that "the **only real innovations** in fashion come from technology"*

Hussein Chalayan founded his own fashion house in 1994, and presented his first show a year later. This bore as little similarity to the other fashion shows of his time as all his subsequent ones did. Chalayan's presentations are highly complex, staged art events with elements of performance, installation, and technical marvels. There are dresses that appear to glow with pulsating light-emitting diodes or fire laser beams from shining crystals, while others are transformed as though by a magic trick. A typically Victorian dress appears with a high neck and floor-length skirt. All of a sudden, the corsage opens and disappears, along with the skirts; the hem lifts, and the model is standing in a short, 1920s-style flapper dress, without having stirred a finger; the dress moves all by itself. The Airplane collection in 2000 used a similar technique. Where Marilyn Monroe had to stand over an air vent, Chalayan achieved the same effect by using remote-controlled airplane parts on his dresses. The skirt widened and blew upward, thereby exposing as much of the legs as desired.

"The only real innovation in fashion comes from technology," says Chalayan. He has proved this with dresses that can be folded to the dimensions of an aerogram (1999), nylon tulle designs that have been shredded by lasers (2000), hard rubber dresses that can be fitted over the body like sculptures (2003), and inflatable collars that protect or support the neck (2006).

Unwearable? On the contrary, many of Chalayan's clothes *can* be worn. He is always experimenting, in the hope of coming up with possible ideas for the future. When he had to undergo a DNA test, it gave him the idea of investigating the identity of others. For his spring/summer 2003 collection he delved into the culture of the Vikings, Byzantines, Georgians, and Armenians, looking for their quintessential style. His approach to fashion, which is rather like that of a conceptual artist who always goes about a project with a particular idea in mind, Chalayan has been featured in more exhibitions that any other living designer. His work was shown as part of the Radical Fashion exhibition at the Victoria and Albert Museum in London, and in the big Fashion exhibition in Kyoto. He showed his Airmail Clothing in Paris, and also participated in the Istanbul Biennial in 2001 and the Venice Biennale in 2005. The London Museum of Design devoted an exuberant retrospective to the 39-year-old in 2009, with girls watering olive trees or making Turkish coffee and reading their future in the grounds.

All of this brought Chalayan a lot of fame, but little money. In 2002 he and his studio went bust. Undeterred, he continued to make video installations and films. Of course, he also persisted with clothing, launching a menswear collection and opening his first flagship store in Tokyo.

He sees himself as an artist as much as a designer, but first and foremost as a man of ideas. Yet he lacked the financial means to make these ideas a reality. In 2008 Chalayan sold the majority of his label to the sports company Puma, who also hired him as a creative director. At Puma he hopes to design products "which please people and offer them real added value, instead of being things they can only marvel at on the catwalks." It seems that, in future, genuine Chalayan designs will be more likely found in museums.

Forward march!
Hussein Chalayan presents three identical models as though they were being prepared for an operation, with turbaned hair and loose tunics. They formed part of this 2009 exhibition at the Museum of Design in London, the city which has become his beloved adoptive home.

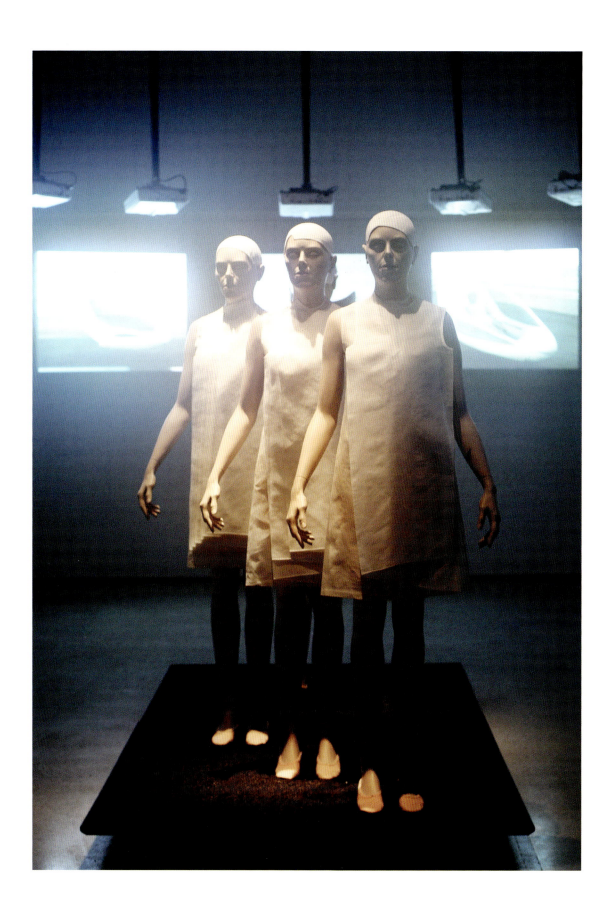

Calvin Klein

The linchpin of Calvin Klein's whole aesthetic is sexuality. Advertising for his underwear, jeans, and perfumes requisitioned gay culture's obsession with bodily perfection and stamped it on the heterosexual consciousness. This was instrumental in softening the deep-seated Puritanism of American society at the end of the 20th century. Since the mid-Nineties, Klein's collections have resembled Japanese avant-garde styles, tempered by the influence of classic American sportswear. His designs have become markedly sharper, more abstract, and more sophisticated. The Bronx-born Klein (b. 1968) founded his own company after doing a degree in design. Like Ralph Lauren, who also came from the Jewish community in the Bronx, in the 1980s Calvin Klein worked his way to becoming a colossus in the world of lifestyle marketing. His chic pantsuits, T-shirt dresses, and perfectly fitting jeans were the embodiment of the main principle of the American Look—that even the most modest item of clothing can be the height of chic, as the key to chic is not what you wear, but how you wear it. In 2002 Klein sold his brand to the Phillips Van Heusen Corporation for $430 million. Today Calvin Klein is the richest fashion label in the world.

Viktor & Rolf

Like Hussein Chalayan and other modernist designers, Viktor & Rolf work with abstract ideas that could easily belong in conceptual art. Viktor Horsting and Rolf Snoeren, both born in 1969, first met at the Arnhem Fashion Academy in the Netherlands. They shared an interest in experimental fashion, and decided to team up together after graduating in 1992. Only a year later the pair won three prizes at the Hyères Festival in France, although they soon realized that accolades do not necessarily translate into success. At first, buyers and the press did not turn up to their shows, even those as original as their Fashion Dreams in Miniature show. Only in 1998, when they were invited to present a couture collection in Paris and proceeded to astound the audience with their voluminous, extravagant creations, did the industry really sit up and take notice. Viktor & Rolf seized their chance. Since 2000, their *prêt-à-porter* collections have not only been fantastic, awe-inspiring displays of creativity, but they have also been wearable. The sculptural element of their work is still there, but they are increasingly bringing in details like ruffles, ribbons, multiple collars, and oversized sleeves, while their smoking suits, particularly the jackets, have razor-sharp, precision tailoring, and come in striking shades such as light pink. In 2008 Viktor & Rolf sold the majority of their company, which still has its headquarters in Amsterdam, to Renzo Rosso of Diesel Jeans.

Akris

Martine Sitbon

It all began with an apron; the indispensible garment of the working classes was produced in great quantities in the 1920s by Albert Kriemler-Schoch and his wife in the Swiss town of St. Gallen, which is famous for its lace. The designs produced by the company today, overseen by the third generation of the family, brothers Peter and Albert Kriemler, under the name Akris, are as simple as they ever were, and are considered to be among the most refined examples of understated fashion in the world. Albert Kriemler (b. 1960), the creative brains behind the company, has always aimed at quality without compromise. He believes that everything depends on the material; he always has to feel it before commencing on the sketches of designs, and he often has fabrics made exclusively for Akris. This results in perfectly tailored, feather-light pantsuits, blazers and outfits that are worn by the likes of Susan Sarandon, Brooke Shields, ex-US Secretary of State Condoleezza Rice, and Princess Caroline of Monaco. For eveningwear, Albert designs spectacular separates made of chiffon, with velvet or St. Gallen lace inserts. For the Akris spring 2010 collection he designed the ultimate minimalistic evening dress, made of beige silk jersey with a turtleneck and long sleeves—unbeatable for sheer chic. It is no wonder, then, that Akris has risen to become the biggest Swiss fashion label.

Flea markets have always had more of an influence on this Casablanca-born designer than her training at the famous fashion school Studio Berçot in Paris. Her designs are just as unconventional, as they always play with contrasts. She might combine a classic gray dress with a futuristic silver vest or a silky smooth draped number with an oversized military overcoat. Martine Sitbon (b. 1951) is like a sponge soaking up all the fashions of the age, from rock music to literature and painting, and pouring them into her personal collections, which she began in 1985. Her work also references her extensive travels in India, Mexico, Hong Kong, Milan, and New York. Her paradoxical combination of male and female elements and the use of unusual materials are the hallmarks of her eccentric style, based on formality and sensitivity, and it has won her a loyal following. She worked as a designer for Chloé from 1988 to 1992, and later for Byblos. She gradually became fashion's best-kept secret, rumored for the designer's job at Hermès or Jil Sander. Instead, since 2002 Sitbon has chosen to concentrate on her own menswear and womenswear lines, although she has had to rechristen her label "Rue de Mail," as her own name, like that of so many designers, had been sold to a financier.

Fashion
for the
A LAVISH LIFESTYLE FOR ALL
masses

The popping of champagne corks ushered in the new millennium—the mood could not have been better: Share prices were the highest they had ever been, and the positive trend in the job market looked set to continue. However, by autumn 2000 things were already starting to go wrong and the wakeup call came when the stock market bubble burst and share prices fell through the floor.

During the last few weeks of "millennium year," George W. Bush emerged victorious from a controversial election campaign to become the 43rd US president. Just a few months later, on September 11, 2001, Bush faced the biggest test of his career when a terrorist attack destroyed New York's World Trade Center, the symbol of American economic power. The Pentagon in Washington was similarly attacked and a passenger aircraft on a scheduled flight, which had been hijacked for an attack on yet another target, was also brought down. The death toll from these combined terrorist attacks amounted to over 3,000 lives and left the whole of the Western world in a state of shock. Stock markets all over the world took a nose dive and on October 7, 2001, war was declared against Afghanistan, with the aim of rooting out the Islamist terrorist groups behind the September 11 attack. The spiraling violence in the Middle East continued unabated and the peace process, which had begun amid such optimism in 1993, broke down. In 2003, the Allies invaded Iraq and toppled the country's dictator, Saddam Hussein. On the day after Christmas 2004, an undersea earthquake triggered a devastating tsunami in the Indian Ocean which left more than 230,000 people dead, mainly in Indonesia, Sri Lanka, and Thailand, a large number of whom were tourists. This terrible natural disaster and a fear of terrorism after 9/11 left many people feeling vulnerable and overseas travel dropped dramatically.

While the economy and the employment situation in Europe was picking up, in 2008 in the USA the subprime mortgage crisis was gathering speed, a crisis which would lead, the following year, to the biggest financial disaster since the 1929 Depression. The fashion industry reacted to all these events with its usual seismic response—in other words, with erratic and jittery volatility. The new millennium has not produced a new style or a brilliant new couture star, but is dishing up instead a succession of reruns: miniskirts, pop art, patchwork, the lingerie look, leggings, punk, tweed, tartan checks, and even

A woman's paradise
Nothing whets the appetite for shopping more than a pair of new shoes, particularly if they are made by a world-famous designer like Jimmy Choo (black strappy sandals, left), Christian Louboutin (blue peep toe, center), or Manolo Blahnik (gold sandals).

Difficult times for politicians

On September 11, 2001, terrorists destroyed the World Trade Center in New York. Less than four weeks later, George W. Bush, 43rd president of the USA, declared war on Afghanistan. The "axis of evil" included not only the extremist Taliban fighters, but also Iraq, against which war was also declared in 2003. All that remained of Saddam Hussein after his overthrow were smashed pictures of the dictator. The devastating tsunami in Southeast Asia, which killed over 230,000 people the day after Christmas 2004, was not the work of man. In 2005, Angela Merkel took over from Gerhard Schröder as the first female German chancellor.

fur have experienced comebacks. Designers, due to an increasing lack of confidence, are even losing their individual signature. Armani is now making sexy fashions like Versace, Lanvin is showing Pucci prints, while Valentino is resurrecting the kind of Mondrian-inspired dresses once typical of Yves Saint Laurent. And every one of them is producing trench coats in an effort to cash in on Burberry's recent success story. "Not even professional journalists can tell any more who a garment is made by," complains Suzy Menkes, a leading fashion commentator.

Given that situation, who would still want to invest thousands in luxurious designer fashions? If everything looks the same, one may just as well buy the cheaper versions—an alternative which is rapidly becoming fashionable as more and more stars and supermodels pose for fashion chain stores like H&M, Gap, and Mango and also admit to wearing their unsophisticated designs in private. What is more, some of the greatest designers are not averse to producing special collections for the mass market. Leading the way in this respect was Yohji Yamamoto, who in 2003 produced a combination of sport and couture for Adidas. A year later, Karl Lagerfeld, Chanel's couturier, committed what was—in the fashion world's eyes—the unpardonable sin of creating a limited collection in elegant black and white for the Swedish retail store chain H&M, which sold out within a few hours. This was the signal for all reservations to be cast aside and now an increasing number of designers, such as Rei Kawakubo and Jil Sander, are designing clothes for the mass market.

The previously scorned "cheap is cool" chain stores are now enjoying a huge boost in popularity thanks to such designers. The fashionistas of the world suddenly find themselves differentiating between the styles of different lower-priced clothes retailers, in the same way as they used to do with couture houses. Spanish clothing retailers, such as Custo Barcelona, Zara, and Mango—the latter receives advertising and design assistance from the beautiful sisters Monica and Penelope Cruz—are famous for their colorful and sexy clothes. Miss Sixty, an Italian fashion firm, is renowned for tight hipster jeans. Miss Sixty's role model is Diesel, an international empire, which specializes in jeans and which now comprises elite brands such as Martin Margiela. But it was the

Americans, who are world leaders in marketing street fashions and sportswear, who were the first to establish cult labels like Gap and Banana Republic in the mass-produced market. "What's the point of me developing a second line?" Jil Sander once asked. "It would just end up looking like Gap." In 2009, five years after leaving her namesake company, she designed a collection for Uniqlo, a Japanese retail firm, reflecting her individual style.

Yukihiro Katsuta, vice president of Uniqlo, which owns 810 outlets worldwide, explains this international clothing company's success as follows: "Happiness has a different meaning nowadays— education, a nice home, and organic foods. Yet, people still want to look good. They look for good clothes made of top-quality materials but at lower prices."

It is Katsuta's ambition to overtake the market leader, Gap, and creativity is as important to him as quality. Nor does he underestimate the glamour factor of prominent names, otherwise he would not have sought Jil Sander's collaboration, or had designs by Keith Haring and Michel Basquiat and popular Japanese Manga figures printed onto T-shirts, or engaged stars like Chloë Sevigny for advertising purposes.

Topshop, an English retail chain, placed its hopes in supermodel Kate Moss, a major star in the world of advertising and design. This fashion icon with her casual Bohemian chic guaranteed Topshop a healthy turnover. Naturally enough, many more celebrities have jumped on the same bandwagon. Just about every star whose style gets a favorable mention in the gossip press ends up with her own fashion range— including Jennifer Lopez, Milla Jovovich and her friend, Carmen Hawk, Sarah Jessica Parker, the American actress twins, Ashley and Mary Kate Olsen, Victoria Beckham, and Paris Hilton.

No one needs luxury couture houses like Armani, Versace & Co in order to dress to impress any more— they can find that kind of red-carpet glamour at a much more reasonable cost at the nearest branch of H&M or Topshop. It is called democratization and it is the one really new aspect of fashion that distinguishes the start of the third millenium. It is undoubtedly enticing customers away from the famous designers. "Labels are for bores," is the latest saying. But this applies only to clothes collections.

Shoes and purses are what define the wearer's style and appearance. Gold and multicolored confetti platform shoes by Christian Louboutin leave Manolo Blahnik's purple sandals far behind. There is nothing to compete with vintage Chanel in red.

New It bags followed hot on the heels of each other. Fendi's brown model with big wooden beads caused a sensation in 2006, as did Céline's yellow "Blossom" tote bag in 2009. It was the same with shoes: Louboutin's baroque-style pumps were matched by Jimmy Choo's rainbow-colored strappy sandals.

Balenciaga created a stir with a patchwork tote bag made of ostrich and crocodile leather, while Hermès reduced the famous "Birkin" to a little shoulder bag. And Manolo Blahnik? He introduces sneaker-style laces to high-heeled pumps or embroiders them like brocade.

Shoes first: Louboutin creates the pink peep toe for California, while his platform heels are more suited to gray Paris. Chanel's classic 2.55 returns as a white mini version, while Chloé's roomy "Stock" is just what young women are looking for.

Not without my clutch purse! Quenny and Dorothea resolutely hang on to their delicate purses from Chanel's Cruise 2010 collection. Manolo Blahnik displayed these stilt sandals at an exhibition held in 2003 at London's Design Museum.

Fashion has been relegated to the back seat while **the new trend** for It bags and dizzyingly high designer shoes takes over

It is celebrities who determine the latest trend, whether skintight jeans, a sexy top—or an eye-catching purse. An "It" bag will pep up the cheapest outfit. It began with the long, narrow Fendi "baguette" purse, which, named for its resemblance to a French loaf, was soon to be seen tucked under every fashion-conscious arm. After that, things began to happen very fast: Vuitton updated his logo purses with a design by Murakami, a Japanese designer, who created the notorious multicolored monogram on a white background. Dior launched the "Detective" bag, Chloé, the "Paddington," Yves Saint Laurent, the "Muse," and Balenciaga, the "Giant City"—purses were getting bigger and bigger and soon began to look as if they were designed for vagrants to carry all their possessions around in. Slouchy purses made from distressed leather were known as "hobos" and the best of them were designed by Dolce&Gabbana, Céline, and Prada.

The It bag's most important achievement has been to relegate clothes fashions to a secondary role while simultaneously insuring the survival of established designers. Purses must now bring in the revenues that dresses used to earn. In the past, bags lasted forever and were passed down from mother to daughter, like the Hermès Kelly bag or the quilted Chanel 2.55—which, with its long chain, was one of the first shoulder bags. It bags, on the other hand, come and go with the seasons; They are "in" today but hopelessly outdated tomorrow. A constant succession of new styles perpetuate the hype and in 2007, seven billion (!) dollars were spent on purses in the USA alone. The average American woman buys more than four purses a year— the more expensive, the better. The little limited edition crocodile purses, which Chanel produced for a prestigious department store costing 25,000 dollars each, were snapped up in no time. Rare trophies such as this are always considered a bargain, regardless of the price tag, which is why waiting lists for such items bump up their value considerably. Purse fetishists had to wait three years for a 2006 Fendi "Spy" bag while there was only a two-year wait for a Hermès "Birkin," even though it virtually played a starring role in the TV series *Sex and the City*. A pale green alligator version, donated by supermodel Naomi Campbell, fetched over 28,500 dollars (21,000 euros) at an auction in support of

2007

"Safe Motherhood." Not so much compared to the 100,000 dollars plus (74,000 euros) raised by Jane Birkin when she sold her own bag in 2007—although she did, after all, give her name to this roomy bag, which is still considered number one among fashion editors.

The rapid changes of style and the incredibly high price tags on such purses—an It bag can cost anywhere between 1350 dollars (1000 euros) and 7000 dollars (5000 euros)—eventually led to overkill. Towards the end of the "Noughties" (so-called because of the two noughts or zeros in the year) it began to seem ridiculous to be buying trendy clothes from low-cost retail fashion stores while spending many times that amount on "must-have" accessories. "That is so yesterday," remarks Elizabeth Kiester of LeSportsac in New York, which has been producing featherlight and relatively cheap nylon purses and luggage for the past three decades. Black nylon first became a fashion trend thanks to Miuccia Prada, who created a backpack made from it in the 1980s, which every woman in the fashion business, from editor to salesgirl, simply had to have.

Nowadays, Miuccia Prada's reputation is based on far more than just her minimalist nylon creations. She has other things in mind: "I'm mad about pink shoes."

Shoes are "the next big thing"—but then they always have been, especially if they are graced with stiletto heels—thanks to Ferragamo, who invented them. Manolo Blahnik pushed high heels to their limit, both in terms of price and design, and Christian Louboutin partnered them with red soles, which could not fail to attract attention. Jimmy Choo, another top-of-the-range label, deigned to design a collection for H&M—which takes us right back to the mass-produced market, which now has a finger in every pie. The good thing about this is that it reacts just as irrationally as the haute couture scene: Sneakers with wedge heels (Converse) are suddenly all the rage, or moccasin driving shoes (Tod's), or cheap Swatch watches. Yet by tomorrow everything could have changed again and we may find ourselves forking out thousands of dollars for some status-giving accessory, be it a purse, watch, or jewelry.

But no, it will probably be shoes again...

2009

434

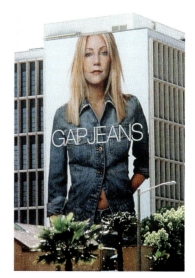

Big names for the mass market

Karl Lagerfeld does not mind touching. In 2004, he created a collection for the H&M chain, which was displayed in the Musée d'Art Moderne in Paris, where model Erin appeared modeling a dinner jacket (above). The use of celebrities to promote their products is now a "must" for all lower-priced labels. The practice was initiated by Gap, which posted a giant-sized image of US TV star Heather Locklear on Sunset Strip. The Spaniards bagged Hollywood star Penelope Cruz (right) as a "testimonial" for Mango, while Uniqlo, the Japanese textile giant, has actress Chiaki Kuriyama (below right) to endorse its products. Miss Sixty (far right) and Zara (below center) have (as yet) abstained from celebrity endorsement, while Topshop engaged Kate Moss not just as a model, but also as a designer (below left).The dividing line between street clothes and designer fashions is becoming increasingly blurred.

THE ART OF THE APRON:
Miuccia Prada

b. 05.10.1949

At first glance, no one would imagine that this woman is Italy's most successful fashion designer. Despite her inconspicuous and relaxed appearance, there is always something that jars slightly, whether it is her long gloves, which reach above the elbow, or a feathery cocktail hat. Usually though it is the unusual shape or color of her shoes. Is this just a housewife who has got it wrong? Her outfit, when all is said and done, is respectable, demure, and covers the knee.

Miuccia Prada's trademark is to add a touch of eccentricity to an otherwise conservative outfit. Even as a young girl, she did not dress like all the others, and certainly did not follow the latest fashion. She found flea market bargains far more exciting, although Miuccia, a daughter of a wealthy family, apparently did wear designer clothes occasionally, particularly those of Yves Saint Laurent. All the more remarkable is the fact that she wore these outfits while distributing pamphlets for the Communist Party, of which she was a member. This was in the 1970s when Miuccia Prada was studying Political Science in her home town of Milan, a subject in which she eventually gained a PhD.

"Fratelli Prada" was founded in 1913 by Miuccia's grandfather Mario and gained a reputation as the most exclusive make of high-quality luggage, some of it fashioned from exotic animal skins, such as walrus. Miuccia, a dutiful daughter, became more and more involved in the family firm, but the thought of becoming a designer never crossed her mind— not even when her design experiments led to unexpected success in the form of a purse, which was young and modern in style yet weighed next to nothing, being made from material normally reserved for packing up the firm's exquisite leather goods. But the real hype began when she produced something as untrendy as a black nylon rucksack, and, in so doing, transformed the traditional House of Prada into the country's hottest label and signaled the beginning of the era of "Pradamania."

In later years, it used to irritate Miuccia that she could not shed the label of techno mini-malism that had clung to her for such a long time, even though the black nylon period only lasted two years. In the years that followed, she unwittingly initiated all kinds of different trends and often appeared to be the lone design force driving Italian fashion forward. Apart from Marni and Dsquared, Milan had not seen any new designers of note emerge in the 20 years since Dolce&Gabbana. All the major innovations had come from Prada.

Miuccia would not have enjoyed such success had it not been for Patrizio Bertelli, whom she met in 1978 and later married. Bertelli owned a leather goods factory in Tuscany and apparently had to talk Miuccia into each new venture. In 1982, they launched their shoe production

---

A nice woman
To look at her, it is hard to imagine that Miuccia Prada, Doctor of Political Science, seen here in 2007 modestly taking her bow after a show, could produce such explosive designs. And yet each of her collections alters the fashion landscape.

Bad taste can be beautiful

In 1996, Miuccia Prada shocked the fashion world with a collection inspired by the dreadful patterns of the vinyl tablecloths of the Fifties and Sixties. The working-class kitchen look becomes an overnight success.

How to cater for all markets

Miuccia Prada's offshoot line, Miu Miu—her nick-name as a child—is targeted at a younger clientele. Shorts outfits with boxer boots for the holidays, belted lambswool jackets and artistic prints—all accessorized with a clutch purse—are typical of this second line (above). What Miuccia Prada began with nylon purses, she continued with leather purses like the 2007 gray Henkel model. Prada is famous for its commitment to art: In 2005, Elmgren & Dragset demonstrate how a Prada boutique can look "in the middle of nowhere" with an installation entitled *Prada Marfa* in Valentine, Texas—a store window, unfortunately closed to would-be shoppers. Miuccia is pushing ahead with her main Prada line: a midriff-revealing shorts-cum-skirt for summer and thigh-high angler boots with knitted shorts worn over a cardigan for winter 2009.

Confusing insights

Prada turns common sights upside down—as shown above in Seoul where a fashion installation inside a rotating transformer adopts all kinds of new forms. Left, Prada's flagship store in Tokyo, enclosed within panels of glass, was designed by Herzog & de Meuron.

What's that perching on my shoe?

With Miuccia Prada it is always worth looking at the shoes since these are her greatest passion. Her Miu Miu line includes a pair of Art Deco-inspired python-skin sandals with a dragonfly perched on the front. In comparison, her patent pumps with the dark red toecap (shown on the right) look positively decorous. Winter is not the best time for shoe fetishists, however, as even Miu Miu recommends thick socks to go with this warm wool coat with its nipped-in waist. Still, the purse is made from gilded leather!

Despite her harmless appearance, Miuccia Prada's work is **deeply subversive**

business, a natural progression for a firm that was already making leather luggage. Somewhat more unusual was the introduction of a ready-to-wear line for women in 1988, but it was with this that Miuccia really hit the bull's eye.

The line she developed, however, was not uniquely Prada. On the contrary, her signature came to be more about turning the clock back with references to the past. It was not uncommon for her designs to look odd at first—inelegant, outdated, or even downright repulsive. One only has to recall her 1996 collection, which was inspired by plastic tablecloths and curtain material typical of the 1950s and 1960s. She herself commented in an interview that "I don't make chic clothes any more—on the contrary, I make ugly clothes from ugly fabrics, bad taste in fact." Was this some kind of crazy housewife trying to turn her apron into a new fashion trend? Well, she succeeded! These "impossible" designs, if nothing else, forced the fashion industry to look to Milan to see what the future had in store.

Miuccia Prada, who resembles an inoffensive teacher, became a radical fashion philosopher. "The bourgeois lady is finished," she announced in 2005, introducing a range of provocatively childlike dresses of hand-painted cotton and papery taffeta with beadwork on rough patches of tulle, looking as if they had been sewn on by children. The same year, she produced an unbelievably extravagant creation in the form of a skirt made entirely from peacock feathers—a piece of decadent luxury.

The 2008 autumn collection symbolizes the bourgeois look taken to its limit: Ruched blouses and simple dresses in black or beige lace fabrics made the models look like matrons. The industry was not altogether impressed: "They look like something your great-grandmother would wear"—but soon young women were seen dressed from head to toe in lace, for Prada also released matching shoes with rigid ruffles and purses printed with lace designs.

For her offshoot line, Miu Miu (her nickname as a child) launched in 1993, Miuccia repeated the theme but in heavy guipure lace, worn over tight bodysuits, or cycling shorts and shirts. Miuccia, a mother of two, is particularly fond of this young line and sees no reason why she should change her style. "I am many different women, depending on the situation and mood. Prada and Miu Miu are the two poles of my universe."

The more affordable Miu Miu line, her menswear line introduced in 1994, and the Prada Sport range launched in 1997 mean that Prada products cover every sector of the market. It is Miuccia's philosophy that "clothes should make sense," as she once remarked. "The best indicator of this is the sales figures." These were boosted even further by a range of cosmetics and by buying into prestigious labels like Jil Sander and Helmut Lang. Prada was all set to become an avant-garde luxury firm and planned to list part of the company on the stock exchange. The terrorist attack of September 11 and the subsequent collapse of the US market put an end to such plans, however. The Sander and Lang labels were sold again, and Prada still has considerable debts. There are rumors that a Qatar investor may come to the rescue of this elite label.

Miuccia's creative energy continues undiminished, however, and, despite the crisis, she is still helping other creative protégés. In 1993, she and her husband set up an art foundation. Fashion was the central theme of the *Prada Marfa* project, an installation in Texas by artists Elmgreen & Dragset, and of the Prada Transformer project with top architect Rem Koolhaas in Seoul. Generally Miuccia is a very discreet patron: "I hate the idea of creating art in order to sell bags."

Subtle progress
Who would realize at first glance that Miuccia Prada was risking a step into unknown territory with this design? What looks like classic couture, is actually modern embroidery: The black silk coat is decorated with individual plastic fringes.

THE MULTITALENTED CHAMELEON:
Karl Lagerfeld

b. 09.10.1938

Karl Lagerfeld often responds to questions with a typical sound bite, such as "You have to already have style in order to buy it," or "Scandals only hurt those who don't have any." His own maxim at any rate is: "One has to constantly reinvent oneself." To do so, one needs neither spare time nor muses, since the "ideas come while you work."

It's easy for a genius like him to talk though, isn't it? Oh well: "Happiness is a question of will!" If you regard all this as something of a psychogram, you are not all that far off the mark. Yet very little is known about this jack-of-all-trades of the fashion industry. Despite the fact that no one talks faster or more volubly than Karl Lagerfeld (and in four languages no less!), he still manages to divulge very little about himself or others. He is the subtlest backbiter in the fashion industry, a world where a sharp tongue and homosexuality seem to be *de rigueur*.

There are no hard facts about his date of birth (was he actually born in 1933?), or about his family (was his mother really an intellectual, and his father a self-made millionaire, who owned Glückskleemilch GmbH, a firm which produced condensed milk?), or his education (did he ever go to fashion college?). Even journalist Paul Sahner was unable to elicit the real facts for his book entitled *Karl*—which is perhaps one of the reasons why it is as entertaining as the man himself.

Let us stick to what we do know: Karl Lagerfeld, at a very early age, demonstrated a considerable talent for drawing and a great interest in clothes. His design sketch for a coat won him first prize in a talent competition organized by the International Wool Secretariat. At the award ceremony, 17-year-old Karl Lagerfeld found himself next to Yves Saint Laurent, two years his senior, who was the winner in the cocktail dress category. These two up-and-coming designers were to have a profound influence on fashion during the second half of the 20th century.

Lagerfeld began an apprenticeship with Pierre Balmain, the master of traditional couture. From 1958 he spent five years at Jean Patou, the oldest fashion house in Paris, where he was bored to death—"only two haute couture collections a year!" In 1963, he set up in business on his own and made sure that henceforth, he no longer had time to be bored. He began designing clothes right, left, and center, even leotards and pantyhose for dancers, not to mention clothing for the Monoprix supermarket chain and for Gadging, a lower-priced brand. When, more recently—in 2004—he worked for H&M, it caused a scandal, yet 40 years earlier, no one had batted an eye: "Being a fashion designer was a miserable profession, badly paid," he recalls. So he bit the bullet and accepted every commission that came his way. Sometimes he has been known to produce 17 different collections a year, no two the same.

Pristine image
Karl Lagerfeld plans his appearance down to the last detail. He needs an image that is easily recognizable and yet represents several different fashion houses at the same time. Dark glasses, white powdered ponytail, and a high stand-up collar are his trademark.

Italian one day, French the next

German-born Karl Lagerfeld can relate to different types of clientele. For Fendi in Milan, for example, he creates clothes for young women; for Chanel, on the other hand, he pushes fashion to its limits, positioning the famous logo on the tiniest piece of fabric.

All kinds of trimmings
Coco Chanel once invented a braided trim for her tweed suits. Karl Lagerfeld's cropped biker jackets have a plain border and are worn with glittering shorts. Alternatively, his designs may feature floral trims, here adorning midriff-revealing white silk satin "torero suits."

Staying in shape
Karl Lagerfeld's dresses for his 2010 summer collection keep their shape even if no one is wearing them: The design on the left has been created like a lavishly embossed outer case, while the tightly belted design on the right is kept in shape by stiff ruches.

"Whatever you want" seems to be the theme that runs through Karl Lagerfeld's many labels

Unlike his highly neurotic rival Yves Saint Laurent, Karl Lagerfeld enjoys creating, and claims he never experiences stress. While Saint Laurent was building up his own fashion house, plagued by much mental anguish, Lagerfeld was using his talents to make other houses great.

The fashion house of Chloé, for example: Here Lagerfeld's designs, inspired by London's street scene, were delicate and poetic, lively and young. They transformed Chloé into the first luxury house to specialize in ready-to-wear fashion. He remained in charge of design there for 20 years and then, after a break of nine years, returned to Chloé for a further period from 1992 to 1997. During the same period, he began to collaborate with the Italian fashion house of Fendi—and still does to this day—designing a range of luxurious, featherlight furs, which could be thrown on as casually as if wearing fur were the most natural thing in the world. He did, of course, design the ultimate It bag, known as the Fendi "Baguette." Not to mention that other fashion icon—the model #101810 camel-hair coat for Max Mara, new versions of which are always appearing. His real achievement, however, is his reincarnation of Coco Chanel: Just like Mademoiselle Coco in her day, he spurns convention and looks for fun and total freedom. He has produced innovative variations on her signature tweed suit with its braid trim, including mini versions, some laden with gold chains or strings of pearls, or even pared down to just a jacket, worn with leggings or jeans. The Chanel logo of two interlocking "Cs" can meanwhile be found on motorcycle jackets, lingerie, bikinis, shoulder bags, moon boots, sneakers, pantyhose, and coat linings. And the traditional Chanel camellia has lost its innocence and become a kind of punk accessory, while today's street girl wears a belt incorporating a holster for the inevitable bottle of water. The classic twin set and "little black dress" have been frequently "reinvented" by Lagerfeld for Chanel's ready-to-wear line and he has been breathing new life into the label since 1983. As far as Chanel haute couture is concerned, meanwhile, he is regarded as the *grand seigneur*, upholding the traditions of this fashion house and catering for the discreet charm of the bourgeoisie, using nothing but the most lavish fabrics and most expensive craftsmanship in the fashion business.

He often seems to have treated his own label, on the other hand, like a poor relation. His collection was once known as "Lagerfeld Gallery," then "Karl Lagerfeld," and since 2012 it has simply been called "Karl." Despite the fact that he is perhaps less motivated by fame and money than his competitors, he has nevertheless long since surpassed them all in every respect. His energy is boundless: His passions include photography, which he took up in 1987, and every year for the past 20 years he has compiled a photography book (published by Steidl). He owns a bookshop, has renovated and redesigned numerous houses and apartments, only to give them up again after completion. Does he have any time at all for a private life?

In 1989, one of Lagerfeld's oldest friends, Jacques de Bascher, died of AIDS. He has always denied that he was also his lover. Instead, he offers another sound bite: "Say goodbye and get over it." Lagerfeld, probably the most high-profile designer in the world, hides behind his high, stand-up collars and dark glasses. He is an observer, not someone who joins in. In a world of drugs and alcohol abuse, he remains sober and disciplined. This is one reason why he is quicker to tap into the spirit of the times than others. He spotted that the focus of the new millennium would be on reduction. In 2000, he lost around 92 pounds (42 kilos), apparently so that he could fit into the ultra-slim suits designed by Hedi Slimane for Dior Homme. In other words, he reinvented himself yet again. It is only the legacy of Mademoiselle Chanel that he will follow faithfully until the end.

Jack-of-all-trades
Karl Lagerfeld has been a spectacular success with Chanel—Mademoiselle Gabrielle could not have done a better job herself (above). At the same time, he is constantly raising the profile of his own collections (below left) and also gaining an international reputation as a photographer (below right).

Isaac Mizrahi

H&M

Very few designers enjoyed such a promising start to their careers as Isaac Mizrahi, born in New York in 1961, who was a hit from the word go. From his very first show in 1987, the press fell in love with this cheeky, witty, and lively graduate of the Parsons School of Design—whether because of his cheerful designs or his entertainer-style qualities. Whatever the reason, he was so well received that the big luxury houses began ordering from him. Despite this, his sales did not live up to expectations, not even when Chanel provided the label with financial assistance. Although Mizrahi was bursting with ideas, he proved unable to develop an instantly recognizable signature line. In 1998, Chanel withdrew its support and Mizrahi was forced to close his fashion house. Four years later, he began designing for Target, a lower-price brand name, tripling its turnover in five years. He was helped in this respect by his numerous film and TV appearances—in the mass market, celebrity status is clearly far more influential than the art of couture. In 2004, Mizrahi began making custom clothes for former clients, who were prepared to spend at least 5000 US dollars on a dress. He once again launched a label of his own. In 2008, the Liz Claiborne retail chain poached him from Target and appointed him creative director, signaling the start of a contest at the lower-priced end of the market as to who could attract the most prominent celebrity designers.

The maxim of fashion retailer Hennes & Mauritz, better known as H&M is "fashion and quality at the best price". Founded in Sweden in 1947, this low-priced fashion chain has developed over the past two decades into the favorite label of all young fashionistas. H&M not only have a reputation for their low prices, but they are also known for getting new trends onto the market more quickly than expensively produced designer fashions. Since 1987, Margareta van den Bosch has dictated the style of the collections—initially as chief designer, then as creative advisor. Her greatest coup was to enlist Karl Lagerfeld as H&M's designer, a development that had all the impact of an earthquake in the fashion world. Since then, no holds are barred: Cheaper brands can afford big names, established designers are becoming involved in the mass-produced market, and lower-priced brands are seeking admission to the higher echelons—in 2007, for example, H&M introduced its COS line (short for Collection of Style), a higher-quality and higher-priced range, which it sells in its own stores. H&M is proud to include some top names among its designers, such as Rei Kawakubo, Madonna, Kylie Minogue, Sonia Rykiel, Jimmy Choo, and Roberto Cavalli (above). Sweden obviously has a gift for offering customers quality at a reasonable cost: IKEA revolutionized the furniture market, ACNE revitalized the jeans scene by introducing red seams.

Gap

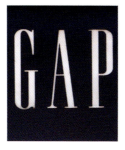

Michael Michalsky

The first mass-market clothes retailer to achieve cult status with fashion fans was Gap. Launched during the 1969 "summer of love" in San Francisco by Doris and Don Fisher, Gap developed into the world's largest retail chain, maintaining its position up until 2009—when it was superseded by Inditex, a Spanish group, which was also responsible for the Zara outlets that were popular in German-speaking countries. The Fishers started out with the aim of closing the gap between clothes that were reasonably priced and clothes that were wearable. In true hippie style, their objective was to produce a pair of well-fitting jeans and once they had created these, they wanted others to reap the benefit. T-shirts could likewise benefit from some improvement, as could sweaters, shirts, and jackets... In no time at all, they had produced a collection of desirable basics, designed to appeal to anyone who wanted quality at a reasonable price. Gap's reputation grew with each of its ambitious publicity campaigns, which, over the course of the years, have starred no less than 308 celebrities, including actors and actresses, athletes and intellectuals, all of whom claimed to wear Gap basics, adapting them to suit their individual styles. The Gap group now comprises the Banana Republic—affordable luxury for a more demanding clientele—and Old Navy—sportswear for families and young people.

At the age of 13, Michael Michalsky, who was born in Göttingen, Germany in 1967, read an article about Karl Lagerfeld which persuaded him to become a designer. After finishing high school, he trained at the London College of Fashion and he began his career as design manager at the Levi's jeans company in Germany. In 1995, he moved to Adidas where he implemented some radical changes. His most brilliant idea was to bring in top designers such as Yohji Yamamoto and Stella McCartney. It was not long before the three white Adidas stripes began appearing not just on sportswear, but on pop stars and rappers, from Madonna to Run DMC and Missy Elliott; music-lover Michalsky also appointed this female rap artist as a designer. When he left 11 years later to launch his solo career, he had transformed Adidas into a luxury lifestyle brand name, much sought after by celebrities and fashionistas. His next job was to revitalize the ailing MCM luggage label and he was responsible for introducing a design and fashion collection by Tchibo, the coffee-roasting company, which has since become Germany's largest textiles company. For his own firm, which has its headquarters in Berlin, he has created the Jeans M67 line, a sportswear collection called Michamic, and also a luxury brand called MICHALSKY. Helped by the good advice of stylist Claudia Englmann (*Vogue*), he aims to compete with the likes of Jil Sander, Hugo Boss, and Prada, thereby covering the entire fashion spectrum.

Fashion for tomorrow

AUTHENTIC, ECCENTRIC, ECOLOGICAL, AND VINTAGE

In November 2008, Barack Obama became the first African American to be elected president of the USA. His campaign slogan "Yes we can" stirred up people's hopes and a belief that this dynamic 47-year-old would indeed be able to bring about the promised "changes" within a short time. But even Obama cannot perform miracles and the financial crisis, which the US property market had been facing for several months, culminated in September in the US investment bank Lehman Brothers filing for bankruptcy, affecting countries all over the world. "Bankster," a contraction of "banker" and "gangster," was coined as the new key word of the year and politicians discovered that no one trusted them any more. Despite Obama's diplomatic talks offensive, there are still no moves toward peace in the Middle East or Afghanistan. Nor is there any improvement in relations with Iran or China. The Copenhagen climate conference in 2009 achieved no real progress—and the decade ended in uncertainty, disappointment, and a deep fear of further terrorist attacks.

Even the fashion industry no longer had any clear guidelines to follow. There has rarely been a decade during which, despite so many different trends, nothing really new has been created—apart from the obvious exception of "techno couture," which automatically adapted to every new demand. It's true that the Berlin Fashion Week is now giving Paris, Milan, London, and New York a run for their money and hoping that it will soon be able to rekindle the reputation it held during the 1920s—but this dream is not likely to become reality. The problem is that clients are increasingly bored: More than 500 collections are produced each season, making the international market less and less transparent. Thus a new phenomenon of polite disinterest has emerged, known as "fashion fatigue."

If you are buying new clothes, you at least want to be able to do so without a guilty conscience. Clothes should not pose a threat to the environment and if luxury is the name of the game, then at least it should be "green luxury" made from natural fibers or recycled material. Ideally, leather and fur should be boycotted altogether. The only designer in the world to stick to strict vegan principles is Stella McCartney: Each of her collections demonstrates that green is anything but bourgeois. Shopping should also be fun, but Europe's leading trendspotter, Li Edelkoort, believes a general weariness began to set in during the early 2000s: "Wherever we go, things just look the same—the same stores, the same products.

Here comes the future

Tavi Gevinson of Illinois started her own fashion blog, "Style Rookie," at the age of eleven. Despite modestly describing herself as a beginner, she soon became a fashion professional. Taken seriously by the fashion world, she was given a front-row seat at all the shows. In 2011, aged 15, she established her own online magazine, "Rookie".

Trying to find something different is like hunting for butterflies."

Yet that is exactly what fashionistas want—to catch the fashion equivalent of a rare peacock butterfly. This is why they are increasingly ignoring the main brands, beginning to avoid such blatant status symbols like It bags and viewing every fresh hype with healthy skepticism. They are moving away from the prestigious main shopping streets and have begun exploring old-fashioned crafts, authentic folklore, extravagant vintage fashions, and new designers. For example, two sisters in Pasadena, Kate and Laura Mulleavy, who were producing extremely individual pieces to a couture standard, have now been "discovered" and have now launched their Rodarte line in New York. Such unique designs are regarded as something special for fashion-conscious women to wear to demonstrate their particular style on special occasions. Jeans and basics are considered perfectly adequate for day-to-day wear—simple well-made chain-store products, without a designer label. But these are ideal for teaming with unusual finds. Turning up dressed like a bird of paradise all the time would be just as boring as wearing nothing but designer outfits—"so yesterday!"

Not even America's new First Lady Michelle Obama submits to being forced into the narrow confines of a specific dress code. Not only does she appear at official events with bare arms—a breach of protocol contemplated by only very few of her predecessors—but she has also hit upon a way of combining elegance and comfort: Michelle Obama simply dons a comfortable cardigan when she is cold or wants to cover her well-toned arms. She seems to have completely rejected the idea of the customary jacket. Nevertheless, she was still able to hold her own next to French president Nicolas Sarkozy's wife Carla Bruni, who, on the face of it, favors the "Jackie O" style of simple shift dresses. The two First Ladies seem to have a shared preference for flats to avoid appearing taller than their husbands.

It is often heard said that fashion should be more geared up to real women. Many mothers and doctors, in particular, feel that skinny models can be potentially dangerous role models for young girls. Starving oneself in order to reach a desired Size 4 dress size can, all too often, lead to anorexia.

Alexandra Shulman, editor-in-chief of the British edition of *Vogue*, was the first to call for a boycott of underweight models. *Brigitte*, a popular German women's magazine, goes one step further: From 2010, it will avoid using professional models and only photograph fashions worn by normal women with normal figures. The successful advertising campaign by Dove, which caused considerable controversy in the media, proves that "real" women can look just as beautiful as models.

The trend away from skeletal models back to women with proper figures has led to a revival of the supermodels. Linda Evangelista, Christy Turlington, Naomi Campbell, Claudia Schiffer and co. are now in their forties with more mature faces—as well as bodies. And yet they still earn huge amounts in advertising and appear perfectly credible as wearers of luxury labels and are certainly more glamorous than the pitifully skinny models.

The realization that allure is not necessarily a question of age is gradually getting through to people. Iris Apfel from New York, who was born in 1921, would not be seen dead in beige or gray, traditionally worn by elderly people. This petite lady insists on wearing strong colors and prints, her trademark oversized, round spectacles, and a good deal of jewelry. "With good-value fashion chain stores like H&M, there is no longer any reason to be badly dressed," she claims. Iris Apfel, interior designer and antiques dealer, has always had a gift for combining old and new, expensive and cheap. In 2006, the Metropolitan Museum of Art in New York staged an exhibition of her fashion style, a look which more and more people are imitating.

Elderly style icons are also a favorite subject of Ari Cohen, a young New York photographer. Since 2006 he has been photographing stylishly dressed "silver agers" on the street and introducing them in his blog, advancedstyle.blogspot.com, to an ever-growing circle of followers. Art Cohen's favorite model was actress and publicity icon Mimi Weddell who died in 2009, but even unknown senior citizens, as long as they are stylishly dressed, are immortalized through Cohen's camera. Nowadays, Internet blogs seem to wield more influence on fashion than traditional media. Designers like Marc Jacobs and Dolce&Gabbana have realized this and welcome

All geared up for change

Trendspotter Li Edelkoort (above left) has identified two
distinct directions in fashion: on the one hand, a desire for
well-made basics and on the other, a hankering for individual
designs. Fashion blog pioneer Diane Pernet offers "A shaded
view on fashion," as her blog is called. The election of US
President Barack Obama raised hopes for "change." His wife
Michelle and Carla Bruni-Sarkozy have already instigated
some welcome changes: First Ladies are now showing off their
figures. "The German Fräuleins," Angelika Kammann and
Alexa Meyer, have received enthusiastic acclaim in New York,
translating their German ethos into flattering cuts for women.

In the city or deep in the provinces, bloggers are everywhere

Anyone can become a fashion icon: In 2006, at the age of 85, Iris Apfel, a New Yorker, was feted as a style icon when the Metropolitan Museum of Art held an exhibition of her clothes. In 2004, "real" women were chosen to pose for the camera in a publicity campaign launched by the Dove cosmetics company—with great success. Scott Schuman went out on the street to photograph unknown people whose style caught his notice, and exhibited them on his popular Internet blog called "The Sartorialist." Schuman is considered the top fashion blogger—but Tavi Gevinson comes a close second. This teenager with her own unique style assiduously studies all the fashion magazines and offers outspoken critiques on the fashion brands.

bloggers as guests at their shows. Bryan Boy, Tommy Ton, Garance Doré, and Scott Schuman, for example, found themselves, much to their surprise, in the front row at the 2009 D&G show, alongside the chief editors of *Vogue* and *Vanity Fair* magazines. What is more, several fashion journalists devoted a good deal of time to their appearance each day in the hope that they might find themselves featured as trendsetters on one of the blogs.

The most famous blogger of all is Scott Schuman—"The Sartorialist"—who, after 15 years working in various branches of the fashion industry, abandoned the business in order to concentrate on photography. Since 2005, he has publicized his street-style snapshots on the Web and is himself astonished at the success of his blog. Not only is his blog regularly visited and quoted, but he finds himself frequently invited to contribute to other blogs, such as Style.com, or help produce video films. He writes his own page every month for the US edition of *GQ*, and is also working on his first book. The Sartorialist cites photographer Bill Cunningham, who has been recording the New York street scene for over 35 years, as his greatest role model. This hard-working photographer can justifiably be described as the true forerunner of all bloggers. He is not considered one of the paparazzi as he has never "hunted" celebrities, only people with style and good taste.

One of the first fashion blogs was set up by Diane Pernet. This American fashion icon, with her signature piled-high hair and dark, butterfly-shaped dark glasses, spent 13 years as a designer in New York, moved to Paris 20 years ago, and went online with her blog, ashadedviewonfashion.com, ahead of everyone else. Diane, a woman of uncertain age, who dresses exclusively in black, is the World Wide Web's equivalent of Suzy Menkes, the famous fashion editor. Not least, of course, she's a role model for the next generation. The youngest rising star among the bloggers is a 13-year old American girl, who calls herself "tavi-thenewgirlintown" on blogspot.com. This precocious teenager with orthodontic braces not only offers excellent styling tips but is also extremely blunt when it comes to judging new designer collections.

Probably one of the main advantages of the Internet is that no one need be afraid to say what works and what does not—regardless of a designer's fame (or publicity outlay). If zippers fail to work, *décolletés* do not look as they should, or heels are unable to survive an evening's dancing, it will undoubtedly be reported on the Internet. It is all the more baffling, therefore, that so many fashion houses still do not check out their clients' views given the fact that 85 percent of the clientele in the luxury sector access the ratings sites and other similar information platforms. Burberry is an exception in this respect—it was the first leading label to set up its own community portal. Artofthetrench.com is a social networking site offering customers the opportunity to share their individual stories and experiences with regard to the classic Burberry trench coat. The site quickly became as much a cult as the garment itself.

Unknown or even undistinguished products can acquire overnight status via the Internet—trade in secondhand clothes, for example, is particularly well suited to the Internet. As soon as old tracksuits started selling for high bids on eBay, a retro cult developed for "Adidas originals." In the case of vintage fashion, which is much in demand, the Web is still the main marketplace for buying and selling this type of rarity. Designers, who can only produce their elaborate couture in small quantities, likewise find the Internet the best selling platform. Consequently, couturelab.com has become a veritable Aladdin's cave for individualists seeking unique bargains. Anyone with more time than money should consider seeking out a local dressmaker who can make individual garments to order, particularly since "local fashion" is likely to be the next big trend—this does not mean minor-league, ethnic fashions, but something that is locally produced and entirely individual, which is the product of mutual discussions between the designer and client, or a design which at least reflects its roots. In New York, for example, "The German Fräuleins" Alexa Meyer and Angelika Kammann have had a good deal of success with their "typical German" fashions. Wolfgang Joop, on the other hand, did not seem to find his true direction until he turned his back on the Big Apple and returned to his home town of Potsdam. His Wunderkind label is a sensational new approach to German fashion and the most exciting style that Berlin has seen since the 1920s.

BACK TO HIS ROOTS:
Wolfgang Joop

b. 11.18.1944

Wolfgang Joop was not a child prodigy, at least not in the eyes of his father Gerhard. On returning from a Russian prisoner-of-war camp in 1952, he felt his son had been spoiled by his mother and aunts. Admittedly, he could draw well but he lacked discipline. He passed his high school diploma, but abandoned his studies of advertising psychology, which he began on his father's encouragement, as well as his own chosen career of art teacher. He was so multitalented, good-looking, and anxious to please everyone that he found it difficult to settle on one course.

Eventually he was given a push in the right direction. Together with art student Karin, whom he married in 1970, he entered a fashion competition run by *Constanze* magazine and won the top three prizes. This led to a job as fashion editor, but this did not last very long either. Wolfgang Joop dreamed of the freedom of an artist but carried on earning a living as a journalist and designer. Since he could write (a gift he inherited from his father, editor-in-chief of *Westermann-Hefte*) as well as draw, he became involved in reporting and sketching at the Paris fashion shows during the 1970s. Wolfgang and Karin, who also worked as a journalist, made a strikingly attractive couple in their secondhand clothes and caught the attention of the fashion industry—but they were too shy at the time to capitalize on this. They also had two daughters, a situation which kept these two young parents pretty much tied to home. Jette, who was born in 1968, is now a successful jewelry designer in her own right and Florentine, who trained as a sketch artist, was born in 1974 and opened a restaurant in Berlin early in 2010.

Wolfgang Joop caused his first sensation in 1978 with a fur collection. The *New York Times* described his designs as typically German, a "Prussian" style of fashion. He may not have been too pleased about this back then when he was still trying to take the world by storm but today he is proud of the comment. By spring 1982, he was ready to present his first ready-to-wear women's collection and three years later, he launched his first menswear range. It was when he launched his first perfume with its accompanying publicity campaign that he really began to attract the attention of the fashion world—and from then on he began writing his name in capital letters, followed by an exclamation mark: JOOP!

Wolfgang's career took off. He was bubbling over with ideas, which led to the creation of various products. JOOP! soon became a lifestyle brand, encompassing the entire fashion spectrum, from jeans to jewelry to glasses. But Wolfgang Joop himself did not quite seem to be fulfilling his full potential. At any rate, a unique Joop brand—be it Prussian or otherwise—did not emerge.

Success at last
Wolfgang Joop was always a restless spirit who liked to experiment, as demonstrated by the diversity of his fashion designs. It was only after he settled in Potsdam, where he grew up, that he finally found his own unique style in Wunderkind.

Nice and healthy

In 2009, to the surprise of the fashion world, Wolfgang Joop embarked upon a joint venture with Medi, a company specializing in medical equipment, aimed at adding a touch of glamour to compression stockings (left) and an osteoporosis corset (right).

As fragile as porcelain

This blue and white toile de jouy print resembles fine Chinese porcelain—but don't worry, fragile bones are protected by Mediven support pantyhose, which have a strategic gap over the knee, or support socks.

The world of Wunderkind

Many visitors to the Wunderkind headquarters in Potsdam
are reminded of the blue flower of romanticism. It begins in
the principal rooms of the Villa Rumpf, a house which once
belonged to artist Fritz Rumpf and was used as a salon by the
Expressionists. Wolfgang Joop has had the villa meticulously
restored and furnished in his own eclectic style. The room,
which is flooded with natural light, serves both as a reception
area and show room. He has reserved the name Wunderkind
for a second villa in Potsdam, which he uses as a private
residence.

Sara for

Wunderkind 2008

The turning point

The Wunderkind spring/summer collection of 2008 marks Wolfgang Joop's final step to freedom. Liberated from managerial constraints, he was finally able to allow his fantasy free rein and create what he considered to be a fashion that reflected German sensibilities. Not long before this, he had discovered his neighbors in Potsdam, Gisela and Hans-Joachim Sander, to be ideal financial partners. Joop's extraordinary talent as an illustrator was highlighted in the "Eternal Love" exhibition in Rostock's Kunsthalle in 2009.

*Living in Potsdam again, where he had lived as a child, awakened all Wolfgang Joop's **creative forces***

As a personality, however, Wolfgang Joop maintained a very high profile and was recognized as stylish, witty, and mischievous, as well as the best sketcher and a master of the pithy remark—Karl Lagerfeld was the only designer who could hold a candle to him.

It was Wolfgang Joop's goal to conquer New York and he was helped in this respect by Edwin Lemberg. The two of them have been partners for 30 years, fuelled initially by passion and later by common interests. Wolfgang Joop went through a wild phase when he allegedly indulged in everything from alcohol to drugs. At some point, however, he decided he had had enough of it all— including what JOOP! had become: an assortment of designer products, for which he supplied the designs and handed out licensee contracts. JOOP! no longer produced any of its own goods for sale. In 1998, he sold 95 percent of his stake in JOOP! to the Hamburg firm Wünsche AG, and sold the remaining 5 percent in 2001, at the same time ending his involvement as design director.

What followed was a story of renaissance. Wolfgang Joop, who tried hard to be everybody's darling, went back to his roots. At the beginning of the new millennium, he returned to Potsdam, where he was born and where he had spent his early years. His character and artistic tastes were influenced by two main factors: a love of nature and the rural countryside around his home town, and the elegance of Sanssouci Palace, close to where he grew up. He adopted Villa Wunderkind on Lake Heiligensee as his private residence and turned Villa Rumpf into his firm's headquarters. As far as Wolfgang Joop was concerned, it was always the Golden East, rather the Golden West that he yearned for, so that for him it was a thoroughly welcome homecoming. He renovated the Bornstedt manor house, with its countless happy childhood associations, and installed his mother Char-lotte there, a stately, personable, elegant woman. She lived there until her death on May 3, 2010 at the age of 94 years. His daughters, Jette and Florentine, also have their own rooms there and his former wife, Karin, has a small house in the grounds, making it a real family home. So-called "Nibelungen loyalty" is an ancient German virtue, which can certainly be ascribed to Wolfgang Joop. Once he embraces someone as a member of his "clan," as in the case of his partner Edwin Lemberg, for instance, he will always stick by them.

Meanwhile, his hard-working nature, his penchant for slightly dark romanticism, his inner turmoil, and striving for higher things can also be described as "typical German" sensibilities. All these are embodied in Wunderkind, and it was no accident that he chose a name for his new label that could not really be translated yet resonates well all over the world. Wunderkind has become Wolfgang Joop's unique signature style: a subtle play between soft, dreamy designs and precise tailoring, more of a work of art than a dress. His couture designs cost at least 1350 US dollars (1000 euros), but luxury, as Wolfgang Joop remarks "cannot be democratized."

In 2004, he presented his new label in New York for the first time, and from 2006 to October 2010 he showed his collections in Paris. The year 2011 was once again a difficult year. Investors kept withdrawing, two boutiques were closed down but eventually Joop was able to buy back all of the "Wunderkind" branches and is once again sole proprietor of his brand. Joop presented his 2012/2013 autumn/winter collection at his Potsdam Villa Rumpf. It would seem that he has finally arrived. Admittedly, fashion is an international business, but the more global the market, the more fascinating is a style that does not try to deny its roots. This was Wolfgang Joop's chance. He no longer needs an exclamation point—his designs are for those who travel between different worlds, who get diverted from their course, yet still reach their destination.

Felt and seams
A felt blockprint dress worn over a silk chiffon blouse with matching cotton jersey pantyhose. Also for Wunderkind's winter 2009 collection: dark animal prints by Hamburg artist Gregor Törzs on crêpe de Chine.

ON A GREEN MISSION:
Stella McCartney

b. 09.13.1971

As a child, Stella McCartney had two main interests: fashion and animal welfare. Both of these were inherited from her mother Linda, who had a wardrobe full of beautiful Chloé dresses and was a committed animal rights activist opposed to all types of animal exploitation. Stella, the second daughter of photographer Linda and former Beatle Paul McCartney, grew up as a strict vegetarian. She decided at a very early age that she would never compromise her strong convictions, not even for the sake of the most fantastic fashion in the world—which she herself intended to create.

Even more problematical than the preconceptions that "eco-fashion" was baggy and uncool, were the reservations about Stella herself. What could anyone expect, after all, of someone born with a silver spoon in her mouth, and who was a habitué of the Portobello celebrity party circuit? Admittedly, she had graduated from Central Saint Martins, but to be appointed at the tender age of 26 as chief designer for the top French brand of Chloé (her mother Linda's favorite label) could surely only be a result of her connections with the international world of show business—and to be sure, people like Madonna, Gwyneth Paltrow, Kate Moss, and obviously her father, Sir Paul McCartney, are in the front row when Stella shows one of her collections. But so what? It does no one any harm.

The Chloé label went back to being the gold mine that it had been under the aegis of Karl Lagerfeld, and Stella was able to prove that she was a master of her trade. Her designs were in perfect accord with the tastes of the young women who are pictured as style icons in glossy magazines. It is hardly surprising that she ended up making friends with many of them and is now entirely familiar with their preferred styles—they like the same sort of clothes that she herself would choose: "Uncomplicated clothes, such as a well-tailored jacket over a feminine dress which can be worn anywhere."

Stella was not a fan of the fashions of the Eighties and Nineties with their deconstructed patterns and unfinished appearance. She learnt her trade in Savile Row, where the best men's suits in the world are tailored. She is adept at creating an immaculately tailored jacket, but would never team it with suit pants—instead she would coordinate it with a delicate vintage-look dress, a style passed down from her mother. The lingerie tops in her first collection were already a hit for

---

With a view to the future

Anyone on the lookout for hot tips about tomorrow's fashions should keep a close eye on Stella McCartney. Beatle Paul McCartney's daughter is a strict vegan and refuses to work with any animal products. Nevertheless—or perhaps precisely because of this—her label is cooler than others.

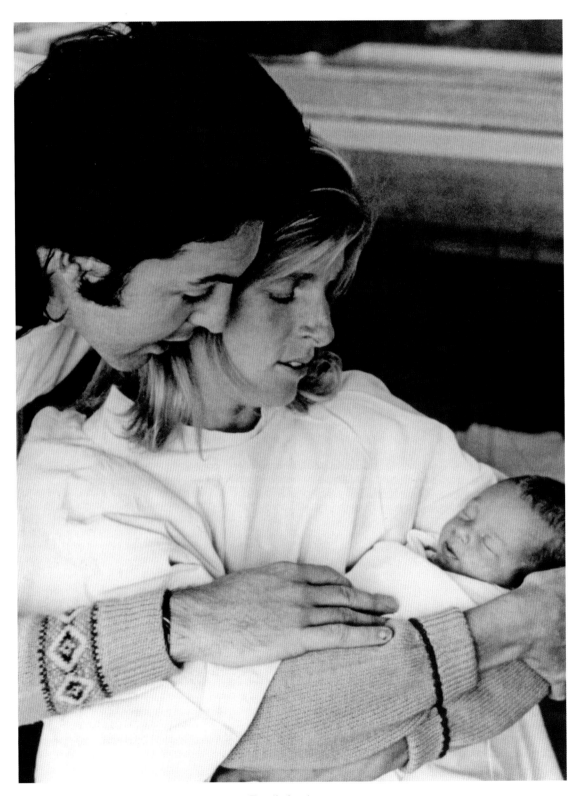

Family business

Stella McCartney was just four days old when she was photographed in the arms of her mother, Linda, under the admiring gaze of her father, Paul. Stella's life is still ruled by the principles which were dear to her mother's heart. Linda McCartney died of breast cancer in 1998.

Friends and family

Her father, Paul, and friends like Gwyneth Paltrow and Charlotte Casiraghi of Monaco sit in the front row at each of her shows. Stella's sexy design style, which gives ruches and frilled peplum a modern look, is on exactly the right wavelength for her contemporaries.

Casual and innovative

As a young working mom, Stella McCartney knows better than anyone that comfort is as important as elegance. In addition to off-the-shoulder shorts-jumpsuits and flattering maxi dresses, Stella McCartney also designs a range of warm sweaters and jackets. Her hottest boots in the 2010 season were completely leather-free, with stiletto heels and a stencil print. For her summer collection, she is designing a wooden accordion-look It bag and large-framed dark glasses.

As the daughter of a strict vegetarian, Stella became a pioneer in *ecological and ethnic trends*

Chloé, but ruches and flowers on their own would not be to Stella's taste either—her fashion has to be "cool," which is why a dress is always combined with a jacket or cozy knitted cardigan.

Stella herself feels that pants are her biggest success: "No one makes them sexier!" And what does she wear with them? Not a blazer, obviously! It has to be something flattering, softly flowering, in order to break up the severe line. "It is balance that makes a design perfect for me." Just how well Stella's determinedly feminine touch has tapped into the current boyfriend fashion trend was recognized immediately by Tom Ford, who himself always has his finger on the pulse of the contemporary fashion mood: He brought Stella into the Gucci group, now owned by the PPR luxury conglomerate, where she has had her own label since 2001. Her fashions are young, light, and flattering—and above all strictly vegan!

It was not so long ago that Stella's "vegetarian shoes" were the object of derision and people scoffed at the "zero energy concept" of her shops. In 2009, however, she became the only fashion designer to be voted by *Time* magazine as one of the "most influential people of our time," since when her business model has been viewed as an example to all and has been instrumental in promoting the growth of a strong movement in support of this ecological and ethical trend. It is worth remembering that Stella designs enduring fashions—from a sense of conviction rather than as a result of deliberation—which is one of the reasons why she can launch one new line after another and open a whole series of shops despite the crisis that other designers have been struggling with since 2008. Stella McCartney also makes ready-to-wear, lingerie, sunglasses, shoes, bags, cosmetics, sportswear for Adidas, and children's wear for Gap—all of them in accordance with her organic-biological principles.

Nevertheless, Stella does not claim to be some kind of missionary. On the contrary, she is delighted whenever she designs a "hot" pair of shoes or purse without customers realizing that they are buying "eco chic": "I'm a firm believer in infiltrating from within." Even father Paul was very impressed by his daughter's endlessly long, tight-fitting, thigh-high legging boots. "I just wish I knew where they ended..."

Stella's shoes clearly tickle the imagination, otherwise they would not be so successful. After all, the bio-degradable imitation leather in her shoes is 70 percent more expensive than leather. But as Tom Ford, Stella's mentor, once commented: "Luxury never goes out of fashion, it just changes its style."

At the moment, it looks as if the future will belong to clothes with moral principles, and this is precisely where Stella is coming from—thanks to her own upbringing and because she wants her own children to live their lives in harmony with nature. In 2003 she married Alasdhair Willis, who is also involved in the fashion industry. Stella prefers not to discuss fashion issues with him since "there is fortunately more to life than fashion." A life with four children is just what Stella had always imagined for herself since she and her husband had planned, right from the start, to follow the family pattern; they each have three siblings apiece.

They also have a dog. Stella, who like her mother (who died of breast cancer in 1998) is an expert in vegetarian cuisine, sometimes makes an exception for him: "On the vet's instructions, the dog gets to eat meat occasionally."

Sweet memories
At just 26 years of age, Stella McCartney was appointed designer of the famous Chloé label. She began designing exactly the sort of clothes that her mother used to wear in the 1970s—loose-fitting, lace-trimmed designs with the lingerie look.

Individu-alism

Jeans

all over the west they wear

LEVI STRAUSS & CO'S
COPPER RIVETED
Overalls.

One day in 2004, sisters Laura and Kate Mulleavy, despite their lack of tailoring knowledge, put together a small collection based entirely on their own ideas and inspired by books and dreams. They named their line "Rodarte," after their mother's maiden name. Once they had sewn ten dresses by hand, they drove from provincial Pasadena to the fashion hub of New York, where they approached a handful of important fashion people and presented them with their elaborate sketchbooks of designs. Their approach could not have been more naïve—but guess what? These two unknown designers were accepted! Soon afterward their clothes were appearing on the title pages of top fashion magazines and were soon being ordered by prestigious department stores. It all sounds like a fairy tale but there is a very simple explanation: In a country famous for practical sportswear and reasonably priced mass-produced clothes, the two sisters' poetic brand of couture fulfilled an unrequited desire for individual extravagance. Rodarte clothes are extremely delicate works of art incorporating unprecedented detail, and often so fragile that you need help to put them on—the perfect garment for special occasions, or the high points of your life. Which is why Rodarte's example is being followed by other designers—even the most sensible woman wants to dress like a princess occasionally.

Safer fashion is for all those who are afraid of making fashion faux pas: Jeans are always acceptable, in every situation. When Levi Strauss created blue jeans in 1873 as work pants for American men, he could never have dreamed that 100 years later everyone in the world would be walking around in jeans. Hardwearing Levis were designed for farm work and because women were always expected to lend a hand, Levi Strauss introduced their first 701 jeans for women in 1934—the traditional 501 was reserved for menswear. However, things did not quite turn out as expected: The farmer's wife in fact wore 501s like her husband, and it was the elegant New York City women, who liked to pretend to be cowgirls while on vacation at the ranch, who were wearing the women's version. Levi Strauss & Co were quick to respond to the city woman's taste and replaced the buttons with a zipper. But people who set store on authenticity still wear classic Levis 501 even now—or designer jeans in stretch material. Jeans have become a fashion product which appeals to every taste and suits all shapes and sizes. And the material from which these hardwearing clothes are made is a dream in whatever form. Denim is the prevailing fabric of the 2010 collections, from Dolce&Gabbana to Jean Paul Gaultier, and from Louis Vuitton to Stella McCartney and Chloé.

Techno couture

Vintage

What began in the 1990s with "magic T-shirts," which changed their color depending on temperature, or else only revealed their pattern when exposed to direct sunlight (and are still one of the biggest selling lines of Nifty Cool Gifts, a US company), grew during the early part of the third millennium into the biggest fashion trend of all time: techno couture made from intelligent textiles, which not only react to temperature fluctuations, but can also save lives. A "life shirt," for example, monitors the heart rate, or can detect dehydration, one of the most common causes of death in old people. Techno couture is also just good fun. Lumalive, a textile developed by Philips, can be activated by remote control into displaying texts and pictures in all the colors of the rainbow. Lumalive integrates LED lighting into fabrics, providing everyone with personal "fixed star" garments, as impressively demonstrated by CuteCircuit's "Galaxy" dress, in which 24,000 tiny colored LEDs, measuring 2 x 2 mm in size, were hand-embroidered onto several layers of organza and chiffon, shimmering and glowing with every movement. And once the batteries run out, 4,000 Swarovski crystals continue to sparkle. Fashion artist Yin Gao, meanwhile, creates dresses that react to light or movement, to sound or air currents—living sculptures which were shown in Basle in 2009.

When Julia Roberts walked the red carpet at the 2001 Oscars ceremony in a vintage Valentino dress, the concept of secondhand took on a new meaning. If used clothes once represented an emergency solution, they were now elevated to a much higher status: Old couture was now the best couture. And Michèle and Olivier Chatenet had a real talent for turning elegant old clothes into coveted new garments. The French couple, who had previously worked for Alaïa, Comme des Garçons, and Chanel, gave vintage dresses a contemporary touch, sometimes just by adding new buttons, or sometimes by taking the original dress completely apart and putting it back together again in a new style. "E2" was the name they gave to their recycling label, launched in 1999 in Paris. Stars including Madonna love their individual garments. The Chatenets do not present their E2 collections at shows in the usual manner, but display them in galleries. Tara Subkoff and Matt Damhave came up with a similar concept when they launched their Imitation of Christ label in New York in 2000. They cut up bargains found in secondhand stores, removed the labels, and created new clothes out of the old fabrics. Their school friend Chloë Sevigny is considered one of the leading style icons of vintage fashion. The whole concept is about far more than just individual clothes—old is good, because it represents a protest against today's wasteful, throwaway society.

BEHIND THE SCENES

The influence of muses and fashion journalists

BERNARD ARNAULT

DOMENICO DE SOLE

KARLA OTTO

PATRIZIO BERTELLI

FRANÇOIS-HENRI PINAULT
AND FRANÇOIS PINAULT

Since 1990, writes the Australian fashion historian Bonnie English in her *Cultural history of Fashion in the 20th century*, there has been a "sea change" in the whole fashion business. This is most evident in the new type of designer that has emerged; where once couturiers could flirt with the public by shunning the limelight and being aloof, now designers have become almost cult figures in their own right, like actors, musicians, sportspeople, and models, and are now all worldwide celebrities. Their carefully contrived image also has to represent their brand, and every public appearance is used to show it off.

This change marked a general shift away from discreet, refined haute couture in favor of the much more publicity-oriented *prêt-à-porter*. Designers and their target audience now live by the maxim that individuality should be acted out in public. This has also caused massive upheavals behind the scenes; there was suddenly a demand for powerbrokers, people who were exceptionally good at marketing and raising the profile of a label, and muses, who provided a new stimulus with their beauty, elegance and, most of all, their originality.

In economic terms, the rumblings behind this radical change had first been heard back in the 1980s, when the luxury goods industry realized that sales from fashion were surpassed by the profit that could be made from perfumes, cosmetics, leather goods, eyewear, or jewelry. Nowadays a collection has two purposes: By itself, it appeals only to a select, extremely wealthy clientele, but as a marketing tool it is invaluable in generating a desire for perfumes, handbags, or sunglasses on the mass market. For small companies, including the many luxury goods companies that have emerged over recent decades, it is becoming increasingly difficult to survive in such a market. By contrast, international companies who present their different brands as though they were completely separate labels, but which actually share suppliers and licensees in order to reduce costs, have only benefited from this development.

Ever more big-name brands are merging with the two industry giants, Louis Vuitton Moët Hennessy (LVMH) and Pinault Printemps Redoute (PPR), rival luxury groups led by Bernard Arnault and François Pinault respectively. Neither

No *éminence grise*

Anna Piaggi, the Italian fashion journalist, was a force to be reckoned with but many people failed to recognize just how great her influence on the world of fashion was.

president had had the slightest thing to do with fashion in their earlier careers. Bernard Arnault, today the richest man in France, started out developing vacation apartments on the Côte d'Azur. In 1984 he founded a holding company and took over the beleaguered textile firm Boussac Saint-Frères; Christian Dior belonged to one of Boussac's daughter companies. After that, one success followed hot on the heels of another. In early 1987 Arnault was instrumental in the rise of Christian Lacroix, allowing the designer to gain a foothold in the fashion industry. In the same year he bought the luxury leather producer Céline and began to acquire an interest in the holding company LVMH, which had also been founded in 1987. It had been formed by the merger of Louis Vuitton and Moët Hennessy, whose directors feared a hostile takeover. Yet only a year later there were massive differences of opinion over the running of the Champagne, cognac, and leather goods conglomerate. The directors of Louis Vuitton turned to Bernard Arnault for help, offering him shares in the company, while the branch of the company producing alcoholic drinks went to the British beer, wine and spirits company, Guinness. It was this chain of events that ultimately allowed Arnault to make his coup d'état. With the support of Guinness and the investment bank Lazard Frères he took a 45-percent share in LVMH, and became the president of the company in 1989, against the wishes of the Vuitton and Hennessy families.

This move may have been controversial, but there is no doubt that Arnault has achieved great things since his accession to power. His

cunning mixture of clever marketing, innovative design, and vigilant monitoring of sales standards and strategies has allowed him to transform Louis Vuitton and Christian Dior into highly profitable companies with a global presence. He has also succeeded in forging a creative association with John Galliano, whose collections for Christian Dior were always frenziedly anticipated. He discovered Hedi Slimane for the Dior Homme line and appointed Marc Jacobs to Louis Vuitton. Both of these designers have since made their mark on fashion through their own labels.

François Pinault was also an experienced business strategist long before he broke into the fashion industry. He began his career in his family's lumber mill, which he sold after his father died, but later bought back. His principle of cutting out the middleman and dealing directly with suppliers and carriers did not make him universally popular, but it did make him rich and influential. Having risen to the top of the lumber business, he turned his attention to other industries. In 1992 he bought the department store chain Printemps, followed by the mail-order company La Redoute in 1994, and founded the Pinault Printemps Redoute (PPR) Group. His next move was obvious, as a long-standing PPR executive explains: "If you have luxury brands, you can make your break by tapping into the American and Asian markets, without having to invest." Pinault's ticket to gain entry to this branch of the industry was practically served up to him on a silver platter, in the shape of Gucci. In 1999 the rumor spread that LVMH president Bernard Arnault was

Power couple
Without the support of the wily businessman Domenico De Sole, Tom Ford's rise at Gucci would not have been quite as meteoric, and he would not have risked founding his own label quite so soon. Here the pair are pictured at the opening of Ford's boutique in Milan.

Jewelry and inspiration for YSL
Loulou de la Falaise was the closest confidante of Yves Saint Laurent and designed costume jewelry for his label.

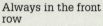

Always in the front row

Bernard Arnault and his wife Hélène are guaranteed the best seats at any couture show, as they own several fashion houses. His biggest star was John Galliano, whom he brought to Dior (below). Frank Gehry designed the museum for his planned cultural foundation (top right).

planning a hostile takeover of the once-beleaguered Gucci company that Tom Ford had restored to its former glamour since 1994. The company's boss Domenico De Sole was under no illusions about the reason why Arnault had acquired a 34-percent share in the company and saw the maneuver as a blatant attempt to neutralize Gucci, one of Louis Vuitton's competitors. He turned to François Pinault, offering him a deal whereby De Sole would mitigate the weight of Arnault's investment by issuing millions of new shares, which Pinault would buy up, thus securing a 40 percent ownership of Gucci. This shady tactic caused Arnault's stake in the business to plummet from 34 to 20 percent. He was furious. The gauntlet had been thrown down between the two titans of the industry, and their dispute was to seep into many other areas of their respective businesses. When LVMH bought the fine wines Château d'Yquem and Cheval Blanc, for instance, PPR acquired Château Latour. In 1998 François Pinault bought Christie's auction house, and in 1999 Arnault followed suit with Phillips de Pury & Company (which he would later sell on in 2003). When Bernard Arnault announced in 2006 that the star architect Frank Gehry would build a cultural foundation for LVMH in Paris, Pinault felt compelled to see through his plans for a modern art museum, originally to be in Paris, designed by the Japanese architect Tadao Ando. These plans had first been mooted in 2000, but had been put on the back burner ever since. Now he bought the luxurious Palazzo Grassi in Venice and commissioned Tadao Ando to make subtle renovations. In 2007 he held

a public exhibition of his personal collection of modern art there. François Pinault has already provided for the future of his company; in spring 2005 he handed over the reins to his son, François-Henri Pinault, although not before ensuring that he was leaving it in a capable pair of hands by thoroughly testing Pinault junior's performance in various branches of the group. François-Henri excelled himself over his ten trial years, and only two years after being appointed to the top job, he surprised everyone with the shrewd takeover of the German sports goods manufacturer Puma. He argued that as a global player it was unrealistic to concentrate only on a small, elite clientele. The German brand, popular with celebrities, formed an ideal bridge between the luxury goods and the business arms of PPR.

Toward the end of the 1990s Prada CEO Patrizio Bertelli also set about taking on new companies alongside the "in-house" brands of Prada and Miu Miu, so as to guarantee good growth potential for the main company. In 1999 Bertelli bought Jil Sander, Helmut Lang, and, in collaboration with LVMH, the ailing Rome-based fur and fashion house of Fendi. Bertelli was not, however, quite as fortunate in his acquisitions as Arnault or Pinault; he did not succeed in dragging Fendi back into the black, and in 2001 he sold his shares to LVMH. The German fashion icon Jil Sander departed from her post in 2000, only a year after the takeover, citing irreconcilable differences. Despite his every attempt to increase profits and reduce costs, the situation remained so disastrous that Bertelli sold the Jil Sander label to the British

Lightweight
Petite, delicate and well connected, Amanda Harlech has been the ideal muse for John Galliano and Karl Lagerfeld.

financial investor Change Capital Partners in February 2006. Things did not go much better with Helmut Lang; in 1999 Bertelli went in with 51 percent, but in October 2004, after several turbulent years, he sold off his remaining shares. In spring 2005 the designer himself resigned from his own label. The brand survived, but was sold in 2006 to a Japanese conglomerate. Ever since then the Prada Group, which includes the footwear brands Church's Footwear and Car Shoe, has concentrated once again on its two core lines, Prada and Miu Miu. By doing this Bertelli has ultimately succeeded in making the once small Milanese leather handbag company Prada into an international business.

Back in 1967, at the age of only 21, Bertelli founded a leather goods factory for belts and bags in his hometown of Arezzo. Ten years later, in 1978, he met Miuccia Prada, the daughter of a prominent Milanese family and heir to her family's small leather goods company. She married Bertelli in 1980, and the couple set about remodeling and expanding the company together. They had an international breakthrough with their glossy black handbags made of parachute nylon in 1985. Their first *prêt-à-porter* collection saw the light of day in 1989, followed by the launch of the cheaper Miu Miu line, which is aimed at younger customers. Prada shops were not set out as pristine sales floors, but rather as creative studios offering a space where customers could pause for a while for inspiration while perusing the clothes and accessories. Top architects were commissioned to come up with the design; Rem Koolhaas designed the flagship stores

in New York, Los Angeles and San Francisco, and Herzog & de Meuron planned the Tokyo store.

One woman in particular helped to raise the profile of Prada to new heights. The German PR and image consultant Karla Otto, who, strictly speaking, did not belong to the company at all, is one of the most influential and independent women in fashion. In 1973, immediately after graduating high school, Otto went to Japan, where she funded her studies by working as a model. This eventually took her to Milan, where she met Elio Fiorucci, whose designs bring a hint of London youth culture to Italian T-shirts, jeans and accessories. In the late 70s, Karla Otto offered to do some press work for Fiorucci, and it paid off; at a time when hardly anyone was actively marketing trends and image, Fiorucci and Otto sparked a global trend, making Fiorucci the emblem of the Pop generation all over the world. After this resounding success, Otto was appointed by Jean Paul Gaultier to manage his PR in Italy. This heralded a major shift in fashion PR. Whereas previously fashion journalists and editors had to travel to the designers' studios in order to find out about and report on the latest collections, and borrow pieces for photo shoots, now the label's press officer was only a short taxi ride away. Her next coup was Jil Sander; Otto brought the label to international prominence and developed concepts for advertising campaigns and boutiques all over the world.

Then came Prada. Ultimately this collaboration ended suddenly after many successful years; Bertelli wanted to buy Otto's company, but the clever PR strategist refused. She

He runs the business, she is the brains

Thanks to her husband, Patrizio Bertelli, the political scientist Miuccia Prada is where she is now. He was the one who persuaded her to make more than just bags, and gradually built up the Prada Group.

Heavyweight

The Australian-born Leigh Bowery had a huge influence on the London club scene and, by extension, on fashion. His "Taboo" club nights overstepped every boundary and gave birth to many new trends. Bowery himself was always a trailblazer.

Like father …
In his career as a lumber
dealer François Pinault was
used to flying around in his
private jet, monitoring his
forest plantation. Later he
managed the luxury goods
company Pinault Printemps
Redoute (PPR).

… like son
Today PPR is run by François-Henri Pinault. His trophies
include Hollywood star Salma Hayek as his wife, and the
Palazzo Grassi as a museum for his art collection.

lost Prada as a client, but the fact that she had turned down Bertelli only increased her clout within the industry. To this day Karla Otto is the sole owner of her company, and thus 100 percent her own woman. Her client list includes Roberto Cavalli, Alberta Ferretti, Pucci, Fendi, Viktor & Rolf, and Hussein Chalayan, plus Karl Lagerfeld's jeans line and sports brands such as Nike.

Besides this novel approach, a direct response to globalization and deep-seated structural changes in the fashion industry, Karla Otto also played a role that had been a vital part of every couture house's marketing strategy since the 1930s—that of the mannequin mondaine. In addition to their house models, the couturiers would choose stars and women from the cream of society to be seen wearing their dresses at social events. Otto, who had retained her size-4 figure since the age of 16, changed her outfit up to five times a day so that she was always wearing the label she was promoting at the time.

For centuries, designers and photographers have been inspired by the breathtaking beauty or exquisite elegance of particular women—most famously, style icons such as Mona von Bismarck and the Duchess of Windsor—or professional models, as explored in the exhibition "The Model as Muse," held at the New York Metropolitan Museum of Art in 2009. The end of the supermodel era in the late 1980s marked a change in the kind of models that designers used; personality now played a more important part in the visual language of fashion and advertising than a symmetrical face.

Muses who had a marked influence

on the signature style of the most renowned designers now included not only classic beauties such as Loulou de la Falaise, who inspired Yves Saint Laurent, or Inès de la Fressange and later Amanda Harlech at Karl Lagerfeld, but also shrill characters whose most conspicuous feature was unrestrained eccentricity. By far the most bizarre of these was the Australian-born Leigh Bowery. In the late Eighties and early Nineties Bowery was one of the greatest trendsetters on the London creative scene. Although he was the exact opposite of svelte, being pudgy and bald, any public appearance by him was a big event. He dolled himself up to look like a wedding cake, wore supersized crinolines with matching face paint, strutted around in a flowery dress that also covered his face, or pitterpattered over the dance floor dressed as a hot pink ballerina with plastic platforms on his feet. In 1985 he set up the still notorious polysexual disco club night "Taboo." Conceived as a purely underground event, these parties soon became a kind of London Studio 54, albeit somewhat wilder and more fashion-conscious than the legendary New York disco. Pop stars and style icons like David Bowie and Boy George, the painter Lucian Freud and the designers Vivienne Westwood, Alexander McQueen, and John Galliano all hung out at the "Taboo" club nights.

In 1988 a London gallery allowed Bowery to really indulge his personality. As a "living work of art" he sat for a week behind a glass screen, changing his home-made outfits every day. His penchant for the extreme—he variously paired hoop petticoats with a steel helmet, wore disturbing masks, squeezed

his massive body into corsets, posed as a club-footed dominatrix in black latex or, when dressed as a teapot, cavorted with an oversized giant spout—had a strong and lasting influence on Westwood, McQueen, and Galliano. The latter dedicated a tribute collection to him in 2003. By this time Bowery had been dead for nine years, having succumbed to AIDS in 1994.

The life of another British style icon, Isabella Blow, was scarcely less flamboyant and tragic. As a 21-year-old Blow went to New York in 1979 to study the history of Chinese art, but quit her studies the following year and went to work for Guy Laroche in Texas. She returned to the Big Apple in 1981 to work as an assistant to the legendary editor of *Vogue*, Anna Wintour, and became friends with Andy Warhol, Jean-Michel Basquiat and Roy Lichtenstein. In 1986 she returned to London as the fashion editor of *Tatler* magazine. By now she was a highly gifted talent scout. In 1989 she commissioned Philip Treacy, a previously unknown milliner, to design her bridal headdress for her wedding to the art dealer Detmar Blow. This marked the beginning of a collaboration that was to become as famous as it was fruitful. Treacy created an array of crazy hats for Blow: a light green orchid with protruding petals; a shiny silver disc that hovered above her head; a tuft of pale pink feathers; or a net of giant dollar signs that fell down over her eyes. Not only did she occasionally let him use her private apartment as a studio, but she also made his hats famous by wearing them so often in public. Other Blow discoveries included the model Sophie Dahl and the designer Hussein Chalayan.

The very picture of Coco
Inès de la Fressange, whom Karl Lagerfeld selected as his first muse, looks remarkably like Gabrielle "Coco" Chanel.

When Alexander McQueen presented his graduation collection at Central Saint Martins in 1994, she bought it in its entirety for £5000, in £100 installments. Yet her star began to wane from 2001 onwards; when McQueen sold his label to Gucci she felt that she had been overlooked, as she had brokered the deal but McQueen did not take her with him. Her celebrity status began to fade. Severely ill and suffering from depression, she took her own life in 2007. The London scene was in shock. "Her appearance and endearing exoticism gave that extra something to any event," recalls the designer Michael Kors.

It was fortunate for everyone, and not just the close-knit circles of the fashion world, that a Grande Dame existed, who was the unchallenged champion of imaginative self-expression – even at a very advanced age. Anna Piaggi is rumoured to have been born in 1931. Yet right up until her death in the summer of 2012, this delightful diva, famed for her soft, blue-highlighted hair, was still causing a stir at fashion events. "She was the world's last great authority on the art of getting dressed," gushes none other than the iconic shoe designer Manolo Blahnik, who got to know Piaggi in the early 1970s when he was her neighbor in the London district of Kensington. By this time the Milanese Piaggi, who had been married to the fashion photographer Alfa Castaldi (d. 1995) since the mid-1950s, had been living in the British capital for many years, working energetically at an Italian fashion magazine, reviewing countless boutiques and, with the eccentric Vern Lambert, ferreting out clothing from the 1920s and 30s at auctions and antique dealers for Lambert's stand at Chelsea's antique market and Piaggi's own wardrobe. For Piaggi was a collector of unusual fashions and an expert at creating striking combinations: "It did not have to be Dior, as far as Anna was concerned," enthuses hat designer Stephen Jones, who created many of her jaunty hats. "She wore shoes from the 20s with Dolce&Gabbana trousers, an ancient Patou coat with a plastic belt and carried a ski pole instead of a walking stick, not to mention her distinctive blue hair, topped with a hat worn at a crazy angle. She embodied all the possibilities that fashion has to offer. Her style wasn't about fashion or making a statement, but rather fun, curiosity, and frivolity." This highly creative approach to the contents of her own wardrobe, which in 2006 held 2865 dresses and 265 pairs of shoes, inspired not only her immediate surroundings but also the man, whom she described as being—along with her husband and fashion expert Vern Lambert—the third most important man in her life: Karl Lagerfeld. At their very first meeting in 1974, he drew a sketch of her—on a paper napkin at a Chinese restaurant in Paris. Many years down the line, she continued to be his muse and source of inspiration; his *Fashion Journal*, published in 1986, documents her phenomenal wardrobe over the course of ten years. Right up until her death, she retained an unerring sixth sense for anything new that might be in the wind—each month she would surprise the readers of Italian Vogue afresh with her features: four pages about a brooch, or about a color, a word, an animal, a tiny detail she had noticed at a fashion show—she

Fashion savvy
Anyone who wants to conquer the market from Milan would do well to entrust their marketing to the German PR guru Karla Otto. Satisfied customers include Roberto Cavalli, who has seen his business really take off in recent years. Fiorucci, Jil Sander and Prada have also benefited from her work.

Poor patron
Isabella is famous for championing hat designers such as Philip Treacy, but she also bought all of Alexander McQueen's first collection, albeit in installments.

A heart for a crown
The American divorcée Wallis Simpson won over the British heir to the throne Prince Edward with her exquisite taste, self-discipline and humor; he abdicated from the throne in order to marry her. As the Duke and Duchess of Windsor, the couple led an elegant life of exile in Paris.

was given a completely free hand in choosing the subject matter as well as its visual presentation. Her publications caused as much of a stir as her sophisticated wardrobe, planned down to the last detail. Fashion historians saw her wardrobe as such a rich repository of fashion treasures that the Victoria and Albert Museum in London—one of the most important museums in the world for design and textiles—dedicated an exhibition to it in 2006.

Of course, the editors-in-chief of the glossy fashion magazines also have a massive influence on fashion, although they do not tend to be muses themselves. One rare exception is Carine Roitfeld, who was the head of French Vogue from 2001 to 2011. As a stylist, she was very much involved in Tom Ford's rise at Gucci; then she successfully shocked the world with her fashion photos featuring models smoking or tied up, commenting with an air of self-satisfaction: "I am the punk of the Vogue family." Franca Sozzani has been just as provocative since 1988 at Italian Vogue, although her waist-length blonde hair still makes her look like an angel. The notorious "Devil wearing Prada" is Anna Wintour, the British-born editor of US Vogue. Despite her tough reputation, she has given many talented designers their opening in the fashion world.

To this, however, former Vogue editor-in-chief Diana Vreeland (d. 1989) remains unsurpassed as a style icon. Although no beauty, she was eccentric, witty and imaginative. Her motto was, "Don't worry about looking vulgar; looking boring is much worse." Vreeland organized the first big fashion exhibitions to take place

at the Metropolitan Museum of Art. She was discovered by Carmel Snow, the legendary editor who made Harper's Bazaar the leading fashion magazine in the world from 1934 to 1958, before her former apprentice Vreeland overtook her with Vogue. Yet although the editors-in-chief can deploy an array of enticing images, the person with the greatest influence in fashion is, astonishingly, the journalist Suzy Menkes, who has only words at her disposal.

After studying English literature and history at university, British-born Menkes (b. 1943) turned her hand to journalism. She has exerted a constant influence ever since taking up the job of fashion critic at the International Herald Tribune in 1988, and is the only person who has the power to make or break careers with a single review. Thankfully, she is incorruptible and always open to new ideas. "It would be a miserable world if there was only sensible clothing," she says, with the wisdom that comes from 40 years of reporting on fashion.

Claudia Teibler

A fixture on the "best dressed" lists
Mona von Bismarck started off with nothing but her beauty; money got her through her third marriage—and a noble title through her fourth.

The power of the media
Legendary editors-in-chief: Carmel Snow of Harper's Bazaar, Diana Vreeland of US Vogue (top left and right) and Carine Roitfeld, up until 2011 of French Vogue (below left). The longest serving Vogue editors-in-chief are Anna Wintour (center right) in New York and Franca Sozzani (below right) in Milan. The woman with the most influence is fashion critic Suzy Menkes (center left).

INDEX OF NAMES

INDEX OF NAMES

SUBJECT INDEX

SUBJECT INDEX

PICTURE CREDITS

Charlotte Seeling

After completing her training, Charlotte Seeling spent many years working as a freelance journalist before becoming chief editor of various magazines, including Cosmopolitan, Vogue, and Marie Claire in Germany and Marie France in Paris. Since the mid-90s, she has been concentrating mainly on her work as an author.

Claudia Teibler

After gaining her doctorate in the History of Art, Claudia Teibler has worked as an editor and freelance writer for newspapers and magazines, including AD Architectural Digest. Since 2008 she has also written several books and thoroughly enjoys her work as an author.

Markus Thommen

Markus Thommen has worked as art director for various magazines, including Cosmopolitan, Harper's Bazaar, GQ, Brigitte, AD Architectural Digest, and Park Avenue. He has also been involved in new project developments for Condé Nast, Bauer, and Holtzbrinck and worked for various companies directing the artwork for catalogues, posters, and advertising. From 2008 to 2010, he was creative director for Traveller's World.

Antje Blees

Antje Blees studied Communication Design before being appointed art director for s.e.p.p. and doin'fine. Since 2005 she has been studying German and American literature at LMU Munich and has taken part in various local exhibitions of painting and photography.

Elisabeth Alric-Schnee

Elisabeth Alric-Schnee studied graphics and fashion in Paris before beginning work for ELLE international. Love brought her to Munich and the German edition of ELLE. She now works as freelance picture editor for various clients and is also developing a fashion collection of clothes for children.

Thanks go to **Florian Seidel**, whose black-and-white images are reproduced on pages 2/3, 6/7 and 500/501. In 2009, this Munich photographer and video artist was awarded the New York prize for the best international short film for his movie "Die Sau ist tot."

© h.f.ullmann publishing GmbH

Original title: *MODE. 150 Jahre—Couturiers, Designer, Marken*
ISBN 978-3-8480-0614-4
Author and editor-in-chief: Charlotte Seeling
Co-author (chapters: "Challenging Legacy" and "Behind the Scenes"): Claudia Teibler
Art direction and Design: Markus Thommen
Layout: Antje Blees for Markus Thommen
Picture editor: Elisabeth Alric-Schnee
Proofreading and index: Christina Kuhn
Cover design: Benjamin Wolbergs
Cover photo: © ullstein bild/Granger Collection
Lithography and image processing: Frank Kreyssig, Heartwork
Project management: Isabel Weiler

© Sevenarts Ltd. All rights reserved/VG Bild-Kunst, Bonn 2014: Erté, work, p. 44; © Succession H. Matisse/VG Bild-Kunst, Bonn 2014: Matisse, Henri, stage setting for a ballet, p. 42; © VG Bild-Kunst, Bonn 2014: Chagall, Marc, drawing, p. 44; Cocteau, Jean, poster showing Tamara Karsawina, p. 44, dress, p. 87; Moholy-Nagy, Laszlo, Bauhaus poster, 1923, p. 45; Bérard, Christian, dresses shown on string puppets, 2 illustrations, p. 81; Fini, Leonor, flacon "Shocking", p. 91; Poiret, Paul, self-portrait, p. 18, Empire-style dress, p. 28, interior, p. 29, window display Boutique Martine, p. 29, perfume flacon Rosine, p. 29; Braque, Georges, birds (adaption by Laurent), p. 156

© for the English edition:
h.f.ullmann publishing GmbH

Special edition

Translated by Susan Ghanouni and Maisie Fitzpatrick in association with First Edition Translations Ltd, Cambridge.
Edited by David Price in association with First Edition Translations Ltd, Cambridge.
Typeset by TheWriteIdea in association with First Edition Translations Ltd, Cambridge.

Overall responsibility for production: h.f.ullmann publishing GmbH, Potsdam, Germany
ISBN 978-3-8480-0763-9

Printed in China, 2014

10 9 8 7 6 5 4 3 2 1
X IX VIII VII VI V IV III II

www.ullmann-publishing.com
newsletter@ullmann-publishing.com
facebook.com/ullmann.social